A FIELD GUIDE

TO THE AESTHETIC

EXPERIENCE

A FIELD GUIDE TO THE AESTHETIC EXPERIENCE

Jerry Farber

An *Interval* Book

ACKNOWLEDGMENTS

"Driving to Town Late to Mail a Letter": copyright 1962 by Robert Bly. Reprinted from SILENCE IN THE SNOWY FIELDS by Robert Bly, Wesleyan University Press, 1962, by permission of the author.

"In the morning dew" from A HISTORY OF HAIKU, VOL. I, by R. H. Blyth. Publisher: The Hokuseido Press. Reprinted by permission of Heian International, Inc.

From "Terence, this is stupid stuff" from "A Shropshire Lad"—Authorised Edition—from THE COLLECTED POEMS OF A. E. HOUSMAN, Copyright 1939, 1940, © 1965 by Holt, Rinehart and Winston. Copyright ©1967, 1968 by Robert E. Symons. Reprinted by permission of Holt, Rinehart and Winston, Publishers.

From "The Faithless Wife": Federico Garcia Lorca, THE SELECTED POEMS OF FEDERICO GARCIA LORCA. Copyright © 1955 by New Directions Publishing Corporation. Reprinted by permission of New Directions.

From THE MISANTHROPE, translated and © copyright 1954, 1955 by Richard Wilbur. Reprinted by permission of Harcourt Brace Jovanovich, Inc.

First two lines of "The Barrel-organ" from COLLECTED POEMS IN ONE VOLUME" by Alfred Noyes. (J. B. Lippincott) Copyright 1906, 1934, with extensions, by Alfred Noyes. Courtesy of Harper & Row, Publishers, Inc.

First stanza of "Daddy" from ARIEL by Sylvia Plath. Copyright © 1963 by Ted Hughes. By permission of Harper & Row, Publishers, Inc.

From "Burning the Small Dead": Gary Snyder, THE BACK COUNTRY. Copyright © 1959, 1965, 1968 by Gary Snyder. Reprinted by permission of the author.

From "Lapis Lazuli": W. B. Yeats, THE COLLECTED POEMS OF W.B. YEATS, Macmillan Publishing Co., Inc. Copyright 1940 by Georgie Yeats, renewed 1968 by Bertha Georgie Yeats, Michael Butler Yeats and Anne Yeats.

From "Nineteen Hundred and Nineteen": W. B. Yeats, THE COLLECTED POEMS OF W. B. YEATS, Macmillan Publishing Co., Inc., renewed 1956 by Georgie Yeats.

PRINTED IN U.S.A.

ISBN 0-943292-15-8

First Edition: August 30, 1982
Library of Congress Catalog Card Number 82-83129

Box 9747
North Hollywood, California, 91609

An Interval Book

For Judy, Eric, Bob, Catharine, Anne, Maddie

CONTENTS

PREFACE

I suspect that, to most of us, nothing could seem more idle than a theory of art. "What is art?"—the question is not one of your more urgent intellectual problems. Not only don't we need the answer in order to live our lives, we don't even seem to need it to appreciate works of art. And we certainly don't need it to make them; the world is full of artists who couldn't care less about aesthetic theory. In fact, if art itself is "impractical," then aesthetics is doubly so. So we leave these questions to philosophers—those custodians of the impractical—and go on about our business.

And yet, oddly enough, this very lack of interest in the fundamental questions about art doesn't prevent any of us from having plenty of answers. They come unsought. We breathe them in willy-nilly. Who can approach a work of art with anything resembling innocence? Like it or not, doesn't each of us carry around some sort of aesthetic, some store of notions about art? Just listen to what people say:

"Now this kind of painting . . . I don't know. I don't call this art."

"I think it's a really great movie, because it's just so true to life."

"My problem with poetry is I never know what it's trying to say."

"We're starting Kimberly on piano lessons. I think that's so good for a child."

"You want to know what kind of people we are? Look at our architecture: McDonald's, Jack in the Box . . ."

"The trouble with her new album is that it's the same old stuff. She's playing it safe. She's not *going* anywhere."

"Great artists are never appreciated in their own lifetime."

I want to suggest that each of us encounters a work of art—*not* theory-free and with total independence ("I know what I

—1—

like, that's all")—but rather on the basis of general assumptions about art, assumptions which we may not even be able to verbalize but which tell us something about what art is and is not, what makes it good or bad, how it gets created, what we're supposed to do with it, what its relationship is to our lives. These assumptions are usually not the result of any conscious theorizing. As I said, we breathe them in. Or—to come at it another way—they're put on us.

Such notions about art—perhaps vague, fragmentary, even contradictory—have much to do with the way we experience it, in the same way that our notions about sex can help to shape our sexual experience. In both cases, with art and with sex, our assumptions derive from many sources. Not only the family, but also churches, department stores, and movie theatres instruct us about sex. Not only teachers, but also society editors and loan officers, copywriters and security guards help to define art.

Now just as we're willing to examine our received ideas about sex and to make the judgment that one notion is more appropriate than another, so, it seems to me, we should be willing to examine and judge our aesthetic beliefs. There was a time when the belief that masturbation would drive one insane introduced gratuitous misery into many an adolescent's sex life. The belief that a poem is a cryptogram or a sort of test track for the intellect is today the sad contribution of a million literature classes to popular aesthetics. To the extent that an assumption about art mystifies us, deadens us, or alienates us—to this extent it is inappropriate.

One reason then for writing this book is to bring some of our aesthetic assumptions out in the open where they can be examined and reconsidered. Although I am proposing a complex and comprehensive aesthetic theory, I've taken some pains to make this theory available to general readers, to all of those who, even if they have little interest in aesthetics as an intellectual hobby, have a real interest in art itself. For specialists in aesthetics or in literary criticism, fine-arts criticism, dance criticism, and so on, I hope that the theory may prove useful as such, and that it may suggest a way of integrating what have been separate and even seemingly contradictory approaches to art. For general readers, I hope that this book, by raising pivotal questions and by challenging common ideas about art, may at the very least provide the incentive for a little spring cleaning. If this book leaves some readers more sensitive, more open to the experience of art, it will have succeeded in a very important way.

A good field guide should be a companion to the direct experience of its subject. And certainly, in approaching art analytically, I have no fears about withering the experience itself, no misgivings about unweaving the rainbow. On the contrary, I've learned that understanding fosters and protects the aesthetic experience. People are sometimes wary about "picking things apart." "Just enjoy it," they say. But often this attitude is merely the reaction not to analysis in itself but to an unwholesome, forced, anxious analysis which is learned in schools and which, instead of serving art, betrays it.

Art theory for me is the aesthetic experience asserting itself and insisting on its own identity. And this kind of experience *needs* to assert itself—because art is so often a captive: a captive to the marketplace—a captive to duty, to fashion, to social and intellectual snobbishness—a captive continually to authoritarian and coercive schooling—a captive to political systems and their instruments of control—a captive at times to philosophy, psychology, history, linguistics, and so on. I don't mean to say that teachers, psychologists, linguists, or historians have no legitimate business with art. Hardly. It is only that their concerns can distort our perception of it, and even have the potential to interfere with its essential, aesthetic function. To the extent that art is captured by non-aesthetic concerns, art theory takes on special importance; to see art clearly is to set it free.

I want to thank the people who read this book in draft form and who were kind enough to give me their suggestions and their encouragement: Nick Nichols, Ita Sheres, Ron Gervais, Anne Thieulle, Larry McCaffery, Maddie Farber, and Judith Bagai. And there is no way a brief acknowledgment can convey the gratitude I feel toward my students, who have been wonderful company in the study of art.

J.F.

San Diego State University,
January, 1982

TO THE READER

There are no footnotes. You'll find a section of Notes and Comments at the back of the book; each of these refers to a passage in the text which will be identified by a page number and a key word or phrase. This section contains a good deal more than documentation, including digressions on matters either too trivial or too vast to be included in the text. You may find it addresses some theoretical questions that have occurred to you in the course of reading the book. In any case, I recommend reading the text straight through and then starting in on the Notes and Comments.

By the end of Chapter Eleven the book is, in one sense, complete: an aesthetic theory has been proposed. What follows in Chapters Twelve, Thirteen, and Fourteen is my attempt to draw out some social implications of this theory. The argumentation in this last section is a little looser, the tone a little more polemic. I'm aware that some readers may largely accept the view of art set out in the first nine chapters and yet find reason to question the social and educational criticism in Chapters Thirteen and Fourteen. This criticism rests in part on convictions that go beyond aesthetic theory.

BOOK I
CHAPTER ONE
"What Is Art?"

"What is art?"

Is this an unanswerable question? Why *should* it be? Other things that we do can be identified with at least some precision: athletics, politics, business, science. Anyone who doesn't know what science is can pick up a dictionary and get a fairly good idea. But art? I won't bore you with dictionary definitions. Suffice it to say that we find ourselves pursuing a series of enigmatic entries: "art" is an "aesthetic object," which has "beauty," which "exalts the spirit," and so on; each term is no more useful or specific than the last. "What is art?" The question is a balloon that wants to carry us up to cloudland, where we sail from one misty abstraction to another. But why?

Suppose we agree that we'll keep the balloon moored, and try to stay down to earth as long as possible. How do you begin? One way is by pointing and listing. A splendidly concrete approach. "Citrus fruits are . . ." And then you don't start talking about exalted spirits; you just start listing: "oranges, lemons, kumquats, limes . . ." If we try it with art, what comes to mind? Could we list the arts—dance, literature, architecture, and so on? Not a bad idea. Here, of course, the problem is where to stop. Someone might even want to leave out architecture. But let's say we keep it. Along with painting, sculpture, music, film . . . What do you think, would you include ceramics? Is there any reason not to? What about tapestry or jewelry? And why not landscaping or ornamental gardening? How about cooking—at least as some people practice it? How exactly do you decide where the arts leave off? For example, if sculpture and painting are on the list, why not include package design? You might object that packages have a "useful" purpose. But then so did two much admired paintings by Watteau which were created to serve as signboards, one for a theatre and one for an art dealer. Not only that, poems have been composed to persuade, music to maintain a work rhythm—and if a cathedral, however beautiful, didn't keep out the rain, its architect would be in real trouble. So perhaps we can't let "usefulness" drive an activity off our list. Besides, all you have to do is stick that nicely designed package on the knickknack shelf, merely to be looked at, and it won't be useful any more. Then there's flower arrangement—not practical at all. Is it art?

Is photography an art? Bookbinding? What about textiles?

So here we are—out of the clouds, all right, and into the fun house of aesthetics. Perhaps we won't ever be able to define the arts by list. But we may have learned something in trying. One problem, it appears, in making a list of arts is that we run into activities that might be seen as arts—jewelry, photography, ornamental gardening—and then again might not. Depending. Depending on what? When is photography an art? Obviously we need some basis for choosing or the whole world will get on our list. You could say, "Fine, let it on"; but at the point when blowing one's nose gets on the list of arts, we're pretty much back where we started. What is art? (Can't you feel the balloon tugging upward? It doesn't seem to like being here on earth.)

Or perhaps we haven't been concrete *enough*. Suppose we let "the arts" go and stay with the individual works themselves. This painting. That photograph. This performance of a song. That building. But here again we still have to decide when to shut the gate. If this piece of free-form sculpture is art, can I then find a nicely shaped piece of driftwood or an interesting stone and display it in a gallery? Will we agree to call it art? Perhaps we will. But what if, as Marcel Duchamp did in 1917, I buy a urinal, call it *Fountain*, and submit it to an art exhibition? The issue here is that of *objets trouvés*—found objects—which began to be offered up as works of art early in this century. Or I could find a sound—say a Datsun pickup going through the gears—put it on tape and claim that it's music. You may disagree. But suppose I keep trying, for as long as it takes, until I find something that you really appreciate. Maybe it will be a tape of waves pounding in the distance as wind and rain start up and the thunder begins to close in. You love it. But you still insist that it's not art, because no artist composed it.

Does there have to be an artist behind a work to make it art? Suppose everyone likes my "nonrepresentational" painting, and then I explain that I soaked hamsters with poster paint and turned them loose on white cardboard? Or what about Bill Strickfaden, a friend of mine who has produced what some people, at least, regard as worthwhile prose poetry on a computer? In other words, does the beautiful driftwood count as art only as long as we think some person shaped it and no longer? That seems paradoxical. Besides, the question "Did an artist create it?" isn't that simple. If we're talking about the "artist's role," can't we recognize a spectrum of possibilities, going from more to less controlling activity, more to less choice? Even with the driftwood, which would lie at one end of this spectrum, there may be some creative activity involved. In the decision to select and display a piece of driftwood—or even to notice it—can we see the function of an artist? Or not? Even in the extreme examples of aleatoric (chance) art, someone sets up the game, the field of possibilities. Bill Strickfaden, for example, gave his computer a complicated set of grammatical rules and a selected vocabulary. And there are many examples to be found in the middle range of our spectrum, such as Merce Cunningham's dance composition *Suite by Chance*, in which, out of a series of prearranged dance movements, the ones to be performed are selected and combined by flipping coins. You see, even if we agreed to exclude works that no artist created, we might have a very difficult time deciding just where to draw the line.

Perhaps, though, we don't have to decide at this point where we stand on such questions. Because I'm going to suggest that, though we've been looking for the definition of art in a perfectly reasonable direction, we have, in fact, been looking in the *wrong* direction.

It's true that when people want to identify art in a concrete way, by pointing and listing, they naturally turn to the various arts or to individual art works. But they always end up in trouble, too. Why? Because the work of art can never be identified on its own, without reference to a perceiver. What tells us that something is art is the response that it evokes. You'll never recognize art by analyzing the pigment, counting the words, weighing the bricks. You have to consider the response. Your own, for example. That's what critics do. They may be informed, experienced, amply supplied with theory; but what they don't have is a box of calipers to measure the "artfulness" of a work. No one has ever found an *objective* set of criteria that can be applied like a gauge or like litmus paper to separate art from non-art.

I want to suggest that there's an excellent reason for this, an excellent reason why we can't test for a work of art as we can for the presence of an acid or of chicken pox. *Art is essentially a way of perceiving and responding.* Objective criteria for a work of art would be as hard to establish as objective criteria for "a sexy person" or "delicious food"—and for the same reasons. When we try to identify art by making a list of the arts or of art objects, we're looking in the wrong place: out there; we need to begin by looking *in here.*

The response which enables us to call something art—the *aesthetic* response (if I use the term, it's with a promise to bring it closer to earth than the dictionary does)—is an iffy business. For one thing, even the most widely recognized masterpiece may not inevitably produce this kind of response, may not work on everyone who perceives it. Obviously. During summer months in the Louvre, all you hear is "Where's the *Mona Lisa?*" People file past it continually all day long as though it were a president's coffin. What are they feeling? "Well . . . so that's it. I thought it was bigger." Tens of thousands. Hundreds of thousands. Does it "exalt the spirit" of every foot-weary tourist? No, you can be sure it doesn't. Here's an even more pointed example. Many years ago I took three close friends to see one of my favorite movies, *L'Avventura.* I was reasonably confident they'd love it. The four of us, I thought, had fairly similar tastes in movies. Well, you know the rest. My friends groaned, yawned, muttered, shifted in their seats. Asked if we had to see the whole thing through (I was seeing it for the fourth time.) Were sure I was playing a practical joke on them.

No need to dwell too long on this familiar scene. There is much more impelling proof that we've been looking for art in the wrong direction.

Let's say that you're looking at some paintings, each of which pleases you very much. Obviously, your response will vary from one painting to another: one may give you a sense of movement and conflict; another may strike you as contemplative and still. But isn't there also at the same time a more general kind of response that is evoked by every one of these works, a response that you associate with the experience of enjoying paintings? And haven't you felt a similar response—perhaps even a stronger one—on some occasions when no painting at all was present? The kind of experience that you associate with art, don't you sometimes have it when you're looking at an actual landscape, or at the ocean, or at an unusual and dramatic arrangement of clouds in the sky? The sort of view that's likely to evoke this response may vary, of course, with individuals, although some scenes—the obvious examples—seem to work on most of us: splendid sunsets, a road lined with autumn trees, fields of flowers, the full moon emerging from clouds, trees silhouetted against a twilight sky.

We may also take this kind of pleasure in looking at certain objects: crystals, natural gemstones, rocks and rock formations, driftwood, seashells. Or natural "dance": a certain person's walk, people hurrying past our window on a rainy day, birds flying, cats stretching, elephants walking, giraffes running.

We don't need a work of art in order to have the kind of response that such works can awaken. And this is not simply a question of our noticing scenes that "look like a painting." Artists can, it's true, turn our admiring attention to a particular kind of scene or body type or quality of light (as both Oscar Wilde and Marcel Proust observed). But it would be stretching the point to say that we only appreciate in nature the kind of scene that we've already enjoyed in a painting. Because we also so often discover our own personal art in the natural environment. What's more, an artist's work may have the effect, not so much of opening us up to particular scenes or forms, as of opening us up, period. I've walked out of galleries and art museums and had a four or five-minute period when *everything* I saw was art, a brief aesthetic jag when people and concrete joined in colored patterns, and the sky fit like fragments of blue tile between the leaves of trees. I've left modern-dance concerts and, for a time, perceived all of my movements as dance: walking down stairs, zipping up a jacket, driving the car.

Sometimes I respond in this way simply because someone has showed me something. "Look at those rocks over there!" "Have you been listening to all the *sounds* on this train?" A couple of friends in Los Angeles, both painters, used to do "pick-ups" endlessly. "Pick up on the lunch counter at Newberry's." "Pick up on that broken window." Things were never picked up simply because they were strange or unexpected; it was always tacitly understood that something was to be picked up as image. I was living in Pasadena near what I regarded as a huge eyesore, the electrical generating station—a weary jumble of big, bare machinery. One of these friends and I went walking in the early evening. He picked up on the place immediately and led me to look at it in a completely different and a more pleasing way. I wondered then if creating art might sometimes be no more than pointing.

Then, of course, there are the natural experiences that don't need to be pointed out, that worked for me when I was a child, and continue to work (as long as I don't lean too heavily on them). One kind of music: the sound of a car or truck outside on a main road late at night, emerging from the distance, sweeping by, then slowly disappearing. Or the sound and sight of water in motion: streams, rivers, falls, fountains, even (no, especially!) juice being poured from a pitcher. Fire. Sunsets, of course, and pre-dawn landscapes. A flock of birds in flight. Patterns of sunlight on the wall.

Not only are there special situations which tend to be aesthetic for me, there are special tools that encourage this kind of response. Windows often do it. I remember sitting indoors one afternoon looking out a small window for a long time at leafy pepper tree branches waving in the wind. Also, walking past lighted windows at night. In fact, one can find framing devices of all sorts: holes, leafy vistas, narrow spaces between buildings, what have you.

Lovely: through the hole
in this shoji-screen
the Milky Way

Silence and semi-darkness often prepare the way for an aesthetic response. Or stepping outside after spending the entire
day indoors. Any change in weather can do it—or being in a
new locale—or even going without sleep. Some drugs may do
it on occasion—for a particular person at a particular time—
but I'm unaware of any drug which is consistently and reliably
"aesthetic."

What is most important to understand is that, given the
right frame of mind, the right conditions, virtually anything
might be perceived aesthetically. If there are limits, they may
be set by the degree to which a perception threatens or
disgusts us. But aside from that, what door slam, what dirt
clod, what outbreak of zits might not give some one of us—
temporarily receptive to it—a moment of art?

Now where does all this take us in our understanding of art?
First of all, we discover that, in art, the individual perception/
response is of fundamental importance. We may agree, for
excellent reasons, to call certain objects and performances
works of art (and I want to insist early and often that I'm not
trying to minimize the importance of these works of art). But
we know that an aesthetic response in a particular person and
at a given moment is not guaranteed by the work of art. The
aesthetic response is, on the one hand, never inevitable, even
for Masterpiece X, but on the other hand always possible, even
for Junkheap Y. We know that this response can occur without
a work of art in an endless range of possible situations. Some
natural objects, scenes, and events are more likely than others
to evoke it, but apparently there are few indeed that we can
exclude—few indeed (none?) of which we can say, "No, this
could never be perceived aesthetically." The right frame of
mind, the right mode of consciousness can extract a moment
of art from almost anything. That's why trying to define art on
the basis of objects, and objects alone, will always leave us
confused. If we're trying to identify art, what we *must* identify,
must understand is the actual experience. When we can
understand it and can do more than label it "aesthetic," then

perhaps we will have found a workable approach to the question: "What is art?" And *then* maybe we can take another look, a more productive look, at the work of art itself.

Try to observe your own aesthetic experience. Not merely the particular quality associated with a certain scene or dance or piece of music, but the *general* underlying quality, the common denominator that allows you to call all of these experiences aesthetic. Is there such a thing: a general quality common to all of our aesthetic experience? If so, it's certainly not easy to examine. If you're paying attention to yourself, you're not perceiving the object attentively. And if you're focused intently on a scene or on some music, then you're not paying attention to yourself. Certainly it's easy enough to say, "What a peaceful scene," or "This music makes me want to dance," but is there nothing else that we can describe—no common quality—nothing "aesthetic" left over after the peacefulness here and the liveliness there have been duly noted?

Compare this kind of experience with others; the others are likely to be much easier to pin down. No matter what frightens you, for example, fear itself is a common denominator which is easy enough to be aware of and even to describe. In fact, often, to be afraid is to be acutely and painfully aware of one's own almost stereotyped physical reaction. Likewise, though sexual feeling can attach itself to an endless number of objects, the turn-on itself remains distinct and identifiable. Even less somatic kinds of experience have a fairly distinct character. Learning, deciding, regretting: each is a certain kind of thing that you do, the essential character or structure of which is obvious. But what, beyond mere perception, is aesthetic experience? What happens to us in the presence of art? How strange that we *recognize* the experience and yet we can't describe it.

No wonder attempts to understand art so often begin with art works. The personal experience itself evaporates under our gaze; nothing remains but the object. Perhaps this is why some theorists—particularly in the eighteenth century—have simply assumed we possess some sort of aesthetic sense or "taste," corresponding to the other senses and especially to that sense from which aesthetic taste borrows its name. An understandable but erroneous conclusion. If there's a quality that enables us to identify "aesthetic experience," we need to look further for it.

In art, we're poured into the object. The qualities that we notice are—or at least seem to be—qualities of the object itself: an exciting novel, a majestic building, a sensual dance, a despairing play. If we insist on turning inward, if we ask, "All right now, what's happening to me as I look at this sketch"— the experience we're pursuing disappears. *Aesthetic* consciousness and *self* consciousness stand at opposite poles; as we move toward one, we abandon the other. This can be true even, say, in dancing, where the dancer may be simultaneously perceiver and object. Aesthetic satisfaction in dancing is not automatic; it comes, finally, when you pour your self into kinesthetic image, into space and time, shape and motion.

This difficulty we encounter in trying to perceive our own aesthetic experience, this barrier at which theory so often turns away to pursue art in objects, is actually, when you approach it in the right way, no obstacle at all. This, in fact, is where the answer lies. How can you observe yourself at the very moment when you've given yourself away? Art, as personal as it is, as close to your own experience, as evocative of feeling as it is, becomes art only when it releases you from your self. But we don't want to start drifting back up into cloudland. What, exactly, such a statement means and doesn't mean needs to be clarified in very precise terms.

We need to make sure that the terms that come easily to mind don't lead us astray. It would not, for example, be true to say that aesthetic perception releases us from the self if "self" refers simply to what is personal. After all, I see a painting in the light of my own personal history, my own knowledge and my own temperament. The particular complex of feelings that it arouses is my own. I doubt that you and I will ever see this painting in exactly the same way. So there can be no question of escaping self if the word refers to an individual accumulation of experience, an individual way of responding, and so on. No—the burden I temporarily lay down in aesthetic experience is that of self-*responsibility*, self-*concern*. The self from which we escape in art is not the self that houses our individual past but the self with an individual claim on the future.

Terms which have been used in the past to describe this aspect of aesthetic experience—"disinterestedness," "psychic distance," "aesthetic attitude"—have invited misunderstanding. With this in mind, let me try to explain as clearly as possible just what I mean by *self-concern.* What I have in mind is a process: the way the brain continually monitors perceptions to see how they can be used, what they may point to in the way of a possible effect on our future. This is close to what, in her theory of emotion, Magda Arnold calls "appraisal":

> When something is perceived, remembered or imagined, it never remains an isolated bit of knowledge. Rather, each object is immediately seen in relation to ourselves and is evaluated as good, bad or indifferent for us. In everyday life, the appraisal of everything we encounter in its relation to ourselves is immediate, automatic, almost involuntary. What is "good" in some way (significant, useful, beneficial) is attended to and striven for; what is "bad" (harmful, annoying) is avoided or overcome; and what is indifferent (insignificant, unimportant, useless) is simply disregarded.

She adds: "This appraisal complements perception and *produces a tendency to deal with the object in some way*" (my italics).

What I call "self-concern" examines the present in light of a personally-centered future, or rather of various possible futures. It is a monitoring, appraising process that "looks out for Number One." Ordinarily, we are in business for our selves, each of us continually protecting this precious self, pursuing goals, striving. When we notice anything, we notice it in the light of this continual striving. Our eyes and ears—our senses— are, ordinarily, working for the self that strives.

But aesthetic perception is time out. It's the great exception. We're no longer obliged to perceive everything in light of the effect it may have on us. Naturally, we continue to recognize things according to how we know them, both intellectually and emotionally. A bronze lion may be ferocious. The last scene of a movie may be tragic. But we don't have to do anything about either the lion or the tragic events. We're on vacation. We've brought along all of our knowledge and experience, even our feelings. But we've left our responsibility back at the office. And this is the beginning of understanding art, of grasping its essential quality—the very quality which is so hard to observe, because it's as much an absence as a presence. Kant calls aesthetic satisfaction "disinterested." Not *un*interested, but *dis*interested, which means having no axe to grind, no *self*ish concern.

Without any axe to grind, without striving, we no longer perceive things instrumentally, as the means to some feared or desired end; instead we perceive things as ends in themselves. My back yard, for example, is often just plain oppressive—one responsibility too many. There are rose bushes which were planted by the people who were here before and which we have left to the mercy of bugs, dogs, and dry weather. There are ragged curls of eucalyptus bark all over the grass (which ought to be cut). There are fruit trees which feed the birds while we buy peaches at Food Basket. There are dog turds. But at times, especially when the light is right and I am right, I just *see* the yard—as it is, not as it ought to be. And it looks very very good. (Someone might point out that, if we cleared away the junk and took better care of the rose bushes, we would be granted an aesthetic view of the yard more often. Perhaps— but this question is reserved for another chapter.)

As we begin to understand what happens—or doesn't happen—in aesthetic experience, an important corollary question presents itself. Why do we *enjoy* art and seek it out? Will we finally be forced to invent some basic drive, like hunger or sex, in order to explain our satisfaction—some "art instinct?"

I don't think so. Whatever else it may do for us, aesthetic perception always, by its very nature, offers us the pleasure of a respite. And this kind of satisfaction, as we all know, can be enormous. Carrying your own weight around, for example, requires an effort of which you're not ordinarily aware until it stops; then, after a day on your feet, bed can be an intense pleasure. Have you ever noticed people half-standing and half-floating in a swimming pool, letting their limbs go slack and weightless? Watch them, up to their necks, loosely bobbing, with absent, even blissful looks on their faces. But a far greater burden than the weight of your own body is the responsibility for your own self. And in both cases the burden is there, the effort must be made whether you are directly conscious of it or not.

Get yourself born human and you inherit a heavy responsibility. You have to stay alive, keep healthy, satisfy your needs for food, sex, love, self-esteem. Deal with your anger and your fear. Try to make sense out of your surroundings—if possible in a way that will make them tolerable, but some kind of sense at least, in any case. Handle the endless stream of threats, not only to your physical well-being but also to all of the persons, places, institutions, ideas, causes with which you have chosen to identify yourself. Self-concern, which is the price we pay not merely for life but for our celebrated consciousness as well, can show itself in the most subtle as well as the most obvious ways. Under its impulse we experience triumph and despair. But it can also carry us through a card game or guide our seemingly aimless fingers as they flip through a magazine at the supermarket.

Born under this burden, we carry it through life. Do we ever—short of death or buddhahood—set it down? Yes, we can and we do, frequently. That very release is what occurs when we perceive aesthetically. No wonder art is universal. No surprise that the human race is addicted to it. Nor is aesthetic experience to be seen as offering merely a "negative" kind of satisfaction. It is not merely the absence of self-concern; it is, as we will see, the opportunity to be alive in the freedom which that absence provides. Wake up some morning after a bout of stomach flu to find your fever broken and nausea gone, and you know what exquisite pleasure a return to simple good health can provide. Naturally, aesthetic release can vary in degree and scope from one occasion to another, from one moment to the next. When it is most nearly complete, we seem to merge with what we are perceiving: the sky, the novel, the song; all responsibility for self seems to have vanished. Of course we value this experience: it's time out. On the other hand, it's easy to see why we can't simply *stay* with our aesthetic experience forever; the demands of the self are much too pressing to be set aside for very long. As a matter of fact, it's worth noting that, even during aesthetic perception, our sense of self-responsibility is never completely out of action. If we're watching a movie and we smell smoke, sooner or later we'll start to think about getting out of the theatre. Even on these psychological holidays, there has to be someone, a skeleton staff, on duty—just in case. Furthermore, it's not only some stimulus *outside* the aesthetic frame, like smoke in a theatre, that can set off the alarm. If the movie itself becomes too personally threatening, we may lose our capacity to respond to it as art.

I remember once in the middle of a romance when it seemed that I was, at twenty-nine, discovering jealousy for the first time. Awful, virulent, paralyzing jealousy. It happened that I had assigned *Othello* that semester in a literature course. But I couldn't go through with it. The play was too depressing for me even to read, let alone teach. What a time! I stayed home as much as possible and listened to jazz on the radio all day—where I heard my unhappiness mirrored in a less threatening way. Perhaps if I could have handled *Othello*, it might have done me some good.

In making the distinction between self-concerned perception and aesthetic perception, we need to bear in mind that it is not, very roughly speaking, the *content* of our experience that separates aesthetic from non-aesthetic, but the *mode*. Art is not relegated to some filmy, delicate realm of refined experience; it can cover the very same range that self-concern does. Art can show us not only what we want the most but also what we fear the most. What makes the difference is the absence of responsibility for one's self: a responsibility which is not to be seen as an abstract idea or a "thing," but rather as a characteristic mode—of neural activity, if you like—which in some perceptual situations is virtually abandoned.

Between a newspaper and a good short story, the difference lies in the *way* we read or are led to read, not necessarily in the subject matter. With the paper, we glance around at headlines, looking for what touches our concerns, either directly or through ego-identification; we read each story just as far as is dictated by hopes, fears, libido, anger, and so on. Even what we consider "mere curiosity" often turns out to be an instrument of self-concern: we're curious about a sweepstakes winner or about scandal in high places but not so likely to be curious about the previous day's high and low temperatures in Helsinki. With the newspaper, our purpose is *extractive.* With the short story, however, though similar content may be involved, we lose our restless desire to extract parts from the whole; the perception becomes an end in itself. Libido, aggression, and so on may be called into play but we are no longer their agent; we simply perceive them, *out there* in the story. With personal goals temporarily disengaged, striving stops. Occasionally, of course, we may read a newspaper story aesthetically, particularly if it's very artfully written. We lose ourselves in it, with its imagery and rhythms; we actually see it happen. Someone might have to be very high to do that with the stock market analysis or weather report, but the growth of literary journalism over the last twenty years or so has made it more likely for us to run across occasional feature stories which encourage an aesthetic response (what "encouraging an aesthetic response" entails is something that needs to be looked at, and will be in subsequent chapters).

For another example of the difference between ordinary and aesthetic perception, consider perception that has a sexual content. Under ordinary conditions, I find that sexual attractiveness is always a challenge to my self-concern. When I'm ogling, even though the possibility of a more intimate contact may be flatly ruled out, something in me *wishes* that it weren't; something in me is left, even if ever so slightly, off balance and wanting more. Sex in art, on the other hand—if the art is working—is just there. I can be aware of sexuality and appreciate it, but without the least sense of personal frustration, personal deprivation, or personal challenge.

Similarly, someone's death, in a movie, may evoke my sadness, but it's not a personal sadness because the loss isn't personal. It may evoke much stronger feeling than the death that I read about in the paper of, say, a scientist or an artist whom I've never met or even seen; yet the second death may be felt as a personal loss in a way the first could never be. The movie death makes no challenge to my self-responsibility nor does it make any claims on my future. We perceive death both in everyday life and in art; it is the mode of perception that changes.

So art is, in its subject matter, by no means to be counted on as an escape. Those things that most directly concern us are, in fact, the enduring content of—to choose one art out of many—poetry:

> But is there any comfort to be found?
> Man is in love and loves what vanishes,
> What more is there to say?

If we can make art out of what threatens or saddens us, there remains another question to be considered. Can we perceive something aesthetically if it simply doesn't interest us? After all, our perceptual field is crowded with things that are unrelated to self-concern. The people we scarcely observe on the street. The trees, sidewalk, telephone poles that we see but don't notice. The thousands of items in a market only fleetingly imprinted on our retinas. The background noises that we scarcely hear. These are all registered and then discarded. If one of the people on the street is a friend, if the telephone pole is leaning dangerously, if the product in the market is a new one—then we may notice. Otherwise nothing. Would it be true, however, to say that all of these things are perceived free of self-concern? No, they are not outside it; they are the *discards* of an active, functioning self-concern, and thus scarcely noticed. In aesthetic experience, on the other hand, we are attentive—so attentive that at times we seem to merge with what we are perceiving. The absence of self-concern is an open door, through which the intensity of our response allows us and encourages us to pass.

Some readers, incidentally, may be thinking at this point that although art may be *perceived* in the absence of self-concern, it could hardly be *created* that way. Actually, the artist has a double relationship, both instrumental and non-instrumental, to the work. But I'd like to ask readers to suspend their judgment on this matter until Chapter Ten, where it will be taken up in detail.

Are there other ways, aside from art, to reduce self-concern? Death seems effective, and, short of that, people have used deadening drugs: narcotics, barbiturates, tranquilizers. But even the tranquilizers, which leave cortical functioning more or less intact, interfere with a good deal more than self-concern; ordinarily they diminish our ability to respond intensely to anything, including art. In fact, it doesn't seem to be self-concern itself which is affected as much as the capacity to feel. That is, we're still taking care of business but we're "laid back" about it. In any case, to be psychologically flat is not aesthetic, even if self-concern is flattened out along with everything else. Once again: perception in the absence of self-concern opens the door to art, but isn't in itself the entire experience. One *responds* to a scene or an object or a performance, and, as we'll see in Book II, this response actually becomes a part of what is perceived, and gives the art object its intensity. Far from deadening our response, art liberates it. The aesthetic release, then, is not merely an absence; it is a space within which experience is liberated, and the intensity and scope of this experience establish the dimensions of an aesthetic encounter.

CHAPTER TWO
Image-Making

It's time—"about time," you may be thinking—to turn from the perceiver to the object. If the center of aesthetic experience has been moved inside, what's left *out there*? What does it mean to call something a work of art? Well, for a start, we can take hold of what's obvious: whatever else the work of art may do, clearly it encourages aesthetic perception. Someone *could* theoretically read this morning's want ads as literature, but *Huckleberry Finn* is going to have a much better batting average. The art work doesn't guarantee an aesthetic response in any individual case, but we might agree that it makes this kind of response more likely (if it doesn't, we're not going to want to call it "art"). Fine. But how? How does it work?

Let's begin by reconsidering "natural" aesthetic experience, the kind that doesn't depend upon an art work. Granted that the right frame of mind might turn almost anything into art, why is it that some natural scenes and objects—sunsets, flowers, and such—are more likely than others to evoke an aesthetic response? For example, we can compare two window scenes. In one instance, you look *through* the window for some particular purpose. You want to see if the mailman's coming. Or what those new neighbors are like. Or what that noise was outside. In the other instance, you're looking at the entire window scene itself—that is, at a rectangular image that's sitting there framed in the wall. The same distinction can be made here as was made about newspaper reading in the last chapter. In ordinary perception, our purpose is extractive and instrumental, whereas aesthetic perception is an end in itself. With the first window scene, that rectangular image has no particular interest of its own; what counts is what you can extract from it that relates to your self-concern.

It's like a snapshot where nothing matters but a familiar face: "Damn! Why do they always get me when I'm squinting?" But with the second window scene, the *entire* rectangle draws your attention: the corners, the edges, the dark green oleander in the lower left, the dark cloud bank in the upper right. This second window scene is not like an ordinary snapshot, but rather like a good photograph in which everything is working, in which every element is of visual importance.

When you pay attention to that rectangular image as a whole, you are looking at a scene which is selected and framed according to no instrumental, no practical purpose. Now ordinarily, everything that we're attentive to exists not only in a perceptual context but in a practical context as well—an enormous network of relationships, all founded upon the striving self. But, in looking at a window scene, as long as your attention is paid to that entire image and to its various elements in relation to the whole, then you are perceiving in a way that bears no relationship to self-concern. Self-concern is interested in what can help or hurt. But that exact selection of a piece of bush, a piece of cloud, some sky, a stretch of empty street, an ochre house and part of a blue one—these things haven't been selected according to the rules set up by self-concern. The selection leaves it cold.

The edges outlining a window scene that you look at for its own sake are edges that sever it from the practical context. When it's cut loose in this fashion, when it can neither help you nor hurt you in any instrumental way, then we can be justified in calling this scene an *image*. Not because it's an illusion, or a mere optical likeness of something else. But because, having been detached from that network of practical relationships, it has for you only a perceptual importance. It's just visual. That's all. Naturally, your eyes will shift their focus within the image, giving special attention now to this, now to that element, in the context of the whole. This doesn't in any way break the integrity of the entire image; it's privileged space, and you can move freely within it. But should your *self-concern* focus on any element within it, the scene dissolves as image and falls back into the practical context. The spell breaks. The postman appears under that piece of cloud bank and it occurs to you that he may have a check you've been waiting for or a bill you were hoping wouldn't arrive this week. The image gives way. The rectangle fades as an object of attention and gives way to the man in the blue hat bearing his good or bad news.

But we're still merely on the edge of the inquiry: why *would* any particular scene draw our attention as a visual whole? You could look out of a dozen windows in the course of the day—none of them revealing anything of practical interest to you—and of that dozen perhaps only one might call forth some degree of aesthetic response. This is our question. Why one scene rather than another?

In order for us to see it aesthetically, a scene must appear detached from the practical context. But this alone is not enough. Obviously, the scene must draw our attention as well. In fact, if it held no kind of interest at all, it wouldn't be detached so much as discarded—along with everything else we scarcely notice. So, to work aesthetically the window scene must simultaneously (a) draw us in, and (b) cut itself loose from the practical context. Book II will deal with (a): how an aesthetic object draws us in, calling forth a complex thinking-feeling response. In this chapter I want to look at (b): the means by which an aesthetic object leads us to perceive it as an image. Obviously, though, the aesthetic experience is a unified one; (a) and (b) are truly separate only as ways of talking about it. If we divide up the experience in this way in order to achieve a clearer understanding, we're going to be obliged to put it back together again before we're done.

How then might a window scene—or any scene—encourage us to detach it from the practical context? To begin with, window scenes, and many others as well, are *framed*. And they may be framed more or less sharply. The more a scene contrasts with its visual context—as does a brightly lit window that you see from the street at night—the more this frame serves to detach the scene and give it a visual autonomy. In aesthetic perception, framing is of immense value. It cuts the image loose; it cuts us loose.

The scene may also be *patterned* in such a way as to emphasize visual relationships that exist within the rectangle and tie it together into a coherent whole. On a rainy day, for example, you might look out a window and see the enveloping gray light, the wet reflective surfaces, the repeated postures of people hurrying past, hunched and leaning into the rain, the faint pervasive slant of the rain itself. All of these are patterning elements that draw our attention to the purely visual aspect of the scene and that help to gather up its various parts and pull them into one image. Or imagine, in a dim room, a small window that reveals nothing of the outside but blue sky and, below it, dark green leaves against a white wall—fresh, simple, and bold color relationships that make the scene cohere into a single image. Patterning elements in a scene—on the one hand the gray light, the repeated postures and so on, or, on the other hand, the sharply set off areas of blue, white, and green—if they're striking, undulled by habit, and free of any immediate practical significance—can lift a scene out of the world that we have to cope with. And they do this by emphasizing the scene's purely perceptual aspect. To see a scene aesthetically is to peel it loose, as image, from the practical world: non-instrumental pattern loosens it; coherence enables it to come off in one piece, and framing gives us the edges to grasp. Furthermore, framing often *creates* pattern, and pattern, even when it's not outlined, tends to generate its own perceptual frame.

Taking away the window frame, what scenes are good bets to evoke the kind of experience described in Chapter One as aesthetic: free from self-concern and absorbed in the image? A sunset. A tree-lined road in autumn. A mackerel sky. An expanse of clouds seen from above in an airplane. A field of flowers. The woods covered with snow. Trees outlined against a twilight sky. We might observe that these scenes tend to some extent to be temporary and therefore less subject to the erosion of habit. But also, in every case, the scene has elements that give it a patterned coherence which is strongly visual, and not instrumental. What would be an example of instrumental pattern? The way merchandise is arranged in a supermarket. Beans of various types, ranging from large cans on the bottom to small ones on top. Then peas, corn, and other vegetables, and so on. Visually, this *could* be very interesting (try it next time). But the patterns are created for instrumental purposes, and that's the way we usually see them: "Where's the tomato paste? Shouldn't it be with the whole tomatoes?"

Ordinarily, if we pay attention to a road stretching ahead of us, it's because we plan to drive or walk down it or because we want to find out what's on it. But the tree-lined road in autumn, particularly if it's a scene to which we haven't become habituated—with its extraordinary deep symmetrical perspective of vivid colors in a defined range: red, gold, brown— becomes image, takes on a purely perceptual existence for us. Of course, the self that strives could always come back into action at some point and say, "Maybe I could move here. I wonder what houses go for on this street"; but, to the extent that this kind of concern takes over, the aesthetic response is diminished.

Why are sunsets so aesthetically powerful—to the point that they have become a cliché and yet manage to survive it? Part of the answer needs to be postponed for a short while, but much of it should be clear at this point.

First of all, they don't wear out their perceptual welcome. A sunset passes quickly, and good sunsets don't happen every day, even in the best of climates. Furthermore, when they do happen, they can take quite different forms. So a sunset is nothing to which we can easily become habituated. The daytime sky, on the other hand, barring occasional uncommon and strikingly patterned cloud formations, is with us much longer and is, ordinarily, something to which we are quite habituated. In San Diego, where I live, the sky is mostly blue, with clouds here and there—perhaps a little haze or smog. You don't spend too much time looking directly at it unless you've just come back from some place that's always gray. But the setting sun imposes a new and visually striking coherence on the sky. Not only are the colors vivid and unusual but a new pattern emerges: the entire visible sweep of sky and clouds is organized color-wise around a glowing center on the horizon. The sunset sky is a set of fresh and striking color relationships. In giving our attention to these internal relationships which unite the entire visual scene, we isolate it from the practical context; we temporarily stop using perception for extractive, instrumental purposes.

Why do flowers evoke an aesthetic response more consistently and powerfully than, say, ordinary flowerless plants? At this moment I have in sight a creeping charlie, a sweet-potato plant and a peanut-butter jar with a half-dozen chrysanthemums sticking out of it. All of these look good, but it's easy to see why the flowers have, if not for every individual, than generally at least, a stronger aesthetic potential. I'm tempted at first to say it's because of their colors. But, after all, green is a color too. In fact, couldn't you imagine chrysanthemum blossoms of a rich dark green or a delicate pale green? (They would have to be set off, of course, by contrasting stem and flowers—let's say gray.) Green flowers ought to work very well aesthetically (especially well, considering how unusual they would be). So we don't want to assume that red, yellow, violet, and such are more "aesthetic" than green. What's important about the colors, I think, is simply that they're bright and that they contrast with their leafy surroundings—I think of white gardenias against their glossy dark green leaves.

But we can't consider the color of flowers in isolation. What most distinguishes the chrysanthemum flowers from the two plants I see is their clarity of outline and their complex yet strikingly lucid patterns. The creeping-charlie and sweet-potato plants are more vaguely outlined. Even here, against a white curtain, they are not as clearly framed as the flowers would be in almost any location. If it were day and the two plants were set against a bright open window, they might be visually stronger. Now, however, each plant as a whole is a dark jumble, less coherent, much less clearly patterned than the flowers. Equally important, we are more habituated to plants than to flowers. Flowers, like sunsets, know the art of saying goodbye, of making themselves scarce. Green foliage—in bushes, grass, and trees—is everywhere (especially in a warm but not arid climate like this one). Finally, although both house plants and flowers are "impractical," flowers have the advantage of being, if possible, even more so—more removed from the likelihood of any relationship with our self-concern.

It's interesting to ask oneself which house plants are *most* likely to evoke an aesthetic response. For what it's worth: several persons I've asked (myself included) have voted for some sort of fern. This, of course, fits very well into the overall analysis, since most ferns are more clearly outlined and strikingly patterned than other plants, and also—for the last two hundred million years at least—are not as common.

It might appear that I have been trying to do in houseplants by comparing them to flowers. But this is because the comparison so far has been on a necessarily limited basis. Houseplants (which, of course, may well bear flowers) have special qualities which are not at issue right now. I've avoided considering our *affective* response to flowers and plants—the feelings and associations that may be awakened in us by orange blossoms or a tulip or a room decorated with an abundance of healthy leafy plants. At this point, I've been concerned only with the common *visual* characteristics which we can abstract from the entire set of scenes and objects that are likely to evoke aesthetic perception.

When visual elements call attention to themselves, not as signs that there is ego business to be transacted, but as a coherent, self-contained, fresh, and immediately perceptible pattern—a pattern which corresponds at the moment to no practical purpose—then we have a situation that may encourage aesthetic perception. I say "may encourage" because there is more to it than this. But without this basis, an aesthetic response is not ordinarily to be expected.

Let's look at a situation where the necessary conditions are not so likely to be met. Let's say that I'm standing at the busy intersection of College and El Cajon Boulevards in San Diego. Now ordinarily, I would be on my way somewhere and would not be looking around much at all. But today let's say I'm waiting for a bus. What I see is a visual jumble: cars, buildings, people, signs, street lights, newspaper machines. Whatever visual patterning and coherence the scene has is thoroughly deadened by experience and exists for me only in instrumental terms: the traffic light, for example, is where you look when you want to cross. The painted lines merely identify and limit my path.

The atmospheric light is neutral and familiar. Colors and shapes seem disparate, unrelated, uninteresting. If I attend to this scene at all, it will be on a purely practical basis. I focus in on a Taco Bell, realizing I'm hungry. I get annoyed by the exhaust fumes. I look with sexual interest at a woman walking by.

An aesthetic response here is certainly possible but, in simple statistical terms, less likely than with a number of other scenes. I might respond aesthetically if someone led me to "pick up" on some aspect of the scene, or supplied an effective point of view, if I were new to city life (or even to San Diego), or if I were a visual artist and could somehow discover an image in the scene—or impose one—or even if I were developing a verbal rendering, looking for the imagery, the metaphors that would tie the jumble up in one striking pattern. But, all other things being equal, I'm much more likely to respond aesthetically when I'm driving west on Highway 8 at dusk and see the hills topped with palm trees, which make precise black silhouettes against the darkening sky. A little trite perhaps but effective all the same.

This is no argument for "nature" and against streets and such. The most fearsome and crowded of all intersections I've seen, the giant *ronds-points* of Paris, with their ten lanes of drivers hurtling on and off the breakneck carousel, have, to a tourist at least and from a safe distance, considerable aesthetic potential. Or look down any big boulevard at night when the rain has just stopped and the air is clear. In any case I've no intention of setting up some kind of aesthetic ranking culminating in the scenic views you get on postcards. The question is: what scenes or objects in our visual environment are most likely to evoke an aesthetic response? Setting aside temporarily the question of what is commonly called "content," I suggest that they would be the ones which, to begin with, meet certain basic perceptual criteria. They are visually coherent, with strongly emphasized and immediately perceptible internal relationships. They are often framed in some way. They are not deadened by habit. The overall pattern which they present does not at the time correspond to any instrumental purpose. Under these circumstances, we may see an image which has at the moment only a perceptual existence for us. This image is detached from the world as we normally see it—the world which is an arena for the striving self. And, therefore, we too become detached as we perceive this image. We cease to strive and we just look.

I've done a lot of experimenting with frames. In classes, at times, I've used an "instant art machine," which is merely a piece of cardboard big enough to stand behind, with a portrait-sized rectangular hole cut out and edged in black masking tape. It doesn't give you *Sunday on the Grande Jatte*, you understand, but it does pretty well at producing images. You frame faces in it, full-face or profile. You frame hands, combs, cigarette smoke, kittens, scarves. You introduce an object from each of the four sides in turn and watch the surrounding negative space change its shape. The frame does especially well with faces, de-emphasizing the habitual instrumental context and bringing out visual relationships within the face, and between the face and the surrounding space. You learn to look not through the frame but at it. Try it.

There are other sorts of frames that can be used in similar ways. If you frame a gesture—by calling attention to it, by marking its beginning and end—if you frame a body stretch, for example, then you have a small dance. Oskar Schlemmer, at the Bauhaus in the nineteen-twenties, made dance out of ordinary gestures; he used masks and solid-color costumes, which had a visual impact of their own but which could also be seen as framing devices, separating the gestures from their practical context. There is also the small music that a spun coin makes on a table if you frame it in time as it wobbles and works its way down to a fine silvery vibration. Ordinarily that kind of sound merely means that you've dropped some change. But if you frame the sound by announcing it in some way, and then listen to the full pattern, which is very clearly delineated and fresh and which corresponds to no practical concern, the effect is quite different.

Framing, as I've suggested, plays a double role: it separates what is framed, setting it apart as an object of attention, *and* it reveals pattern, even creates pattern within the frame. It's easy to experiment with this: you make a frame out of your fingers, or, better, cut one out in a sheet of paper, then move it here and there and see what patterns emerge within it.

Having looked among "natural" scenes and objects for qualities that encourage aesthetic perception, we discover, in turning to works of art themselves, these same qualities in abundance. Furthermore, an awareness of these qualities will help us understand the functioning not only of individual works of art but of the various art media as well. Consider, for example, the effect of the musical scale. It definitely doesn't exist within a practical context (unless we're studying music). In the network of relationships woven by our self-concern, there are the sounds of doors slamming and voices saying, "I'd be glad to," but there is ordinarily no C-E-G-C. The scale itself can be seen as a kind of auditory frame, shaping sound, containing it, cutting it loose from the practical context, turning it into image. The scale, moreover, builds into music some very strong, very clear and striking internal relationships, unlike anything you get in naturally occurring sound. In sculpture also, the medium can provide a frame. To see how this frame works, compare a human figure sculpted in wood or stone, metal or clay, with a waxworks sculpture. You may or may not find the wax figure as disagreeable as Coleridge did, but you may still recognize that it has a very limited aesthetic potential. When a figure is sculpted in stone, the stone is a frame which helps us to perceive the human form aesthetically. Lacking such a frame, the wax figure is less likely to appear to us as image. Either, as occasionally happens, we mistake it for a real person, or, as more often happens, we *try* to see it as real, in order to have the pleasure of rubbing shoulders with celebrities or of "being there" at some historical event, or we simply see it as what it is: a more or less accurate, more or less amazing wax copy of a real person. But in any case, barring an extraordinarily artful presentation of the figures, we are not especially likely to perceive them aesthetically, though they may stimulate our imagination and may arouse our admiration or (in Coleridge's case) disgust.

Language is a very interesting medium for us to look at in this regard. As we *ordinarily* use it, language is chock full of pattern that does us no aesthetic good. All this pattern—all these sharply defined and recurring relationships—must be seen as having a basis in the practical needs of self-concern. Language is an instrument if there ever was one. And we're quite deadened to it. We scarcely hear its sounds—just enough to turn them into meaning. And, even with the rich and subtle complex of meanings that language offers us, we tend to understand just enough to satisfy the needs of the striving self.

If you want to hear the *sound* of language, listen to one you don't know. You will have at least one advantage over those who speak it; you'll be able to hear it raw—in a way only small children and foreigners can (not entirely raw, of course, since one hears these foreign sounds through the filter of one's own sound repertoire). How long has it been since you paused, amazed, over the sound of a familiar word? "Mush-room . . . muh—shroom." If you want to avoid instrumentalizing your own language, as far as this is possible, then you must turn to poetry. Here too, we extract meaning from sound, but we're less likely to leave the sound behind as we do so. Poetry, when it's working, makes us much more open to patterns of sound and meaning for their own sake.

Worlds on worlds are rolling ever
　From creation to decay,
　Like the bubbles on a river
　　Sparkling, bursting, borne away.

A poet does for language what the setting sun does for the sky.

But where is the frame here? Is language a frame like the musical scale? Hardly. As I said, language itself is far too practical. But a patterning *and* framing function somewhat comparable to that of the musical scale is to be found in various literary forms. In poetry we find it in rhyme schemes, in the various meters and syllabic structures, in stanza forms, and perhaps above all—in recent centuries as poetry has grown (unfortunately, some would say) more visual than aural— in the short line itself with its enfolding luminous white space. But poets still, thank God, give readings. How interesting to observe them: the immense difference between their intro- ductory comments and the poem itself. See, even with the least stagy of them, how effectively the frame is set, and held, in place.

What frames a novel? Unlike a musical scale, language does not, by the mere fact of its presence, serve to detach a work from its practical context. And the patterning a novel offers, unlike that in painting or even in poetry, may not be immediately apparent as we begin to read it. But what does affect us from the very start is the fictional frame itself. This fictional "as-if"—the storyteller's "once upon a time"—is like the proscenium arch in theatre. But it's not merely out there in the work of art; it's also an expectation that we bring to a literary work. Without this expectation, we may respond in a very different way. The radio listeners who were thrown into a panic by Orson Welles's *Invasion from Mars* had no fictional frame to set between the radio show and their own self-concern. But this kind of misunderstanding isn't common. We are much more likely to do the reverse, "fictionalizing," to some extent, what isn't fiction. A book tends to frame its contents whatever they are. When, on top of this, we have an author using literary techniques such as imagery and sound-patterning (and, more particularly, fictional techniques such as character, dialogue, and descriptive detail, that achieve the vivid presentation of scene) as a way of handling nonfiction material, then we are strongly encouraged not so much to "disbelieve" the book, any more than we "disbelieve" a sunset, as to perceive it aesthetically within this frame that, in one sense, fictionalizes even what we may unhesitatingly accept as nonfiction. Pick up Truman Capote's *In Cold Blood* or Norman Mailer's *Of a Fire on the Moon* or Tom Wolfe's *Electric Kool-Aid Test*—all of which purport at least to be works of nonfiction. In each case, from the very first page, or even from the first few lines, we know we are in the hands of a storyteller and artist; the frame—which we, experienced readers of fiction, cooperate in creating—is set firmly in place. Literature, incidentally, is not the only art in which expectation and belief can play a framing role. What happens to that piece of driftwood that's set on a pedestal in a sculpture exhibit? A certain amount of avant-garde art has involved a redirection of this expectation; thus we have dancers who walk on stage and smoke a cigarette, pianists who sit at the piano and don't play.

None of what I have been describing in this chapter works in an inevitable way. If you're in a very goal-oriented state of mind, neither the novel nor the play, neither the poem nor the sunset may have the power to cut you loose. There may be times when it takes very little to elicit an aesthetic response from you, and other times when *nothing* is able to work on you. Try an art museum when you're famished or have a headache (or, better yet, don't). Some of us, I suspect, may do much better with natural scenes and objects than we do with poems and paintings, simply because we are fortunate enough never to have been tested or graded on our appreciation of mountains and rivers.

Sometimes practical relationships can aesthetically neutralize something that others might appreciate. To me, the hopelessly cluttered desk in my office is a daily rebuke; someone else might see things in it that I never will. On the other hand, I like to stand back and look at the great collage that a magazine stand offers—but I might enjoy it less if I were the one who had to keep the magazines in order.

CHAPTER THREE
(Sensory Pleasure)

As a rule, when we're perceiving aesthetically, colors, shapes, sounds, and so on seem interesting in themselves—more so than during the course of ordinary experience. Is it possible that there is some intrinsic pleasure in these sensations which emerges more fully when self-concern is suspended? There are excellent reasons to think so—excellent reasons to believe that humans, along with other animals, find pleasure in sensation for its own sake. Think, first, about the evidence of subjective experience. Within moderate limits and subject to the diminishing returns of habituation, we like our skin touched, pressed, stroked; we like to feel our muscles working and our bodies moving; we like to rock, turn, swing. We like the sensations of warmth and coolness, even when we don't "need" them, that is, when our body temperature is already at a comfortable level. We take satisfaction in light, in color, in visual variety and movement. We enjoy sound for its own sake: the sound of rain, rivers, wind, fire; of voices, footsteps, busy restaurants, teeth being brushed—even the sound of traffic if it's not too immediate and oppressive. We enjoy smells—not just the "pretty" ones but practically anything different and distinct that isn't positively revolting: hot tar, laundry soap, shoe repair shops, pages in a new book. We like an amazing number of tastes. We even like being aware of our bodily processes, as long as there's no discomfort or anxiety involved: digestion, elimination, blood circulation.

The notion of a pleasure to be found in pure sensation, in the active process of being alive, has always seemed suspiciously attractive—even romantic—to me. And so I've resisted it, dismissing the various cases one by one. Touching, I tell myself, is sexual. Taste has to do with hunger. Enjoyment of a particular smell is either instinctual or learned by association.

And so on. But the subjective evidence covers far too wide a range to be easily argued away. And, alongside it, there has been an accumulation of experimental evidence as well.

According to Donald B. Lindsley, a psychophysiologist, research points to the existence in infants of a "sensory hunger."

> The nature of the activity of the infant suggests that it is partly to satisfy a striving for sensory stimulation. Reduction of sensory stimulation when an infant is wide awake often leads to crying and restlessness, as if he were struggling to attain more stimulation. Restoration of mild and gentle stimulation usually quickly restores the equanimity of the infant.

A British psychologist, John Boddy, recently surveyed the evidence for "stimulus seeking" drives and came to a similar conclusion: "It appears that higher organisms experience a need for patterned stimulation at an optimum level." Boddy speculates that this kind of drive, by exposing us to "a wide range of stimulus patterns," may encourage perceptual learning in humans and may also help neural structures to attain their full development.

Some interesting work in this area has been done with animals. H. J. Campbell discovered that fish would repeatedly give their skins a mild electric tingle by swimming across a light beam that had been set up to trigger the charge. He got similar results with a crocodile:

> Like most of its kind, its life is predominantly sedentary. I have frequently thought it dead when finding it in exactly the same position in the morning as it was the night before. It shows purposeful activity on two occasions only. The first is when my assistant proffers its thrice-weekly feed of lean steak, and the other is when there is a chance of obtaining an electrical fondle.
>
> There are two to three inches of water in its tank and from time to time a set of goal post electrodes is placed in the water at one end of the tank. When this is done, the crocodile lumbers off the stone slab on which it spends many hours basking in the warmth of a lamp. It trundles slowly through the gap between the electrodes, ponderously turns and sets off back again. On good days it will do this some fifty times in fifteen minutes, which is tremendous physical activity for a crocodile, comparable only to the energetic activity of capturing prey.

Subsequently he gave rabbits and monkeys the chance to turn on a bright light. Again the animals seemed to relish sensory stimulation. It took the monkeys three days to learn that touching a probe would turn the light on for a few moments and that they would have to keep touching it to get more light:

> On about the fourth day the monkeys touched the probe some two hundred times in fifteen minutes, and within a week they reached out and grabbed the probe before it could be pushed through the bars. After that they touched the probe at a fairly steady rate of about three hundred to five hundred times during a test session.

Campbell found that the monkeys would behave the same way no matter what the lighting in the laboratory and at any time of day. He also found that when he changed light colors, the monkeys took longer to become satiated with the stimulation. Ordinarily their special interest in turning on the light would disappear within two hours. But when the color of the lamp was changed every fifteen minutes, they would keep on for up to four hours. He also discovered that the monkeys would go out of their way to procure a medium-pitched sound—although they were not as energetic as they had been with the light.

It could be argued that part of the animals' pleasure in these experiments came simply from causing the stimulation to happen, from producing results. And this may, in fact, contribute to the satisfaction involved in such experiments. But the fact remains that laboratory animals will not consistently press bars, touch probes, etc., to produce just any events. Campbell, for example, found that lamps of lower wattage produced considerably less response. The intensity of stimulus appears to be what these animals were after.

If we put this kind of experimental evidence together with our own subjective experience, we're led toward the conclusion that sensation is pleasing for its own sake. Within limits, of course. Every sense seems to have an optimal range. Very faint sounds may be unsatisfying, very loud ones painful. Bright glowing, scintillating colors seem intrinsically more pleasing than flat dull ones, which provide less neural stimulation. We are especially fond of stained glass, gems, fire, fireworks, light shows, teleidoscopes (all of which offer patterns that shift to some extent and therefore resist habituation). But when the stimulation gets too intense, the fun dies down. Walking from darkness into bright sunlight with wide-open pupils is not pleasant.

The phenomenon of satiation helps to explain much of our response to sensory stimulation. There are processes, built into our perceptual apparatus at various levels, that tone down and even eliminate sensation. In vision, for example, the receptors in the retina itself gradually taper off their response to a continued stimulus—and the same sort of thing occurs at higher levels in the brain. The result of all this is, among other things, a diminishing reward from any sustained source of sensory enjoyment. This helps to explain how, on the one hand, we can become temporarily habituated to, even bored with, attractive colors, a pleasant smell, or our favorite record, and, on the other hand, we can feel a sensory delight in a change of weather, an unaccustomed smell, or variety and contrast in color.

Somewhere along the line it will be wise to remind ourselves of the obvious: there's more to sensory plesure than this simple innate tendency to enjoy stimulation for its own sake. Other, more specific drives—such as sex, hunger, and thirst— focus our attention on particular *kinds* of stimulation and do so in a more imperative way. In addition, we pursue some very specific kinds of sensation because we've learned to like them. Haven't you ever become fond of a melody, a scent, or a color combination that you've learned to associate with someone you love?

And in between the more direct sensory goals connected with basic drives and the learned sensory goals that we have acquired by association are some preferences that have an ambiguous status. To consider just one example: what leads us to enjoy the smell of jasmine? Like many other flower scents, it seems to have a special, preferred sensory status. Such scents may well serve to bring on the bees, but on what basis are *we* attracted? Do we have a built-in preference for these fragrances, and, if so, what biological function might that serve? Or is our response at least partly learned? Could it be that a jasmine scent attracts us because of some synesthetic connection with sweetness of taste? (Sweetness in taste itself is less puzzling: in biological terms a built-in preference for sweetness draws us toward high-energy foods—an arrangement which may make less sense in the supermarket than it once did in a natural environment where sweetness and pure caloric energy had not been abstracted from their nutritional setting.)

In opposition to the drives and learned preferences which impose a particular focus on our "sensory hunger" are the innate and learned aversions which, in a given instance, will cancel it out. Most of us, for excellent biological reasons no doubt, will be led to pass up the sensory stimulation of raw sewage, if it is at all possible to do so. And we each have our individual learned aversions as well. I can't stand the sound of certain new words: "funding," "streetwise," "workaholic" (merely to write them makes me shudder).

The point, I hope, has been made. The concept of "sensory hunger" does not fully explain preferences for sensations that are the objects of specific drives or that have been enhanced by association, but it may well account for our pursuit of sensation in general, and our special fondness for sensation which is well defined, intense (but not to the point of discomfort), and fresh (that is, unhabituated).

It could be objected that "sensory hunger" implies a kind of striving (Lindsley, as you may have noticed, uses the word in describing infant behavior), and that it is contradictory to introduce striving into the aesthetic experience, which I've described as a release from striving. But striving is effort toward a satisfaction *which is not yet at hand*. The baby, deprived of adequate sensory stimulation, may well strive. But sensory hunger would find *immediate* satisfaction in the aesthetic experience itself. Clearly, someone could strive in order to be in a position to experience art: walking to a library or a gallery, buying tickets for a concert or a play. The need for aesthetic release, like the need for sensory pleasure, can lead us *toward* the work of art, where, in the presence of immediate satisfaction, striving stops.

Actually, this notion of direct sensory pleasure fits very well into our overall view of aesthetic perception. Consider how much of our satisfaction in sensation is inhibited, even cancelled out by a continual concern with other matters—by our imposing need to take care of business. Stepping out of doors isn't always a delightful sensory bath. Wouldn't *that* be nice? But we have a lot on our minds. General sensory stimulation is not ordinarily our highest priority. Certainly, it's easy to see how a sensory hunger might be useful to the species. It not only exercises and develops our nervous system; it also gets us moving and into active contact with the environment. However, you can expect that this kind of general low-level pursuit will give way in the presence of other needs. Am I going to relish the sound of the voice that insults me? How fully do I appreciate the bright blue, yellow, or red of the cosmeticized yogurt that's being sold these days? Am I satisfied by the smell of a freshly printed memo from the chancellor warning against reckless experimentation in the classroom?

How many of our perceptual moments do we fully enjoy? So often there's too much distraction, too much static. A slight sore throat or perhaps fatigue. The vague awareness of tasks to be done and bills to be paid. Tinges of resentment, sexual stirrings, competitive leanings. Endless scheming, problem solving, fantasies. There's usually something else for us to do besides simply looking around. And yet at times we do just that, and, to some extent, we enjoy it. The question of degree is important here. It could be that, most of the time, the need for sensory stimulation is satisfied at moderate levels in a way that brings us little conscious satisfaction. Perhaps this sensory stimulation is likely to be pleasurable for its own sake only in certain situations: when it takes an unaccustomed form or is particularly intense, or when we have been previously deprived of fresh sensation, *or* when the clamor of self-concern has been temporarily stilled.

In aesthetic experience, the release from self-concern rescues our sensory pleasure, which might otherwise be overwhelmed by the pressure of ego business. I'm not arguing that sensory pleasure is flatly incompatible with self-concern, only that this pleasure is vulnerable to it and is easily preempted (especially in persons who lead high-pressure lives, dominated by goals and deadlines). One of the chief virtues of art is that, by suspending self-concern, it allows our natural appreciation of color, sound, movement, and so on to emerge fully and freely. We appreciate more in music than patterns of notes. We take pleasure in the sound itself: the rich blare of a trumpet, the sudden onslaught of bongos or a tabla waking up the body like a sharp spray. Buildings surround us, are "too much with us," in fact. But a fine architect knows how to rescue our pleasure not only in buildings but in the very color and texture of material: wood, brick, stone, glass, concrete. And, whatever else it may be, a good color movie is always a light show. Generally, of course, sensory pleasure plays only a part in the aesthetic effect. The kind of perception in which little more happens than the liberation of sensory pleasure can, if you like, be seen as the threshold of art. At its bare minimum, let's say, art rescues sensation.

Also, though we may be tempted to view sensory enjoyment as a pervasive, characteristic element in all art, it is clearly more important in some areas than in others. A novel—its imagery notwithstanding—doesn't provide the kind of *direct* sensory pleasure that we get from music, painting, architecture, dancing, and so on (or even from poetry, where we are more likely to be conscious of sound). That sensory pleasure is universal in art is at least open to question. For this reason, I suggest that, while we recognize, parenthetically, the often very important role of this kind of pleasure, we don't insist on it as an essential ingredient in all art.

II
CHAPTER FOUR
A Painted Fear

A flower isn't merely a perceptual event, a pattern of colors and curves, a sensory snack. It happens within us in a way which can't be comprehended in purely visual terms. Each kind of flower has its particular mood, its feeling. There are chrysanthemums and birds of paradise, sunflowers and magnolias, bluebells and roses, poppies, tulips, water lilies . . . each has a character which is not reducible to particulars of color, shape, and pattern. Each resonates within us on its own private frequency, awakens something in us which is unique. In Chapter One we looked at art as perception in the absence of self-concern, and in Chapter Two we considered ways in which this kind of perception may be encouraged by the art object. All of this, however, leaves us still far short of the mark. We've abstracted from aesthetic experience to arrive at a useful but still empty form—like an empty cake pan. But the cake is still missing.

Aesthetic experience is not merely perception. If music draws your attention, you don't just hear it; your feelings are awakened. If a painting interests you—or a flower or a piece of sculpture—you don't simply see it; you *respond* to it.

But art involves our feelings in a special way. Sometimes in ordinary experience it happens that we let our own response color what we're perceiving. For example, we say, "That apartment looks so sad with all the furniture out of it." The sadness is actually our own response but, to some limited extent, we seem to see it in the apartment. In aesthetic perception, however, what is only a tendency on other occasions becomes fully realized. The perception calls forth an immediate response, which may involve recognition, association, feeling, and so on. And this response is *perceived*—or, if you like, seems to be perceived—in the object. A series of musical tones awakens associations with folk dances and calls forth feelings of exuberance and celebration. But I don't experience these associations and feelings as *my* response to *that* series of tones. I simply hear them in the music, and I would unhesitatingly describe it as festive, joyful music. Actually, joy and sadness are human emotions; they reside in me not in any sounds, but they are *referred* into the image, and I hear them there.

There's nothing very strange about this sort of projection. We do it often, in a small way. When you're weary, the world tends to look weary as well. But what happens in art goes beyond this. Typically the perceiver, for some period of time—whether it be a moment or an hour—*disappears* into the image. All gone. No one home. There are, of course, situations, such as that of "critics" and even that of artists themselves, which set up a counterforce to this gravitational pull that the art work exerts. But more of that later on.

There's no denying that to take up the question of emotion in art is to look through not one but two glasses darkly. If "art" is a problem word, so also are "emotion," "feeling," and "affect." There's been endless debate over what these words may represent, and how they are to be distinguished from one another. Some psychologists have even suggested dumping these terms altogether and starting over without them. What does seem clear by now—to me at least—is that the sort of experience we normally refer to as "emotional," or even more generally as "affective," is (a) complex and (b) not neatly separable from "non-affective" experience. Feelings appear to involve many areas of the brain, and often, through the sympathetic nervous system, the whole body as well. And feeling, or emotion, is not isolated from knowing; in fact, the kind of experience that we call "emotional" is in several ways a cognitive experience.

First of all, emotion is *aroused* on the basis of what we know. In order to be afraid of a certain animal, I must not only know that it's there but also believe that it's dangerous. Last year I was out for a walk with my daughter Annika, who was a year and a half old at the time, when two large dogs ran up to us snarling. I might have expected her to be more scared than I was. But she smiled and said her version of "doggie," while her father alone was frightened. Knowing, however, isn't merely a trigger, the stimulus for subsequent emotion. It is an important part of our total emotional response. As I pointed out in Chapter One, there is often an almost stereotyped reaction of which we are aware when afraid, whether of snarling dogs, suspicious noises at night, a belligerent drunk, an alarming bodily symptom, or a roller coaster ride. But our actual emotional response in any particular instance will include and be shaped by our understanding of the entire context, and will certainly be affected by our reflexive attitude toward our own response, regarding its appropriateness, its possible effect on our behavior, and so on.

In addition, the entire affective experience itself can be seen as a way of knowing; that is, the fact that you are having a particular "emotional" experience tells you something about the situation. An important part of what you know about a person, for example, is how that person makes you feel. Finally—and here we approach this issue from the other side—is there any occasion when experience is so purely cognitive that we can say it is totally free of any affective element whatsoever? Or would it be wiser to see experience as a very complex matter, involving *many* components in a balance which is always shifting along not merely one continuum but many, so that a segment of experience can be labeled as "knowing" or "feeling" only at the price of considerable distortion? If this is so, then our response to art would likewise never be one of pure feeling on the one hand or pure thinking or knowing on the other.

An obvious point, maybe, but a useful one just the same. Understanding the complexity of emotional experience, for example, may save us from having to ask ourselves whether aesthetic emotions are "real" emotions or not. Obviously, what we experience during, say, a frightening movie scene has something in common with fear in non-aesthetic situations. Obviously also, something is missing.

Ordinarily, emotions or feelings involve our sense of the self as an ongoing institution *with a claim on the future*. Self-concern, which is simply our responsibility for that institution, faces the future vigilantly, and is continually prodding us to make plans and to form expectations. Now suppose we hear some good news—or some bad news. The news is "good" or "bad" precisely because it speaks to our self-concern in some way. Our "emotional" response to this news will be a complex process of knowing-feeling that *centers on the institution of self,* and is likely to involve some reconsideration of what can be expected in the future.

But what happens in art? We understand the situation in a different way, and so our response takes a different form. What we perceive in art appears as *image,* divorced from the practical context and from any future outside of itself (novels, symphonies, films, and so on have only an *internal* future). There is no self-responsibility involved, nor is there any direct challenge to our plans and expectations—we perceive the image without having to *do* anything about it. In other words, some very important components of ordinary emotional experience are missing. And yet we do feel—but in a way which lacks its usual connection with the ongoing future-binding institution of the self. Caught, by art, within that frame which divorces it from the striving self, our feeling has, in fact, *no home but in the aesthetic image.* And that is precisely where we perceive it. This is why we can truly enjoy tragedy, death-bed scenes, mournful music. I think of Hokusai's famous *Great Wave off Kanagawa,* which depicts a lovely enormous wave curling its tendrils menacingly over a small boat. The painting may or may not arouse stirrings of fear, but if it does, the fear is out there, detached from self-concern. It is a painted fear—and we can contemplate it free of charge: the image of fear but with no personal consequences to threaten our self-concern. Why else would blues music be so well loved? The blues, when you have them, are something to get rid of; they're no fun at all, until you hear them as image—*out there.* (One question that will be taken up in later chapters is exactly how it is that in situations which don't touch our self-concern we can be led to feel at all.)

Ordinarily we're caught up in "the pursuit of happiness"; that is, we pursue only a half of our range of experience and we run from the other half. But how marvelous it can be, how exhilarating, to stop running and to contemplate not only the lights but the shadows as well. What we perceive, for just a while, is our life redeemed: we perceive sorrow and joy alike, in the silence of non-striving. And both of them, for the moment, are satisfying. Satisfying, that is, provided that what is ordinarily threatening to us doesn't break through the aesthetic frame to the point that we begin to experience fear, let us say, or sorrow not in the object or performance but in our own threatened and striving selves.

Someone might balk at this point: "Fine, but what if you're in a good mood and things are going pretty well for you? Why would you need to redeem tragic feelings that you don't even have?" It's an excellent question, *assuming* that, at a time when things are going well, we really are untroubled by the tragic side of life. And some people do operate on this assumption. They try as much as possible to keep looking at the bright side of things, and they have little patience for tragic art of any kind. A. E. Housman let this objection be made in his poem, "Terence, this is stupid stuff." Terence is berated for his mournful poetry:

Pretty friendship 'tis to rhyme
Your friends to death before their time
Moping melancholy mad:
Come, pipe a tune to dance to, lad.

Terence's rebuttal takes up most of the poem. His argument, essentially, is that the sad verse is a way to "train" for bad fortune, a sort of prophylaxis against suffering. And he tells about the king, Mithridates, who more or less immunized himself against certain poisons by regularly taking small but increasing doses of them. The result?

They put arsenic in his meat
And stared aghast to watch him eat;

Terence concludes:

—I tell the tale that I heard told.
Mithridates, he died old.

But I think there's more to say in behalf of tragedy than that it's a preventive medicine against future sorrow. Even in the present and even when things are "going well," it may be that the somber side of life is not so easily put out of mind. The very notion of looking on the bright side implies some awareness of another side from which one chooses to turn away. Even if you lock all your skeletons away in a closet, you can't help passing that closed door, which may in time become more ominous than the old bones themselves.

Really, it's no wonder that tragedy has occupied so high a place, in Western art at least, for so long. If respite from self-concern is the most basic and pervasive source of aesthetic satisfaction, then tragedy, at some risk of course, may offer the most thorough respite and the greatest satisfaction.

Joy, laughter, and simple good humor, it could be argued, don't need to be redeemed, are as satisfying outside of art as in it—more satisfying, in fact, precisely because they're more "real." But these feelings have their own aesthetic claim to make, and are not so ready to be elbowed aside by the haughty muse of tragedy. Adults especially, because they know too much and worry too much, often find it difficult to surrender themselves wholly to joy and laughter. We may think we do—until we look at happy children. Within the privileged frame of art, however, we can indulge in this kind of experience more freely. There's still more that can be said in behalf of at least some upbeat art. The joy of small children tends to be exclusive; it is a joy which, locked in the present moment, simply doesn't know about unhappiness. Older children and adults also can experience this, but more and more we lose the ability to live one moment at a time. We become familiar with another sort of joy, one which is nagged at by insecurity and doubt; this joy *wants* to be exclusive, but can't quite manage it. But there is a third joy which has given up exclusivity, which to some extent comprehends other, darker feelings. This is something that we find especially in certain works of art where joy has in some way encountered the opposing aspect of things, where the good humor that the work arouses in us is more likely to have conquered, transcended, or even included "negative" experience than to be merely exclusive and unaware. Like most people, I expect comedy to offer good humor, laughter, and a happy ending, but I also know that my own favorite comedies—such as Molière's *Misanthrope* and Schnitzler's *Reigen* (*La Ronde*)—are those that sail fairly close to the wind.

Such comedies are complex and can evoke a response which is also complex. It's been convenient, up to now, to talk of clear-cut and simple feelings: joy and sorrow. But we need to recognize how subtle and many-faceted our response to art—this knowing-thinking-feeling response—can be. In this connection, I remember seeing, in 1972 I think, James Cunningham's bizarre and satirical version of *Swan Lake*. The details are hazy now. I remember that Prince Siegfried had, instead of a crossbow, one of those toy guns that shoot sparks. The evil Baron von Rothbart was wearing nothing but a posing strap and a cape. At one point Siegfried and the Swan Queen sat down and spoke with each other, very much like dancers on a break between rehearsals, talking about their personal hassles. What was my response to all this? Nothing, I assure you, that can be described in simple terms. There was, as a personal setting for the experience, the residue in me of a great many performances of *Swan Lake*; there was a complex tangle of attitudes, at various levels of consciousness, not only toward *Swan Lake* and its particular brand of romanticism but also toward classical ballet in general and toward romanticism in general. There was my longstanding awareness of the incongruity between ballet dancers on stage, who are like a race of gods, and the scrawny sweat-drenched mortals you see in class. There was a sense also of the incongruity between cultural and aesthetic ideals of the late nineteenth century and those of the late twentieth century. Imagine! *Swan Lake*, this incredible tableau: Siegfried, all aristocratic elegance and virility, encountering his true love, all regal grace and melting, quivering femininity—then their dark nemesis bursting on the scene, a melodrama villain. This incredible tableau surviving— more than surviving—into the age of Woodstock and *Ms.*, Grand Union and Andy Warhol. In its way Cunningham's dance harvested *all* of this. The experience was funny; it was deep; it was liberating; it was shot through with dissonance, conflicting feelings of aspiration and resentment, belief and suspicion. It was very personal. And yet, personal as it was, I didn't experience this response as anything separate from the dance. I saw it in the dance.

But complexity, though it may have been particularly apparent in my response to Cunningham's piece, is hardly limited to this kind of sophisticated parody. Consider your aesthetic response to any work of art—any painting, let's say. How much there is that feeds into this response. How delicate, variegated and changeable it is. For this very reason, the words you find to describe it may be few and fumbling. To describe, even partially, what happens in aesthetic experience is an "art" in itself.

What I've tried to establish in this chapter are a few very general points about our aesthetic response: (a) it is both cognitive and affective; (b) it has some similarity to the way we respond in ordinary experience, but differs in being free of self-responsibility; (c) it tends to be perceived in the aesthetic image; (d) it can be satisfying whether it involves "positive" or "negative" feelings; (e) it tends to be subtle and complex.

Now let's take a closer look.

CHAPTER FIVE
Resonance

A red traffic light means "stop," and that's that. Almost always. On a few occasions, however, I've found myself looking more closely, more intently, if only for a few seconds, at this red light that is holding me up. What I've experienced on these occasions is more than mere sensory stimulation. Still, it wouldn't be true to say that the red light sends me off on any train of thought; I remain right there in the visual image itself. It's the color that draws me in—rich and glowing but, more than that, with a kind of depth, with a special quality of feeling, almost as if it were alive. Ordinarily this red circle would be a very modest element in my visual field. But on these occasions, as I look, there seems to be so much in it; I sense something vast—a whole mode of life—and yet concentrated purely in this color: something dynamic, unnameable and utterly beautiful.

I've chosen to examine this kind of experience not because it's unusual, but because it happens to all of us at times and because it illustrates, in very simple and pure form, a kind of response that has considerable aesthetic importance. Each of us will find a ready example. Not a red light, perhaps, but a piece of cloth or wood, a glimmer of light on water, a splash of color somewhere, a sound or a smell. You're out walking at dusk. A lighted bus passes you with people on their way home. As you look, this everyday moment—and with it life itself—seems extraordinarily vivid, precious, abundant. Something has drawn you in, and seems, for that moment, emphatically rich and alive. In such experiences there is, I think, a key to understanding how we respond to works of art.

In the case of the red light, what seems to happen is that the color, rather than merely becoming attached in my mind to any *particular* meaning or memory, is free to resonate through a whole tract of past experience, a whole range of contexts in which I've experienced a similar kind of color. It's not that the red light reminds me specifically of cherries, say, or of a bright red soft drink I loved when I was little, or of imitation rubies or stained glass, or even of other traffic lights, but rather that some experiential quality—affective certainly but cognitive as well—arising from *many* contexts is evoked by this color and is what I perceive in it. The red light is like a sound that echoes back from countless unnamed experiences, the combined echoes giving it a rich complexity and a quality of profound involvement in life. This kind of experience—which I will call "resonance"—lives only in the image itself and dies with it. It can never be reduced to a particular significance which could then be stated conceptually; on the contrary, this resonance stands in contrast to recognition, which is a way of processing a perception by pinning it down to a concept, a particular identity.

Resonance and recognition: two ways of responding to what we perceive. Recognition, of course, has its own crucial role to play in art—in, at least, a great many works of art. In art as in ordinary experience, recognition involves perceiving something, translating it into a concept or identity, and responding accordingly. I look at a painting of a house standing in an open field. What my optical apparatus passes on are colors, shapes, edges, and so on. Recognition translates these into "house": a concept that has been abstracted from and imposed on my remembered experience. And this concept, "house," conditions, contains, and organizes my perception. I see the house as a house, not as a white and red hole in the sky, not as an explosion on the field. Recognition is a matter of reading signs. The colors, the arrangement of windows, etc., can change, but a certain constellation of signs will always give me "house." Should these signs themselves be somewhat altered, I may get "shed" or "castle." But if I'm to recognize, something has to be defined: my perception has to be pinned down with a concept, a specific identity. Ordinarily we can name what we recognize, and even when there is no name, we can easily attach one that will serve ("the guy with the stooped shoulders," "the plant with the fuzzy leaves"). This name, this identity enables us to detach the recognition from the perception, to keep the concept and let the percept go. That's why recognition is static, not dynamic; when you have it, you have it and that's that.

Resonance, on the other hand, does *not* involve pinning a perception down. On the contrary, it has the irreducibility of living things; it's characterized by fluidity and even by an amazing elusiveness when we try to capture it conceptually. When we experience resonance in its simplest form, as with the stoplight, what we're aware of is a sort of tone, a depth, which we perceive in the object and which is fluid, shifting, dynamic—growing stronger or weaker, altering as the object changes or as our attention grows or fades or changes its focus, *or* as various areas of experience within us begin to resonate more strongly or to fade away.

I see resonance as an essentially aesthetic kind of response because it doesn't seem to happen—at least not intensely—when self-concern is on duty. It happens in free time. I find myself momentarily free to play with the stoplight, or rather to let *it* play inside my head. Somewhere within, no doubt, I recognize the light as a traffic signal, and will be ready to start up again when it goes off. But for the moment that's of little importance. The glowing circle of red glass resonates within me: here, there, wherever the experiential context is properly shaped to receive it. Who knows through what depths it resonates, what bypaths of analogy and association it follows—what taste of spicy red candy sucked thin and glowing against the light; what signs of vitality and excitement—red light says *ON*—in cars, stoves, stereos, recording studios, grandparents' old radio; what fervor of devotion in cathedral windows, shining blood of Christ, robes and jewels that grace Van Eyck madonnas. But on no *single* experience, on no single type of experience, does the red light come to rest, unless I actually force it to do so. What is it then that I sense? What am I conscious of? The color itself, but saturated with feeling and with something which, if it is too unformed to be called "meaning," is nevertheless an awareness that goes beyond mere affect. The more purposefully I pursue this resonance, the more likely it is to weaken, whereas if I let the color take over, looking becomes contemplation, my breathing slows, the image remains alive, mobile, emergent.

Apparently we can re-experience some of the quality of an experience without remembering the experience itself. We get the juice without the orange. And when a number of related experiences are evoked, we get a quality which draws from all of them, but not as an abstraction—nothing dull or static—a quality, rather, which hovers over this shifting aggregate of experience, gathering more strength now from one area, now from another. If one particular past experience is activated, we get memory. If a concept is activated, we get recognition. But when, in an aesthetic situation, experience humbly and anonymously contributes its quality to perception, we get resonance. Though the experience that contributes to resonance is not consciously remembered, we may well be able to bring some of it to light if we have reason to try. Some of this experience, however, may not be so easily recoverable—because it's buried far in the past or because it is, for one reason or another, locked up in the unconscious.

I'm sure that some of what we sense on these occasions may come from the intrinsic quality of, say, a color itself. Sensory stimulation and the satisfaction it brings can be an important part of the experience, particularly if we're looking at vivid glowing color. And, beyond that, who can say that the wavelength, the intensity, the precise texture of a color don't have an evocative power of their own, entirely independent of remembered experience? Are there direct connections between color or shape or sound on the one hand and feeling on the other? Are some responses of this type built in, fulfilling some adaptive function? Perhaps. But even so, this would be only a base on which experience then begins to build. A lifetime of experience prepares the way for our resonant response. A pure bright yellow may feel sunny and exuberant. A warm dusky gold has connections not only with the metal, gold, and other precious objects, but also with autumn and with late-afternoon sunlight—and therefore with feelings that can be rich, mellow, and slightly melancholy all together. And, obviously, because resonance derives from our experience as individuals, a given color may resonate quite differently in two persons who have grown up in very different locales: one, perhaps, in a land of pastel springs, russet autumns, white winters, and summers with long golden afternoons—the other amidst blue sea and sky, brilliant flowers, green cascades of foliage all year round. And what of a third person who has grown up with the cement and asphalt grays of a big city and for whom the brightest colors are those to be found in stores and on posters? Culture is as important as geography here: the sound of a koto has an "exotic" quality to me, whereas to a Japanese it might sound merely "old-fashioned."

I've said that resonance, unlike recognition, can't simply be named or abstracted from the perception. We can talk about it, of course. We can approach it. But the words we find may well seem like clumsy and lifeless fragments that do more to betray than convey the experience itself. If we want to give some sense of the area that resonates, we can pile up associations in a list as I have done, hoping with these clues to put the reader or listener in touch with resonant feelings that may be at least somewhat similar. In fact, if we want to communicate resonance, what we need to do is not to try to name a resonant experience but to make it happen, to recreate it. And for this, language as it is ordinarily used won't help us. Only when it becomes an aesthetic medium can language begin to evoke resonance.

To understand how language can do this, we have to look more carefully at the relationship between resonance and recognition—since language, whatever resonance it may on occasion evoke, is obviously, as language, rooted in the act of recognition.

Let's begin by observing that something which we recognize can also, at the same time, evoke a resonant response. I recognize the red circle as a traffic signal but, on this occasion, that recognition doesn't dominate my response as it might if I were eager to get through the traffic as quickly as possible. It's unlikely that I would ever be so absorbed as to miss the functional meaning of a traffic signal, though like others I have had moments when I was resonating so fully to the *sound* of a person's speech that I momentarily lost its meaning. More often, the very opposite happens: recognition occupies our attention so fully and exclusively that any possible resonance is forestalled. In ordinary life, recognition is always moving to adjourn perception, always ready to pass on to something else: "OK, it's a tree. That's that. Next, please!" But this doesn't have to happen; we can respond resonantly either to an abstract painting *or* to a portrait, provided that we can do without recognition in the first case, and that we don't, in the second, let it close us off to the painting in front of us.

The importance of recognition varies from one art to another. Even in the nonrepresentational arts, we may recognize red as red, cement as cement, a violin as a violin, a rondo as a rondo, and so on. Still, what we expect in the way of recognition depends on the kind of art we're perceiving. With theatre we expect to recognize something other than what's actually there in front of us. This is true even of absurdist theatre: the character on stage may be frying Band-Aids in butter but we still see a *character*. Paint can just sit there and be what it is, but actors act. Question: what would theatre be without this recognition of something which is "represented?" There are names for it: "performance art," "happening," etc. When it comes to the art of mime, our need to recognize is even more imposing. There's plenty of room for ambiguity in theatre, but we want mime to be lucid. Lucidity is built into mime technique. Otherwise what would mime be—if it weren't obliged to represent anything? Dance. But one could easily argue (I would be glad to) that mime *is*, also, dance, that theatre *is*, also, performance art. All art is abstract art.

Recognition, then, is important, to varying degrees, in the arts. Often it serves as a basis for resonance. I began this chapter with a very simple illustration: a glowing circle of color. But resonance is not always evoked directly by perceived color, sound, and so on. Resonance itself can rest, entirely or partly, on recognition. My resonant response to a still life, for example, isn't based solely on color and shape; my recognition that the colors represent apples and pears plays an essential role. Recognition enables us to create a representational image, which is an interpretation of the perceptual image. And this representational image has its own possibilities for resonance, which go beyond color, shape, texture, and so on. A face, a landscape, an interior can take on that depth and intensity, can give us the sense that we are seeing something alive, inexhaustible, and unnameable. Recognition turns paint into trees, fields, farmhouses: a detailed landscape. Then it stands discreetly aside and allows this landscape, this painted image, to resonate in us, to take on vastly complex experiential quality which alters its balance from one moment to the next, which cannot itself be recognized, which is not to be pinned down with anything so static and lifeless as a name or a statement of its "meaning."

When we turn to literature, we're struck by an immediate difference. In a painting, whether it's representational or not, there are always colors and shapes that we may be able to resonate to directly without any intermediate recognition. But when we get to printed words, *everything* that happens has to be built on a base of recognition. That is, I just about never have a resonant response to these little black squiggles on the page—there would have to be some very fresh and striking typography involved, that's for sure. What I do with print, literary or otherwise, is simply recognize the squiggles and translate them into words. And, at this point, we find ourselves actually moving away from perception—at least in the ordinary sense of the term. The squiggles are there, but they're of no particular interest, aside from my translation of them. Perhaps, in a way, I hear the words—I seem to hear the ghost of their sound—but there's certainly no sound coming from the printed page. Essentially my perception has been translated: into patterns of meaning and ghosts of sound. What is there at this stage to resonate to? Read this sentence—is it resonant? Not too likely. But now, at this very point—out of these words, which have led us away from perception, and with the help of these ghosts of sound—it's possible to build: an image. And this image may, if the words are right and if we're receptive, turn out to be dynamic, untranslatable—and resonant.

Look at the squiggles that follow this colon: "eyes". Between the quotation marks you recognize an English word. It names a concept which can be abstracted from the marks on paper and which you can, more or less, define. If I make it "their eyes," we still have recognition without much in the way of an image: no more than a brief sound pattern and an imprecise fragment of meaning. But suppose it is:

Their eyes mid many wrinkles, their eyes,
Their ancient, glittering eyes, are gay.

That's another story. Now we have an image. And should we respond aesthetically, as well we may, this image, created by recognizable English words, becomes something which is not itself to be recognized, nor to be traded in for a concept, but is, rather, to be contemplated, as it resonates through various tracts of our experience and gains depth from them. And, needless to say, if we put Yeats's two lines back into their context at the end of his poem, "Lapis Lazuli," the resonance will be much richer still, more intense, more complex.

Granted that recognition can take the life out of things we perceive—

"Daddy, look at *that!*"

"Oh, it's just a bug."

—and reduce them to useful, hard-edged concepts. But it can also work the other way around. The recognition of signs, such as the letters of the alphabet combined into words, can lead to the creation of a vivid image, which we experience as being much more alive than the signs themselves. "Image," of course, doesn't *necessarily* imply resonance. The language, as we ordinarily use it, is full of images. If someone says to me, with annoyance, "I was waiting on that corner for an hour!" I may well get some sort of image, but very likely without resonance. I simply recognize this image in terms of its significance for me.

"Image," we should be aware, has many meanings. We can talk about images at every level of perception, and even beyond perception: from entirely "out there" to entirely "in here." What's on the movie screen or in the mirror is an "image," but so also is something that I've concocted in my head, without any perceptual stimulus at all. There is a series of possibilities involved. Image can refer to a visual likeness out there in the environment. It can refer to a more or less uninterpreted sensory pattern that comes from our eyes (or other sense organs) through special sensory processing centers into the brain. This would be an image without recognition (though, actually, what the sense organs themselves perceive and pass on is *affected* by what happens "higher up"). But the word can also refer to something that has been interpreted by recognition: not merely the pattern but, let's say, the landscape with its trees and farmhouses. Then there's the image which our brain concocts in response to perceptual signs of a wholly different nature: letters on a page. "Glittering eyes"—here we have an image which is not really perceived in the sense that the previous types are. And yet, in another sense, it *is* perceived; we do experience poems, novels, and such as "out there."

Now with images, at more than one level of perception, we have options. We can simply recognize them (or extract their significance—something which is akin to recognition but at a higher level). Or we can respond resonantly. Or we can do both, provided that the recognition doesn't lead us away from the image itself. On the lower level, our recognition can help to create an image at a higher level: colors become trees; squiggles become glittering eyes. And at this higher level, we again have the same options. When we're talking about an image based on recognition, it may not always make sense to speak of "recognizing" it, since that work has been done. But what we can do at that point is, as I've said, akin to recognition. Confronted with the landscape or the "glittering eyes," we can attempt to extract significance from them. To the extent that this attempt lets us stay right in the image, it's compatible with a resonant response. But to the extent that it takes us *out* of the image into a purely conceptual, nameable significance, it is absolutely incompatible with resonance. Instead of merely talking *about* the landscape, I try to "name" it, to translate it into a concept, to recognize what it "represents": "This painting represents the essential violence [or "tranquillity" or "indifference"] of Nature." There, I've pinned it down like a butterfly. But how diminished it becomes, how static, how lifeless. To repeat: we can talk *about* the painting—productively and endlessly. Through this talk we may well succeed in seeing it more clearly and opening ourselves up to it more fully. But when we try to convert the painting into a concept, it dies. I see this happen all the time in school-damaged persons, who try so doggedly to turn literature into pure significance that they lose the resonance—and, instead of hugging this lively and beautiful creature, they're left with their arms around a skeleton. No wonder they don't want to read it.

This isn't the place, however, to get into that (see Chapter Fourteen). Nor is it the place to explore at any length the ways in which literature evokes resonance. But we can at least take a brief look at a few of the resources literature has in this area.

Metaphorical images in literature operate in a way that is particularly favorable to resonance. They do much more than name something; by overlapping two terms, they give us an image of experience that has depth, reality, and a kind of fecundity. In a good literary metaphor this overlapping defines an area of experience so rich, so subtle and complex that no amount of non-metaphorical descriptive detail could ever evoke, even if it filled paragraph after paragraph, what the metaphor can evoke in relatively few words. Look at the metaphor which opens Sylvia Plath's famous poem, "Daddy":

> You do not, you do not do
> Any more, black shoe
> In which I have lived like a foot
> For thirty years, poor and white,

What listing of qualities, what attempt to *name* the experience could illuminate the particular range of thought and feeling that this metaphor does?

In one of Spenser's sonnets, the speaker tells us what it's like to go through the ups and downs of love while the woman he loves remains unmoved.

> Of this worlds theatre in which we stay,
> My love, lyke the spectator, ydly sits

He's the actor, going through all the comic and tragic roles; she's the audience, who not only fails to respond sympathetically but actually mocks him:

> Sometimes I joy, when glad occasion fits,
> And mask in myrth lyke to a comedy:
> Soone after, when my joy to sorrow flits,
> I waile, and make my woes a tragedy.
> Yet she, beholding me with constant eye,
> Delights not in my merth, nor rues my smart:
> But when I laugh, she mocks, and when I cry,
> She laughes . . .

A metaphor like this (I include similes, which function in a comparable way) takes two kinds of experience and, by bringing them together, reveals the area that they have in common. It's as though we took two circles and, by overlapping them, made the overlapping area light up (admittedly an oversimplified view, since the two terms can affect each other in a way that goes beyond the notion of "overlap"). And this experiential area which is so suddenly illuminated may well have the kind of plenitude and depth that we have found in resonance. In Spenser's poem love and theatre are overlapped—a very effective metaphor as he uses it. It carries feeling—including that awful feeling of playing to an unresponsive or even hostile audience. It establishes in a vivid way the relationship of the two persons involved: he, on stage, has to knock himself out trying to move her, while she, in the audience, is free to do no more than observe coolly; he's active while she sits idly; she judges while he is judged; he runs the emotional gamut while she retains a "constant eye." This metaphor uses theatre to reveal the overwhelming need of the lover-as-actor to awaken a sympathetic response, as he continues to confront the maddening refusal of the beloved. But more than that, there is within Spenser's metaphor an insight into the essential nature of romantic love—an insight we all catch a glimpse of when we're in love but generally turn our backs on: to be "in love" is to be trapped in theatre, that is to say, in a dramatic, emotional illusion: Stendhal's "crystallization." The lover here is forced to act out the full romantic repertoire. She, romantically uninvolved (at least as he sees her), is free of the illusion and therefore makes a terrible audience—responding so inappropriately that you know she's seeing not the various roles, but the poor naked actor behind them. To see the character rather than the actor, she herself would have to be caught in the illusion, would have to share his script. There is then in the very metaphor a substratum of cold self-knowledge that can be glimpsed beneath the histrionic "lover's complaint."

But we could go on. Good literary metaphors, because they yield, not a concept which is abstracted from experience, but a live portion of experience itself, seem inexhaustible—even when they focus on a quite specific and limited area. Lorca's gypsy making love to a woman by the river at night:

> Her thighs slipped away from me
> like startled fish,
> half full of fire,
> half full of cold.

The "startled fish" are more than a way of establishing a certain visual and tactile image. Nor are they merely to be seen as a "sexual symbol." They bring with them from the river their aqueous environment, which is superimposed on the scene, setting the lovers in a medium which is fluid, dreamlike, and entirely apart.

We should notice also that the overlapping area which a metaphor delineates is not simply revealed for its own sake, but is used to deepen the image of what is being described: the sexual experience in Lorca's poem, unrequited love in Spenser's sonnet, the speaker's relationship with her father in "Daddy."

Metaphors are not automatically resonant (nothing is, for that matter). Some metaphors have mainly a conceptual import; others are too stale to be very evocative. Universities are often, for example, described as factories. And with good reason. But the metaphor by now isn't fresh enough to encourage resonance; its main value is conceptual. And there's something else missing. We resonate not to metaphors but to metaphorical *images*. Resonance needs an image to project into. I'm sure some talented writer could take the factory metaphor, brush it off, intensify its experiential quality, bolster it with a powerful and appropriate sound pattern, and do the job very nicely.

It's no accident that metaphors occupy such a privileged place in literature and that literary theorists as dissimilar as Aristotle and Proust think so highly of them. At their best they force us off the path of mere recognition into the unconceptualized thickets of experience. (That was a conceptual rather than a resonant metaphor.) Tom Wolfe describes a girl with "lips as raunchy as a swig of grape soda." What would you say is the overlapping area here? I don't know. I don't want to know. But it's one of my favorite metaphors.

I've pointed out that resonance is not easy to talk about, that it certainly can't be named, and that what we say about it may seem clumsy and lifeless. Metaphor, I think, is one of the least futile ways of trying to convey a resonant experience (actually, resonance can't be "conveyed," but one can hope to awaken analogous areas of experiential quality). We can assume that many literary metaphors were born in an attempt to evoke some of the resonance in a particular moment of perception that the writer experienced.

It is a beauteous evening, calm and free,
The holy time is quiet as a Nun
Breathless with adoration . . .

Still, metaphorical images are not the only kind with resonant potential. Evocative non-metaphorical language can work
very well. Here is Robert Bly's "Driving to Town Late to Mail a
Letter":

It is a cold and snowy night. The main street is deserted.
The only things moving are swirls of snow.
As I lift the mailbox door, I feel its cold iron.
There is a privacy I love in this snowy night.
Driving around, I will waste more time.

Look at the first two lines: the selection of detail is crucial. Just
as an artist sketching a horse can give us an astonishingly
vivid image of it with just a few well-placed lines, so a few
careful details can create a powerful literary image which
gathers around them, expansive and full-blown. The trick is to
find the details, the words which, in combination, will have
maximum leverage, which will raise up many times their own
weight in experiential quality. Ultimately it is not words that
the poet is working with; in an important sense, the medium
of all art is the brain—and beyond that the body—of the
perceiver.

I can, in drawing, give you a fairly detailed rendering of the
horse, if I so choose, without forestalling the possibility of a
resonant response. Dürer's horses are like this. But drawing is
a spatial art—a drawing makes itself available to you more or
less all at one time. Literature is a temporal art. If a literary
horse were rendered with Dürer's wealth of detail, you'd
forget what the head was like before you got halfway to the
tail. A whole novel can unfold at leisure over hours or even
days. But a vivid, evocative literary image has to have that
spatial all-at-once quality even though its elements are presented one at a time. This makes sequence an extremely
important variable that the writer manipulates. And this is one
reason why the literary image demands details that are few
and artfully chosen. But there is another reason. We see the
image directly in the drawing. There is not the same directness
in literature: here we see the little squiggles on the page; we

translate these into words with their accompanying sound-ghosts, and these in turn get translated into a mental image which is very different from the squiggles that are actually being perceived. What this means is that the writer needs the reader's cooperation in image-building in a way no other artist does. The writer, therefore, mustn't try to do all the work. Our imagination needs just the right amount of stimulation to set it in motion in the right direction. Too many details are deadening.

Excess language, then, is obviously damaging in literary imagery. It dilutes the evocative power; it works against a "simultaneous," "spatialized" presentation by dragging out the sequence; it stultifies the imagination. Not only that, useless language won't carry resonance, which needs to be perceived *in* the words (just as my response to the stoplight was something I saw *in* the light). And because these useless words won't carry resonance, they reduce the coherence of the image, which therefore tends to break up, leaving us with little more than the words themselves. Bly's poem may have a deceptively "prosy" look, but I think it's actually very tight and evocative. Shall we ruin the first two lines to make a point?

It's a very cold night and there's a lot of snow.
No cars are on the main street.
There's no one to be seen.
There's nothing at all moving but the swirls of snow.

Some images which are not metaphorical or which depend only slightly on metaphor have great resonant potential because of their *centrality*. I don't mean the kind of centrality you find in general statements like "You can't win 'em all" — statements that have conceptual validity in a great variety of situations. I mean the centrality of an image which (a) utterly evades conceptual translation, (b) is highly specific, and (c) though specific, maintains contact with a substantial range of experience, but without being tied to any *particular* kind of experience other than the one it depicts.

In the morning dew
Dirty, but fresh,
The muddy melon.

If we read or listen to these lines attentively, we're likely to construct a mental image of this muddy melon in the morning dew. And nothing else. This is no allegory, no coded message. But the image that we get may well be deepened by a resonant response that owes some of its quality to other kinds of experience. Some images seem to be in touch with, to draw from, a greater circle of experience than others do. They are concentrated. They seem larger than themselves. I asked some neighbors, individually, to read these lines. "Do you get an image from them?" I asked. Each did. "Do you get some kind of feeling from that image?" Yes again. Then I asked each if there were any situations, any experiences that might give a comparable feeling. The range of response is interesting.

> When you're dirty and about to bathe. You can even dig being dirty for a while. Also there's an awe that I feel in my own back yard.

> A just-born infant, all goopy and fresh . . . Also, hearing unmanicured folk music from an old woman on her front porch.

> I get smells—things I smell waking up in the early morning: could be trash that needs to be taken out, or flowers. Also, back in Germany in an open-air market in the early morning, with all the fruit and vegetables spread out. And now I remember digging up potatoes when I was little; I get a young feeling. That's what I get mostly: smells and a young feeling.

> Your well-known mean old man with a kindly heart.

> Swimming in Mission Bay. It's dirty but refreshing.

> A feeling of dawn—the taste of tomatoes when you pick them right off the vine.

> The way you feel after sex . . .

> Could be a dog coming in, in the morning, from outside, wet and dirty but refreshed. And I think of wet laundry that's fallen off the line; it's gotten a little dirty, but it's clean.

These would hardly be adequate as "interpretations," but that's not what they are. None of these people *began* by associating anything else to the melon image. It was only when I asked them to explore their own responses that the other experiences came forth. To be accurate, we should say that it's not the image which has centrality so much as the response that it evokes.

Creating this sort of image is a matter of marksmanship and enormous sensitivity. If you miss ever so slightly in one direction, you may have a fine image but one with a very limited range. If you miss in the other direction, the image may have a deadening explicitness. But when you hit the nub, everything vibrates. It is, I believe, a great mistake to call such images "symbols" and then try to pin down just what they "symbolize." Symbols abound in literature, of course, but there is also an abundance of excellent writing that offers us, in place of symbol, this extraordinary marksmanship. And how pointless it is to look for the "real" meaning of such images. Here's another of Bashō's haiku:

> The rains of May
> gathering, swift
> river Mogami

Someone might argue that the river *is* time rushing things off to eternity (or to oblivion). Someone else might insist that the rains are sorrows drawn in to feed the torrent of creativity or growth. Still a third person could see this river as the universal process, within which what is apparently individual loses its separate identity. A fourth person, however, might insist on a more specifically social (albeit anachronistic) meaning: the transmutation of individuals—who are no more than raindrops—into the onrushing and irresistible force of a revolutionary class. It's fun doing these. And perhaps what I'm trying to say is that although certain literary images—in allegory, for example—demand to be decoded, highly resonant images like this one of Bashō's are another matter: here a little interpretation is a dangerous thing. If we choose to do that at all, better to play with it, better to multiply the interpretations, denying a privileged status to any one of them. These parallels may be interesting, but I much prefer the sensuous concreteness of the river Mogami image itself, immeasurably deepened by the resonance that its centrality contributes. We can manage without the parallels; they're just commentary at best. The image is art (assuming that we come to it attentive, wide open, and still).

Literary images have still other resources to draw on that help to evoke a resonant response. And, let's emphasize again, the reader or listener is not to be discounted. It might be possible for someone to respond resonantly to the stalest everyday image, just as someone might remain unaffected by the best of poets. But as far as the writing itself is concerned, whatever contributes to the freshness, the coherence, the evocative intensity of an image makes resonance more likely. In some images, sound patterns play a crucial role. Images that depend heavily on metaphor, selection of detail, and centrality can be translated from one language to another without being utterly destroyed. But images that depend heavily on sound translate only when there is a lucky correspondence between the two languages. Otherwise . . . Here are a few lines by Verlaine, which have great evocative power in French:

> Dans l'interminable
> Ennui de la plaine
> La neige incertaine
> Luit comme du sable.

But to substitute:

> In the unending
> Tedium of the plain
> The shifting snow
> Shines like sand.

just doesn't make it. And there's no point blaming the translator; it's an insurmountable problem. In the French, the rhymes are important; also there's a nice chiastic—or crossed—sound pattern framing the stanza: *able* enn*ui* . . . l*uit* comme du s*able*. Repeated nasals, echoing rhythms, the assonance-rhyme combination of *plaine-neige-incertaine*: all these produce a sort of drone that rises up from the first three lines and that contributes enormously to the power of the image. To try for comparable sound effects, while keeping the plain, snow, etc., seems to be asking more of English than it can deliver. And—to reverse directions—I for one would hate to have to translate these lines by Gerard Manley Hopkins into French:

> And all is seared with trade; bleared, smeared with toil;
> And wears man's smudge and shares man's smell.

How do patterns of sound help to evoke resonance? This is a question that can be more easily answered after we have (in Chapter Eight) considered music and the way it affects us.

I've offered literature, representational painting, theatre, and so on, as examples of art forms where resonance can be mediated by recognition. I should add "natural" aesthetic experience to this list. I can resonate more or less directly to a color or a gleam of light. But I also resonate to what is recognized: a bird's shadow flying over the grass—swaying branches and rippling leaves—the green swing, leaf-shadowed and almost still. With the aid of recognition I construct, out of colored shapes, a representational image—just as I would do with a painting. And this image itself, as long as it resonates, is not in turn to be recognized or converted to significance. I stay with it. I let it come into me to forage and return—return neither with concepts nor memories but with some of the very substance of my life, saturated with feeling, individual yet unnameable and unbounded, out there for my contemplation and beautiful beyond words.

Beautiful no doubt. But anything more? Is there any *knowledge* in this resonant perception of the world around us—or in our response to one of Bashō's haiku? I raise this question because resonance often seems, at least, to carry with it a sense of heightened truth, of accentuated reality—a sense that one is not merely perceiving something out there but really knowing it. The person who responds in this way appears to be totally absorbed in the object; this would support the claim that a very special, unclouded kind of knowing is involved. And yet, on the other hand, the enormous subjectivity of resonance is obvious, should by now be more than obvious. The resonance is an elixir prepared out of my own individual experience. What is it then that I'm knowing so well? The swing (and the river Mogami)? Or just myself?

The answer, I think, has to be: both. My resonant response is a way of knowing something out there in the context of my own experience, my own body. Now that way of viewing knowledge, these days, as the twentieth century draws to a close, is hardly news; someone could point out that *all* knowing—

even the most rigorously scientific investigation of an object—
is ultimately just that: knowing something out there within the
context of our own bodies, our own experience. But scientific
knowledge is characterized by its narrowness, its exclusivity,
its sharpness of focus: The garden swing decreases its arc at
what rate? Never mind the color for now, or how it makes me
feel. Shadows on the swing stand in what relationship to the
leaves and the sun? Never mind for now that the birds are
chirping or that they make the garden seem alive. Scientific
knowledge—in fact instrumental knowledge in general—the
sort that gets us through each day—is built on sacrifice;
there's always an untruth linked to the truth, precisely because
of its narrowness and exclusivity. These instrumental truths—
and thankful I am for them—are in a sense forced on me.
They're what religious dogma might be to someone else: I go
along with them, even rely on them, but on some level I don't
believe them. I don't believe that business about how planes
stay up. I don't believe water is hydrogen and oxygen. That's
just someone's trip—useful but fraudulent. When I perceive
something resonantly, however, it has the wholeness, the
fluidity, the infinite subtlety and the limitless abundance—in
fact the truth—of life itself: "a World in a Grain of Sand." No
wonder the grain of sand seems so especially real.

CHAPTER SIX
Resonance and Reaction

Resonance is not something that we experience all the time. It may be present, to varying degrees, in aesthetic situations, but our ordinary way of responding to what we perceive is quite different. Now I've already suggested how resonance differs from recognition, which is the way we commonly interpret perception by pinning it down to a particular identity or concept. But resonance is an unusual kind of response in *affective* terms as well; ordinarily our feelings are brought into play in a very different manner.

Resonance takes place in the absence—or at least the diminished presence—of self-concern. It has to. Self-concern tends either to discard a perception or to channel it instrumentally: "What can this do for or to me? What relation does it have to my plans and expectations?" But resonance doesn't flow in such channels; a resonant image needs free access to, and free play among, areas of experience that are linked not by any concept or instrumental purpose but merely by the image itself. And the feeling in resonance—its affective content—is likewise cut loose from self-concern. We don't experience it in reference to self; we perceive it in the image.

Ordinarily though, it is this very self-concern that brings our feelings into play. Ordinarily, when we perceive things that affect us—actually or potentially—we don't resonate; we *react*. It is this *reactive* response which needs to be distinguished from resonance on the affective level, just as resonance was distinguished from recognition on the cognitive level.

Let's look at the stoplight once again. If I'm trying to get to the bank before it closes so that an important check doesn't bounce, and if the light turns red just as I approach one of those six-way intersections where you have to wait forever, then my frustrated "*Damn* it!" response is a reactive one. Or we could take another look at the back yard swing. If I were looking for a house, found one I liked and could afford, and then noticed that there was a swing set in the back yard, I might think, "Oh, how great! The kids will love it." In this situation, the swing, like the stoplight that delays me, isn't merely a detached image to perceive; it stands in a real (or apparent) causal relationship to my own well-being. My response to it is likely to be experienced as a *reaction* to what I perceive, whereas resonance is experienced more as a *participation* in it. And that's quite a difference.

Reactive response is the kind of response with which psychologists most commonly concern themselves. It's the meat and drink of psychotherapy. The striving self perceives and reacts, perceives and reacts, celebrating its own separateness and its pursuit of personal well-being.

Reactive response is nowhere near as closely tied to perception as resonance is. We can stay with the perception but we don't usually have to. It's true that very direct, non-cerebral reactions, for instance the pain from an electric shock, may live and die with a stimulus. But usually we can continue to react emotionally to something—an insult, a kiss, a headline in the newspaper—not only after it's gone, but sometimes long after. Perception has brought the ball into our court; the rest—reaction—is up to us. Resonance, however, requires the image. Keeping the tennis analogy, you could say that, with resonance, the two players seem to merge.

OK. Now what I've said so far might suggest a simple arrangement: we resonate to art and react to ordinary life. But this simple arrangement would also be wrong. Because if we were to exclude reactive response from art, we'd have to ignore a great deal of art, including literature. And yet, distinctions analogous to this have been made (for example, by Clive Bell and Roger Fry). I suppose it's tempting at times, particularly for theorists who begin with painting and sculpture, having seen the way color, shape, line, and so forth can in some way elicit a very special "aesthetic" kind of feeling, to want then to exclude those more "vulgar" heavy-duty emotional responses to loyalty and betrayal, defeat and conquest, the fall of princes, and love thwarted and triumphant—

responses, in other words, to the subject matter of theatre, of the epic and the novel, of opera, of film, and of at least some painting, sculpture, dance, etc.

But how *do* we get reactive response back into aesthetic experience if this kind of response is based on self-concern? That's the question, and a careful look at what happens when we read a novel or see a play makes it not too difficult to answer. We respond reactively, but on an as-if basis: *as if* our self-concern were involved when it really isn't. Everyone is quite good at doing this, of course. Precisely how we manage it is an interesting psychophysiological question that I don't think anyone has answered yet. As I suggested in Chapter Four, emotional experience is complex. Fear or joy involves much more than the turning on of some single tap. Obviously when we experience emotion on an as-if basis, some elements of the emotion are retained and others are not.

Teaching improvisational theatre to amateurs, I've learned what astonishingly good actors people are. And this acting we do is very much related to what happens when we respond reactively to art. I can sit here at the typewriter, and—just for fun—begin to laugh uproariously at nothing or to cry bitter tears of disappointment: "Tears in his eyes, distraction in his aspect." And it's not just my facial muscles and the muscles of my body that are involved. I don't consciously decide to let my lower lip get all stretched out and quivery; something's going on inside that makes it happen: not "real" unhappiness because I'm not "really" unhappy at the moment, but still some components of that emotion are obviously available without any appropriate cause and without an accompanying concern about my own well-being. I can do joy or sorrow with equal ease; I don't find myself any more or less eager to do one than the other. But improvisational theatre works even better than this spontaneous "emotion"-making. We do scenes; we get *deeply* involved. We're not just making faces now; there are powerful pervasive feelings for which the scene provides a context. But it's all *as-if.*

Responding to a play or a film is less work. It takes a fair amount of energy to achieve elation or misery from scratch, sitting at your typewriter, and without help. Acting in a play is easier. Watching one is easier still. The performance we're watching helps us enormously; it evokes the emotions and rationalizes them. But here too some components are missing. It may not be too useful to argue whether we should call what we experience at a play emotion, simulated emotion, the illusion of emotion, or, in Hamlet's phrase, "a dream of passion." The question would have to be resolved in a much more precise way than that. But as I've pointed out, there are, ordinarily, components in an emotion that make it "practical," that relate it to our self-concern. Commonly emotion is geared into action in such a way that, when no appropriate action is possible, the emotion is likely to become more intense, even at times overwhelming. These components are missing when we respond in an aesthetic context. The response that we feel doesn't drive us toward action—at least not while we're involved in the aesthetic experience. We're aware of our feeling but we don't have to do anything about it.

Nevertheless, though it may be detached from self-concern, this kind of aesthetic response *is* reactive. I respond to something which has instrumental significance *within a pretend context*, to something which stands in a causal relationship, not to my self-concern, but to the image of self-concern. Reactive responses in art are far more channeled, more clearly defined, more identifiable than resonance is. They are much easier to describe, as are the situations which evoke them. Falstaff appears to have been slain on the battlefield. But then he rises up, having merely feigned death to protect himself. We are surprised, pleased, and amused. The situation, along with our response, can be summarized, conceptualized, in a way that resonance cannot.

Mere recognition can evoke a reactive response; a simple "no" or "yes" on the right occasion will do it. Resonance, however, demands an image. That's why it's easier, using language, to evoke reactive responses than to evoke resonance, which requires us to put words together artfully in order to fashion powerfully evocative images. Consider television dramas, which are not too often the work of highly skilled artists. The average *Lassie* re-run may bring tears to your eyes more easily than many a tragedy which uses language in a far more resonant way. Start with a child and a dog and you're halfway home already. Then all you need to do is threaten their relationship in some way and the Kleenex comes out in a million homes. This is not meant to play down reactive emotion, which can be and has been tremendously important in the narrative and dramatic arts. Aristotle—to cite authority itself—set great store by this kind of response when he analyzed tragedy in his *Poetics*, and not solely in the much-interpreted section on *katharsis*. The discoveries and reversals, for example, that he likes so much as plot elements are a very recipe for procuring intense reactive response. But, as Aristotle himself well knew, there is more to a work of dramatic or narrative art than the arousal of reactive emotion, important as it may be. I hope that the reasons why this is so will become increasingly clear.

CHAPTER SEVEN
The Empathic Focus

How exactly does a work of art, detached as it is from the practical context, evoke reactive emotion—and why is this so easily done? You might think that it would be difficult, not easy, since art, in order to *be* art, must never directly challenge our self-concern. And how is reactive emotion to be kept within the image? This would seem to be a contradiction in terms. I've already maintained that reactive emotion is just that, reaction *to* something, while resonance is a participation *in* it. Why then wouldn't a frightening scene in a movie or a ridiculous situation in a play lead us, through fear or ridicule, to react against what we are seeing, thereby separating ourselves from the image and falling back into the realm of self-awareness and self-concern?

The principal solution to this problem is empathy. And what I'm referring to, I should emphasize, is not the line of aesthetic theory that derives from "Vernon Lee" (Violet Paget) and Theodore Lipps, but simply empathy as it is commonly understood nowadays: a way of feeling with someone else, projecting into another person's position, that involves more actual identification than does sympathy. This kind of empathy does a splendid job of solving the problems that attend reactive emotion in an aesthetic context. Instead of pointing at our own self-concern, it gives us a focus of concern which is within the image and therefore safely detached from the practical context. In *The Charterhouse of Parma*, it's not I who has been imprisoned in the citadel of Parma, but Fabrizio del Dongo; in *After the Banquet*, it's not my husband who has just lost the election but Mrs. Noguchi's. Because empathy focuses our concern within the image, our reactive response can continue to be experienced as *out there* rather than *in here*.

We need, however, to make a clear distinction between empathy in art and empathy in ordinary life. Unlike aesthetic empathy, ordinary empathy is not free of self-concern, even though it may well seem "a step removed." In ordinary life, self-concern spreads out along lines of ego-identification. That is why to share the feelings of a friend is to expose your own self-concern, no matter how guardedly, to someone else's fortunes. You have identified not with an image but with a real person, who exists within the practical context; therefore you have involved yourself. When things get bad, you can't just munch popcorn and watch the show.

As a general rule, empathy flourishes in the dramatic and narrative arts where reactive emotion is also plentiful, and is less common in the arts that rely more exclusively on resonance, such as music, sculpture, and painting. In theatre, in film, in literature, empathy is of the greatest importance, and operates in many ways, some less obvious than others. The obvious examples are plentiful enough: in Hitchcock's *The Thirty-Nine Steps*, which showed last week at my neighborhood theatre, we participate *with* the character played by Robert Donat, who provides, with the possible exception of a very few scenes, a consistent center within the image for our reactive response. I could add an endless list of films, novels, and so on, all arranged in very much the same way around a central, more or less unswervingly empathetic figure. But then there are artists who play with our empathy, manipulating it to achieve more complex results. This is possible because empathy in art is somewhat more fluid than it is in ordinary life. We can empathize with several characters at once, can shift from one to another and back again. In *The Misanthrope*, for example, although Alceste is clearly the central character, Molière arranges things so that we may empathize with another character and *against* Alceste in one scene, and then find ourselves empathizing *with* Alceste in the next. From this balancing arises some of the work's dynamism and also some of its extraordinary depth.

But we can empathize readily even when "characters" as such are not present—for instance with the speaker in a lyric poem:

> Not, I'll not, carrion comfort, Despair, not feast on thee;
> Not untwist—slack they may be—these last strands of man
> In me ór, most weary, cry *I can no more*. I can;
> Can something, hope, wish day come, not choose not to be.

Though I myself may at some time have been attracted by the "carrion comfort" of despair, my feelings here are centered empathically in the speaker, not in myself. In poetry there is always a voice speaking which is not our own.

Fiction typically presents us with characters that, to varying degrees, may attract empathy. But even when no character is on the scene, there is still the narrative persona itself—not the author, but the author's creation: this voice that speaks to us. As a matter of fact, there are literary works where we are more likely to empathize with the narrator than with the characters themselves. This is particularly common in satirical fiction. For example:

> Hardly was Candide in his inn when he was attacked by a slight illness, caused by his fatigue. Since he had an enormous diamond on his finger, and since a prodigiously heavy money box had been noticed in his baggage, he immediately had two physicians near him whom he had not called, some intimate friends who did not leave him, and two devout ladies who had his broths heated. . . . However, thanks to medicines and bleedings, Candide's illness became serious.

In another kind of story we might have some empathic feeling for Candide. But here, it is the narrator's scorn for the physicians and phony friends that we share.

Can you see why, in works of art that involve satire or some other form of aggressive humor, there needs to be a carrier for our feelings who is present in the work itself? Otherwise, we would be invited to feel *against* the aesthetic image, and therefore to pull back from it and into ourselves. In narrative literature, this carrier is very likely to be the speaking voice, or perhaps some particular character whose point of view the narrative takes. In drama and film, however, narration is not common. It's possible that in some films we may identify empathically with a "camera eye" or "directorial point of view," but I think this also is uncommon. How then, in a dramatic work, do we laugh aggressively and yet stay empathically within the image at the same time?

Sometimes, the problem is solved by having characters played off against each other. We empathize with one momentarily and laugh aggressively at the other; then the action leads us to switch roles. The Marx Brothers take turns victimizing each other and everyone else, and scarcely anyone gets off free. Some characters attract little or no empathy; Margaret Dumont, for example, is more or less permanently stretched out on the sacrificial altar, along with a host of hotel-managers, officials, financiers, and stuffed shirts in general. Groucho's hostile wit and randiness draw empathy until the moment comes for him to be undone by Chico's stubborn metalogic. But it's Harpo who plays the empathic trump cards. Glittering with anarchy and grace, he pulls us in, becomes subject as the others turn object.

But then what is to be said about the single comedian, who appears to be both subject *and* object? What about Chaplin, for example? In the opening of *Modern Times*, he's struggling to keep up with the conveyor belt on an assembly line. The co-workers and foreman hardly provide a focus for empathy; the focus has to be with Chaplin, particularly insofar as he's presented here in generally sympathetic terms as a victim of industrial capitalism. And yet, at the same time, he's ridiculous. Can we laugh at him and still keep our feelings in the image while we're laughing? I believe we can. Because there is a kind of laughter which often looks rather like aggressive humor, but which is perfectly compatible with empathy.

Like you perhaps, I'm burdened with a sense of my own clumsiness, incompetence, social ineptness, and so on. These failings may not be sins, but one pays a high emotional price for them, beginning in the early years of childhood. What is it that happens when I see this clumsiness, this ineptness acted out on the screen by Chaplin, by Jacques Tati, or by Woody Allen? Is my laughter aggressive? Not at all. On the contrary, these are "good guys," who provide a focus for my empathic feelings. I'm on their side; I want things to turn out well for them somehow, even though this may not always happen. Their empathic suitability, in fact, is a necessary condition for this particular kind of laughter, which I will call *redemptive*, rather than aggressive, laughter.

There are two contrasting ways of seeing one's own weakness or problem when it is displayed by others. One way involves disavowal of the weakness, and hostility toward the others. The second way involves recognition of the weakness, and some degree of identification with the others. One way says: "If there's anything I can't stand, it's a phony!" The other way says: "We're all such bullshitters, aren't we?" Both offer the kind of immediate ego-gratification which is compatible with aesthetic experience. I begin with a flaw, an inadequacy, which, if I own up to it, will make me think less of myself, and which creates tension and displeasure. I reduce this tension in the first case by denying the problem and turning my displeasure outward, and, in the second case, by sharing the problem and therefore rendering it more "human," more acceptable. In either case, this reduction of tension can take the form of laughter when it is achieved suddenly within the structural context that comedy provides.

As a general rule, aggressive humor and redemptive humor are inspired in comedy by two very different types of comic figure. Objects of aggressive humor may invite a hostile response merely because of their role, e.g., as "parental" law-and-order figures, or because they embody traits we may disavow, such as cruelty or snobbishness, or for both reasons. To see a personal weakness or social failing projected on such non-empathetic figures, on "bad guys," on mere objects, does nothing to redeem it. We laugh with delight to see these figures thwarted; the qualities that they embody are nothing we would want to associate ourselves with. The stuffy bank manager or school principal who gets a pie in the face is more likely to represent social eptness than ineptness, but it's a kind of eptness that none of us wants to be associated with. Woody, Charlie, and Tati's M. Hulot, on the other hand, take on our failings, within the aesthetic image, and redeem them. But only, of course, failings that deserve redemption. Each of these comedians implies a moral system. Woody is neurotic but not wicked. Chaplin gets drunk but is never brutal. Hulot will accidentally knock over your vase but he would never be unkind. In fact, each is, in one way or another, particularly admirable. And the failings that are redeemed are likely to be the ones we have to live with and, in the long run, are willing to live with. Still, the moral system may vary drastically from one comic work to another. There is no official list of "redeemable" qualities. For that matter, it is not just our failings that are redeemed. These comedians take on our reverses, misfortunes, our bad luck. When you need the car most, it won't start. When you want to impress someone, you have corn in your teeth.

In *Annie Hall*, Alvy Singer (Woody) finds himself in a car on a rainy night with Annie's suicidal brother at the wheel. I laughed *uproariously* at the scene. I hate to drive with other people, even under the best of circumstances. And when it's raining and I'm in the right front seat, I get so tense I scarcely breathe—never mind suicidal brothers. Now this scene, of course, could have been done, in another movie, in a non-comic way. There might have been suspense, anxiety, but no laughter. But the comedian's comic style—which can involve exaggeration or understatement or some other kind of incongruous stylization—by its own inappropriateness, makes a certain range of reactive emotions inappropriate on our part. Woody Allen's comic role reassures me as I watch the scene in the car. It's not that I'm reassured that the car won't crash. That's not the point. Maybe it *will* crash. We may see him in the hospital in the next scene. And *that*'ll be funny. Comedy, based on incongruity, always leaves us, not an objective way out but a psychological way out, an alternative point of view. We're never locked in a room with fear or despair or frustration or embarrassment. Because even the comedian's exaggerated response—say, of terror, in the car scene—implies, through its exaggeration, another perspective, a way of looking at the situation from outside. In this way comedy sets up a sort of double frame. There is, to begin with, the aesthetic frame itself; and within that frame, the comic perspective, the alternative or outside view, establishes its own kind of psychological frame.

The aesthetic context frees us from self-concern and, in "serious" drama, it allows us to experience the entire range of reactive emotion free of charge. But comedy preempts much of this reactive emotion before it has a chance to take hold. Instead of fully experiencing anger and sexual desire, we get instant gratification in the form of a pie in the face or a sexual joke, and instant, though temporary, release of tension in the form of laughter. Instead of pity and terror, we get instant relief—again manifested as laughter—when potentially pitiful and terrifying situations are defused by the double perspective, the outside view of comedy. I imagine Woody Allen as Oedipus: "It could have been worse: I could have killed my mother and married my father."

Aggressive humor and the kind of humor that I've termed redemptive are often mixed together in a single work. Most obviously, there can be an encounter between a subject figure and an object figure. In *Annie Hall* again, there's the scene in which Alvy, waiting in line for a movie, manages to squelch the smart-ass film-intellectual who's talking about McLuhan, by miraculously producing McLuhan to tell smart-ass that he's all wrong. Alvy's discomfort when, at first, he has to stand in line and listen to the man's smug lecture, produces redemptive humor. That's life. We've all been there. We can enjoy sharing this discomfort, recognizing it in Alvy. But the squelch is pure aggression, carefully prepared and justified. The film-intellectual's qualities—which you can be sure we refuse to claim—are not to be redeemed but attacked. The scene is a comic version of David and Goliath—always sure to satisfy, since so few of us think of ourselves as Goliaths.

But even a single character can produce a mixture of aggressive and redemptive humor, or can operate somewhere around the borderline. Alceste, whom I've already mentioned, is the Misanthrope. He has impossibly high standards, is continually and uncompromisingly critical, lives in a state of permanent rage against humankind. But these qualities: are they to be redeemed or purged? If we analyze the humor, we find that it goes both ways—with the balance depending to some extent on who is watching or reading—or staging—the play. When he says that he would hang himself for insincerity or that he would like to lose his lawsuit just to prove how wicked men are, Alceste is (to me at least) grotesque, and an *object*. But in the next scene, when a smug and overbearing nobleman insists on reading his own wretched sonnet to Alceste and then, expecting to be flattered, demands Alceste's opinion, the humor shifts. We're back in line with Alvy at the movie. Alceste even tries to temper his words but it doesn't work. This extraordinary attempt at calm and forbearance, though, makes him even more sympathetic—and also pulls the bowstring of comedy back even farther as the scene approaches its climax. The inevitable confrontation occurs. The nobleman has rank and influence but Alceste is wittier:

ORONTE: Others have praised my sonnet to the skies.
ALCESTE: I lack their art of telling pleasant lies.
ORONTE: You seem to think you've got no end of wit.
ALCESTE: To praise your verse, I'd need still more of it.

We're on Alceste's side, and his rage is, for the moment at least, legitimized. But the play has only just begun. The perspective will shift many times more: Alceste is a social critic gone off the deep end, but then, without him, where would we be? I myself love this particular ambivalence in *The Misanthrope* and find it very resonant. If I want to reach for associations, there are a great many at hand. I think of saints and fanatics and the paradox that vibrates between them. I think of a certain very mocking age—was I fourteen?—when people would say: "You just don't know when to stop." I think of Molière himself, the great satirist, finally turning his invincible weapon back on itself.

Alceste is not so much at the borderline between redemptive and aggressive humor as he is an amalgam of the two. Some of the most memorable figures in comedy are of this type. Falstaff is, more or less—but I would guess that time has altered the balance somewhat. Falstaff's "discretion," his reluctance to fight, might have inspired a more aggressive humor in an Elizabethan audience than it does now in me. Proust's Baron de Charlus is a spectacular blend of the two kinds of humor. These characters have a kind of baroque drama and magnificence to them. There is a "stereoscopic" sense of high relief which comes from the two different comic perspectives. Less baroque perhaps, but more recent is Ted Baxter, the newscaster on *The Mary Tyler Moore Show*. Vain, selfish, stupid, and a social klutz, Baxter was a jerk from the word go, but so nakedly human that you couldn't entirely disown him.

Purely aggressive humor may be easier to bring off in literature than in the dramatic arts. No matter how repellent the characters are, no matter how violently they are attacked, the author's persona is always available as a source of empathic focus within the image. Given that focus, the most biting satire is possible. Here is Alexander Pope, trashing a playwright named Moore who had stolen some of Pope's lines. The situation Pope creates is that the Goddess of Dullness has called all her people to a sort of Olympic Games. The publishers are going to have a race, and the prize she has created— as a joke on them—is a dummy, an imitation poet: Moore, of course. Here's Pope's description of this "prize":

> But such a bulk as no twelve bards could raise,
> Twelve starveling bards of these degenerate days.
> All as a partridge plump, full-fed, and fair,
> She formed this image of well-bodied air;
> With pert flat eyes she windowed well its head:
> A brain of feathers, and a heart of lead;
> And empty words she gave, and sounding strain,
> But senseless, lifeless! idol void and vain!
> Never was dashed out, at one lucky hit,
> A fool, so just a copy of a wit;
> So like, that critics said, and courtiers swore,
> A wit it was, and called the phantom Moore.

It is difficult to so dehumanize a character on the stage, although playwrights since Aristophanes have tried. One problem is that theatrical characters have a tendency to draw empathy almost in spite of a playwright's intentions. It's possible, of course, to put so strong an empathic focus on one character that another, antipathetic character will be pure villain, comic or otherwise. But satirists are not always willing to strengthen any character's hand that much.

Is it possible to deliver purely aggressive comedy on the stage, without any empathic focus at all? I'm not at all sure that it is. For one thing, aggressive laughter may tend to pull us out of the aesthetic image if there's no empathetic character on whose behalf the aggressive response is experienced. But also, our tendency to empathize is so strong that we generally take what we can get. If there's no one around who's halfway attractive, we'll find something in whatever wretch or villain is offered us. What are we going to see on the stage, after all, that is totally alien to us? Jarry's King Ubu is the epitome of selfish greed. He's a coward, a liar, a tyrant, a murderer. He's pure id. I have no difficulty empathizing with him, particularly in scenes when there is no real alternative, when he is essentially the only game in town. Is this redemptive humor? I think it is. But everything depends on how you regard Ubu. I have students occasionally who can't help trying to see him in a "realistic" way—this tends not only to forestall any possibility of identification, but also to alienate them from the play itself.

It may be that, if we are led to respond aggressively and if we are resolutely denied any empathic focus within the image, we tend to pull back somewhat and become more self-aware and less intensely given over to the experience aesthetically. Perhaps this explains the tradition of jeering at villains, something which I've seen children do more or less spontaneously at puppet shows. When I try to think of a comic scene with minimal possibility for empathy, I think of Molière's Harpagon, alone on stage in *The Miser*. He's so wretched, so fearful for his money, so grotesque, that at one point he catches himself by the arm: "Give me back my money, you rascal! . . . Oh! It's me" (IV, vii). What's especially interesting here is that Molière, following his source in Plautus, has Harpagon suspect even the audience itself and address it directly—almost an acknowledgment that, for the moment, the audience has lost its aesthetic identification with the image and has been made self-aware.

Aggressive humor presents the same sort of problem in painting and drawing. Satirical works, like those of Hogarth and Daumier, may evoke a reactive response but without offering an adequate focus for empathy. Much of Daumier's work actually does have empathic possibilities, but Hogarth, in many of his paintings and engravings, is as unsparing as his contemporary, Pope. He invites an aggressive reaction to these portrayals of idleness, stupidity, cruelty, and debauch. There isn't much here to hold us in the image but the image itself. And here at least, painting, drawing, etc., have special resources. Hogarth's action, because it is frozen, has a less intensely reactive effect than theatrical action would. And the resonant possibilities of color, texture, line, and such are considerable. So what we get may be a sort of contest between reaction and resonance. If resonance is able ultimately to absorb the reactive response, the image will work well aesthetically. If not, our response becomes more centered in us than in the painting or engraving, and the experience becomes weaker aesthetically, though it may well be satisfying and useful in other ways.

One of Hogarth's younger contemporaries, who was definitely not a satirist, illustrates how works of art can *become* humorous with the passage of time, even though they were not intended or initially received that way. The painter is Greuze, whose highly sentimentalized scenes became popular in an age when sentimentality was the vogue for many Europeans. What he painted was not so much feeling as fashions in feeling—and fashions don't always age well. At the time, the tearstained face, the hand to the forehead, the eyeballs rolled up to heaven were as hip as you could get. For most contemporaries, there was no rift apparent between the pose and the feeling itself. But for later generations the two pulled apart; the pose began to look corny, and the resulting incongruity opened up humorous possibilities. In fact, the conventionalized expressions of feeling that you see in Greuze and elsewhere became the comedian's stock in trade at a later time. And today, you and I, when someone asks, "Was it a boring meeting?" and we feel the need for comedy, put our hands to our foreheads and raise our eyes toward heaven. And yet, scenes of grief have been a fixture throughout the history of European painting, especially religious painting, and, by and large, they have not turned funny. This is because, whatever artistic conventions may have been involved, the representation usually has had a direct connection with our own experience; it's the real thing. Greuze's fate awaits the artists who let themselves be led astray by fashion, depicting not so much what they and others feel and say and do as what they are, at the time, *supposed* to feel and say and do. Look at movies made earlier in this century: the twenties, thirties, or forties; you'll see all this in operation. What ages well and what doesn't? We discover that it isn't by depicting fashion that art becomes dated but by yielding to it. But even

Greuze's fate isn't irrevocable. Perhaps he's been somewhat rehabilitated these days. The age that's just freed itself—or is trying to free itself—from the previous age's fashions has the least tolerance of them; adolescents are more accepting of their grandparents' styles than of their parents'. If Greuze has something to offer as a painter—and he does—then we can learn to take his sentimental poses in stride.

As a matter of fact, this rehabilitating process has been very much speeded up in recent decades. We've learned to appreciate recently outworn fashions even though (and partly because) they're still close enough to make us wince. That's camp. (In a many-layered culture, whose layers change stylistically each at its own speed, camp doesn't even need this double perspective in time. A perfectly new artifact from Layer Y, perceived from Layer X, will do nicely.) Without this taste for camp, we're alienated by the old movie, driven entirely out of the image into our own scorn and embarrassment—or it acquires some interest simply as unintentional comedy. But now we cultivate this irony, this ambivalence. In dance, for example, a choreographer can have his or her cake and eat it too. You introduce into a "serious" work some Vegas show dancing or some tap or a little exhibition tango dancing. You treat it with irony and distance as befits your degree of sophistication, but it also does a hell of a lot for your piece because it's so tight and flashy. The original audience for a work that will later become dated simply accepts it and appreciates it. The subsequent camp audience appreciates it but with an ironic detachment that keeps their hands clean. But there has to be something there besides the fact that it is dated: a style, a special range of color, an extravagant orchestration, a magnetic presence, an enthusiasm or a restraint— something that intrudes excitingly into the range of possibilities open to more up-to-date non-camp artists.

Just what is happening in a camp situation depends not only on the work, of course, but also very much on the perceiver. There appears to be a range of possibilities bounded by two opposite ways of perceiving the work. On the one hand, the perceiver may see the work primarily as a joke. With minimal empathic focus in the work itself, this perceiver would be likely to feel detached from it and to become more self-aware. I picture a *Leave It To Beaver* re-run, playing to a derisive living room audience, who look around at each other, laugh, compete in the search for funny comments. It's even possible for this kind of work to become the center of a kind of participatory theatre, as has happened with cult/camp films like *The Rocky Horror Picture Show* and *Reefer Madness*, where the aesthetic image may spread beyond the original work itself and comprehend the audience, which plays a more or less ritualized part, e.g., throwing toilet-paper rolls in the air when a character says, "Great Scott!"

At the opposite extreme, the perceiver will simply take the work seriously, even romantically, in a kind of infatuation with bygone standards of taste and feeling. A devotee of early musical comedies, for example, may choose to bury himself enthusiastically in that world, which he may well prefer to this one, and simply reject any awareness that particular elements are dated or corny.

Generally, the camp experience is somewhere in between. And here, camp raises an interesting aesthetic question: Is it possible for our ambivalent, ironic response to be satisfactorily contained in the image itself? Or does it always force us, to some extent, out of the work and into self-awareness? Obviously, when camp elements are used in a larger work, as in my dance example, or when the entire work is itself intentional camp (Susan Sontag's distinction between "camp" and "camping"), there is not *necessarily* a problem, since the work seeks to contain the ironic response it evokes. But old science-fiction films—*The Giant Claw, Rocket Ship X-M*, and so on—are not, as a rule, intentionally camp. And when I see them, my aesthetic participation in the image is, I think, necessarily limited. There's just more going on in my head than *The Giant Claw* seems to want to absorb. That's why movies like these are so good to see with friends. We're not back to *Leave it to Beaver* exactly, but some of the response needs to be shared; it has to go somewhere and it can't go into the image; we nudge each other: "You notice the older scientist always has a daughter? Never a son." All this would argue for a somewhat diminished aesthetic involvement and a corresponding emphasis on the audience; thus camp—whether postcard or movie, table lamp or opera—as something especially to be shared. And here also is a reason why camp can work so well as a source of group identity, or clique identity. This energy which is withheld from the image and which tends to spill out among the perceivers makes camp a celebration of its audience, a cohesive ritual and, of course, a kind of membership card.

But to leave the matter here would be to miss a very important aspect of the aesthetics of camp. It's true that camp can evoke an ironic response which forces the perceiver to retreat somewhat from the image. But this bi-valent art can also, in another way, draw the perceiver more fully in. When I look at a fifty-year-old *Bringing Up Father* comic strip, it is the *reactive* elements in the story line (the familiar twists and reversals, the stock jokes) which are most likely to have faded —if anything has faded at all. And what this means is that I'll be more open to purely resonant aspects of the work than I might have been when it first appeared. This resonance may even be enhanced by the sense of intervening time that I get from the comic strip's datedness (Greuze seems much farther back in time than his contemporary, Maurice Quentin de la Tour, whose marvelous portraits don't give me quite that same awareness of the historical abyss). The drawing style, the clothing, the colors, the backgrounds, the way Jiggs and Maggie use language—all of these may be much more fully and resonantly present to me, in proportion as the "official" content of the strip drops away. Of course, there has to be something there to take hold of—that's why one comic strip, one singer, one table lamp makes better camp than another, equally dated. What I'm saying is that camp can provide a frame through which we view a less reactive and more highly resonant image. In time, even "extrinsic" reactive elements can become muted—elements, that is, which derive not so much from the work itself as from the role that it plays in society or in someone's personal life. Architecture that is regarded, when it first appears, as a symbol of "the vulgarization of taste" may arouse a less defensive response when it recedes into history, losing its threatening qualities as it becomes either "legitimate" (the Eiffel Tower) or camp (the old movie theatre that has silver stars on the ceiling and a purple curtain with palm trees). But this glance at the relationship between resonance and reaction anticipates a subject that will be pursued in the next chapter.

CHAPTER EIGHT
Resonant Relationships

How large a role does resonance play in our experience of a work of art? Do we resonate only to certain key elements: a patch of color or a particular figure in a painting, a certain image in a poem? What I've said about resonance so far might seem to support this notion: resonant elements would emerge as high points; they would be jewels in the crown of art. And it's undeniably true that a particular shot in a movie, a metaphor in a story, a face in a painting can stand out because of its particularly vivid and intensely resonant quality. But if we left it at this, we'd be in no position to do justice to the work of art as a unified whole.

First of all, it's important to observe that resonance arises not merely out of particular elements but out of elements in relationship. Even the simplest examples bear this out. The stoplight isn't just a certain shade of red; the color exists within relationships. The light is not only red but round, clearly defined, translucent, set off against the darker rectangle of the light standard. A literary image is compounded out of words in relationship; if some of these relationships were to change, the image would change and, along with it, our resonant response. Relationships have resonant potential, not as abstract concepts, but in concrete form. Let's take, for example, the relationship in size between figure and background in a portrait. In one portrait, a head might very nearly fill the frame. In another, it might occupy only a modest place in proportion to the surrounding space. Each kind of relationship has its own associations in our experience, its own range of contexts. When do faces loom large? Obviously, when we're close to them, but also when we focus on them so intently— whether through attraction, distaste, or curiosity—that what surrounds them drops away. Faces in smaller proportion are associated with other experiential contexts, contexts in which, no matter how intense our interest may be, we're made aware of the intervening distance and surrounding space. Perhaps some social gap separates us; perhaps we are holding ourselves, or being held, at a distance. Also, a larger surrounding space in portraits tends more sharply to delineate the outer surface, even the social surface of the subject. But minimal surrounding space surrenders emphasis to the features and to the inner life. So, each kind of relationship has access to certain areas of experience. The mere relationship alone isn't resonant, of course, or every snapshot ever taken would be also. But the relationship helps to determine the kind of resonance that we may experience when confronted with an aesthetically effective portrait.

Faces themselves, incidentally, are an excellent illustration of the way resonance can arise out of complex relationships. Taken as a whole, a face may well be familiar, evocative of experiences with people who have "that kind of face," and evocative perhaps of other associations, say with some kind of animal. But every face is also new: a unique set of relationships among features which, taken individually, may themselves be familiar. This assertive chin. Those meditative eyes. These flat, exotic cheekbones. That silly smile. It no longer suffices to think of resonance as deriving from *one* element which activates a range of experience for which it provides the common center. Insofar as a face is a familiar type, it may well *be* a common center, but insofar as it offers a new set of relationships, the resonance that it can produce is of a more complex sort. There is no previous experience whatsoever that links together all of these features that we see; we are looking at something new. These eyes activate one range of experience; that chin activates another, and so on. What's the result? Naturally, we don't experience a separate response for each feature. Rather, the various kinds of experiential quality—of knowing-feeling—are brought into each other's presence. Connections are established. Accommodations are instantly made. This range is narrowed; that one is reinforced in certain areas. One range of experience introduces a sense of repose, another a sense of tension; another carries the scent of a certain distant place or of some vanished time. But the resonant response that we are aware of and that we perceive in the face is *one* response, in the same way that the taste of a soup registers as one taste, though its components may be many.

Ordinarily, we don't respond resonantly to faces. We're content to recognize them, either in the simple mode of identifying a particular person, or in the more complicated mode of identifying feeling or personality: "As soon as I saw her, I knew she wasn't going to go for it"—"He didn't look like someone who'd give me any trouble." Or we respond to faces reactively, with fear, delight, jealousy, love. In either case, resonance is unlikely. When we recognize, we tend not to see much more of a face than is instrumentally necessary. And reactive emotion, which is intense but usually narrow, tends to limit drastically the range and mobility of our response. Nonetheless, faces have enormous resonant potential, a potential which art is often able to realize.

Just as the features in a face are related, so a face in a painting can become one complex element in a still larger structure of relationships. And this larger structure can have its own resonance. But this doesn't amount simply to a set of nested boxes, where the resonance from one element disappears in a larger resonance, and so on until we reach the frame, which sets a limit to the increasing scope and complexity of relationships within the work of art. A resonant response is not static. It can change as we focus first on one element, then on another; it can change as we let our attention broaden to include larger relationships (which are finally limited by the frame in time and space) *or* as we let it narrow and dwell on one particular aspect of the work. Our response will not be the same when we're focusing on a particular face as it is when we're more attentive to the painting as a whole. But the resonant qualities of the face will influence our response to the whole painting, and the resonance of the painting will affect our response to the face.

Outside my window is a bottle-brush tree. The blossoms are striking to look at, a bright hazy red; from here they look more like big thick caterpillars than bottle brushes. It's easy to focus in on them and let this very summery redness find its home in me. But even when I look intently at the blossoms, I can't help being affected by the green leaves all around—very green now after one of the rainiest seasons ever. And this color relationship has its own resonance, which I can't express but can only play with verbally: berry bushes, apple trees, Maddie's long-gone Twiggy dress, and certainly—cut out of red and green construction paper: Christmas. This green-red resonance *includes* the resonance of its separate elements but these are present now in a more limited, conditioned way. At moments the green-red fades somewhat and the blossoms alone take over; then it comes back, and the leaves and blossoms become waves within a larger wave. But there are larger waves still. As I allow the blue sky behind the tree to become more important —by moving my head slightly down—the branches and blossoms thrust vigorously into this blue, and the scene takes on a healthy, exemplary, almost touristic beauty. There's a Chamber of Commerce feeling about it. And the season seems more like spring (which it is). Then, if I move my head a little to the right, I get a section of the bottle-brush tree against the beige stucco of my neighbor's house, and the resonance shifts, mellows— becomes civilized, tranquil, and seductive. I can't really describe it, but if I set myself to the task, I could weave various stories around this feeling. One might take place during my childhood in Hollywood after the war, on a warm sunny day in December. Living in a bungalow behind the bottle-brush tree would be an English expatriate who knew Huxley and Heard, or else, perhaps, a German atonalist; and this person— cool and European in the stucco bungalow—would be enchanted with Southern California, and even a little drugged by it. Now, if I choose to focus back on the blossoms and leaves, the green-red resonance will gain importance, but on this occasion with an altered, somewhat more complex tone.

A week later, I look out the window, tired, coming down with a cold. I see the same tree, the sky, the house, but they're dead. The colors are colorless. There's nothing there. Abracadabra!

I have stressed that resonance is much more fluid than recognition, much more fluid than any significance that we may extract from a work. It is never static. At any instant, it quivers, mobile and perfectly adaptable to changes within us and in our perception of the work. Resonance happens in time.

To look attentively at a painting is to explore, not in a sudden flash of perception but over some period of time, our own resonant response to its various elements, to relationships among them, and to the complex structure of relationships that is the entire painting. The painting as a whole may be dominated by one set of relationships which broadly establishes the tone of our response. But as we look at it, other aspects may emerge, and, as they do, the resonance within us changes accordingly. All pictures are moving pictures. All art is temporal. On the other hand, because experienced readers and listeners tend not to lose what they have already perceived of a novel or a piece of music but instead to be aware of the entire work unfolding before them, one could say that, in this sense, all art is spatial. We're drawn to the whole work. It is within this frame that the shifting play of our response takes place. It is this whole that conditions our response to its various elements. It is the unity of this entire work that, when things are working well, harmonizes the various areas of resonance within us and makes of them one continuously developing but still unified response.

An arch may have its own diffuse resonance. But the field of this resonance will be delimited and defined in a particular way if the arch, let's say, encloses a portal at the center of a massive facade, and it will be defined in another way if the arch is one of a series of similar arches in a long arcade. As we give our attention more fully to the entire facade or to the entire arcade—more or less zooming out—the resonance takes on new qualities, as though we were listening to music and the orchestration had become richer, more complex.

It's not surprising that music should supply an apt metaphor here. I suppose there is no art in which the building of complex resonant relationships is more clearly visible than it is in music. This is particularly true of instrumental music, which, when it's not employed to tell a story, is purely resonant. Absolute music, because of this "purity," has much to teach us about art in general. We need, therefore, to look at the way resonance emerges from musical relationships.

Sound a B flat. It's not much by itself. But to go up from B flat to F establishes one kind of relationship, and to go down to the lower F establishes another. These relationships of melodic interval are very simple. They have an extremely broad range of potential association, and for that reason, a single melodic interval by itself is not likely to be very resonant. The interval alone is like the words "their eyes" before Yeats combined them with other words to form the lines quoted in Chapter Five.

But wait a minute. Can we compare a musical interval with any word, no matter how abstract? Words, after all, can be defined, more or less. But try to imagine a glossary for these musical intervals. Can you see it? You'd look up:

and it would say: *See perfect fifth, ascending.* And then you'd look that up, and what would you find? Is this upward movement "happy" or "positive" or something like that? Nonsense, of course. I think of the ascending fifth at the beginning of a folk song, "Wayfaring Stranger," or of the repeated ascending fifths that open a Jewish melody called "Guitar." These are two very mournful songs; they provide contexts in which there is nothing particularly happy or positive about this ascending interval. Nor could our glossary call the descent from B flat to F "resigned" or "sad" or something of that sort. Out of countless possible examples, we can choose the high-spirited dance theme from the last movement of Beethoven's Violin Concerto, a theme in which the descending fourth is a particularly important—and in no way sad or resigned—element.

And yet . . . and yet . . . There's something there all the same. These two musical intervals have evocative ranges which are *not* identical. Movement up, movement down (these very terms are metaphors): we could associate each with an endless list of contexts, but the two lists would not be identical. Neither list, however, can be summed up with any verbal description whatsoever. Naturally, movement down *can* have associations with sinking, falling, weakness, decline, death, and so on. But there are also downward movements which involve concentration or repose or consummation. Movement toward the earth is by no means limited to "decline and fall." We take off our shoes to get in touch with the earth. We get basic and sit on the ground or floor. We approach an earthy reality ("Get down!" someone shouts to a performer) and even a sexual reality ("going down on" someone). Downward movements can be emphatic (foot-stamping, table-pounding); folk dancers stamp and slap the ground with emphatic pleasure (and this may well be part of my associative response to that descending fourth in Beethoven's Violin Concerto). As for upward movement: certainly it can be associated with awakening, arising, growth, aspiration, etc.—all generally "positive" contexts. There are "up" moods, people feel "high," "uplifted," think "lofty thoughts," have "high ideals." But people also "blow up," "screw up," and "crack up." Upward movement can be associated with unsatisfied yearning. And not everything that grows is positive. Anxiety can grow very nicely in music with an ascending chromatic movement. Height, moreover, whatever its advantages, can involve instability and danger, isolation and loneliness (I think of Rilke's "Exposed on the Mountains of the Heart").

What we're led to conclude is that it is only when these simple relationships are set in a larger pattern of relationship that their diffuse evocative potential condenses sufficiently to evoke an intensely resonant quality. With the ascending fifth, for example, it matters whether or not a tonality has been established and how the upward movement is related to it. Also, is one of the tones accented? What instruments are involved? What is the tempo? And of course the interval itself may seem large or small, depending on the melodic context. There is, in other words, no glossary that could be made giving the evocative significance of musical relationships. At most, we could assign each relationship—like each color in painting—a sort of profile created out of a great many associated contexts, a profile which would, of course, vary at least slightly from person to person and culture to culture. Theoretically we could do this. Actually, it would be an endless and pointless job. Still, the notion of such a profile may help us understand the sort of relationship a melodic interval can have to our own experience. Musical intervals are not similar to words. There's no agreed-upon, definable meaning. And the experiential range that could be associated with an interval is much broader and even more contradictory than would be the contexts associated with a single word. But intervals have this in common with words: in isolation they are too vague to be very interesting; it is in combination with each other that they come alive. Resonance is bounded at opposite ends by vagueness and recognition. When our response to something perceived narrows to no more than a particular memory or concept, then what we perceive won't resonate. But, at the other end, our response can be so diffuse, our range of possible association so wide, that no particular experiential quality is involved, or what *is* involved may be too faint, too diluted to matter. Curved lines and straight lines have enormous evocative potential—but only when they are defined in a pattern of relationships. Styles in art have been built on a curvilinear or a rectilinear basis, but a plain curve and a plain straight line are unlikely to resonate.

So musical intervals are put into relationship with each other—both harmonically and melodically—and as they come into each other's presence, the range of possibilities for each becomes delimited. Together, they acquire increasing power to define areas of knowing-feeling—what I somewhat lamely call experiential quality. And this applies not only to intervals, of course. We can add relationships of rhythm, dynamics, and instrumental timbre, until, instead of "descending fourth," we get a violin playing this passage, *allegro* and *piano*, over brief, punctuating cello figures:

The fast 6/8 is a dance rhythm, with its own range of associated contexts. Here its bouncy qualities are particularly evident (especially so, given the reverberating rhythm of the cello accompaniment). The descending fourth leads to a kind of rebound in the ascending triad that follows. If we're going to think of dancers, we might picture a dancer leaping down to spring up again. Or it could be a ball bouncing. It could be a rhythmic sexual contraction and release. Yet this passage isn't any of these things; it merely resonates through areas of experience which are now sufficiently delimited, sufficiently focused to yield up experiential quality, which we hear in the music.

After this melody is introduced on the solo violin, the orchestra takes it up. The solo version sounds, to me at least, gayer and more delicate. If it were played on the piano or the flute or the harmonica, its resonance would shift somewhat in other directions. Every instrument has, for each of us, its own resonant range, which is perhaps more distinct that that of musical intervals. The range is reduced and the resonance is focused when we put the musical instrument in a particular context and introduce an individual listener. Then, instead of "trumpet," we have: a lonely horn—slow, sweet, and blue— singing some hip tune in the city at night: "So-phis-ti-CA-ted lady I know . . . " (it would be hard for me to think of a more resonant sound).

Every element in a piece of music contributes to the complex structure of relationships that resonates in us. Naturally, how much we perceive of this structure is up to us. One person listens to a car engine and hears noise. Another person has learned, through years of listening, to hear the functioning of the engine in considerable detail, and knows which component of that sound comes from the tappets, and even what kind of condition they're in. That same sound is there for both, but the second person perceives it more attentively and more fully. All rock music sounds alike to one person, all chamber music to another.

An interval simply relates two tones. Melody is created by relationships that are more complex and on a larger scale. Still larger forms, like a *theme and variations* or a *rondo*, relate whole sections of a musical work. In music, to perceive the overall structure of a work is to open yourself up to relationships like the ones that exist between various intervals, rhythms, and so on in a melody, but on a much larger scale. These large-scale relationships have their own very important contribution to make to our resonant response. In a drawing or painting or sculpture they may well be obvious, but in a symphony, spread out as they are in time, they're often less so.

The interplay of expectation and discovery is important in our resonant response to music, as it is, though in a different way, in our reactive response to, say, a film or a novel. As we listen to a series of musical tones, our resonant response extends to cover what we expect will come next. This expectation conditions the way we will hear what follows. Larger-scale structural patterns also, as they unfold, set up expectations. The structure of a melody or of an entire composition is not revealed to us all at once; there is a lively ongoing "drama" (but a non-reactive one) in the way our expectations are fulfilled or not fulfilled, are continually being created and revised. This "drama" plays an important role, moment by moment, in our resonant response. At each moment resonance is colored by our expectation of what is to come, and by the way our previous expectation has or has not been met.

I should emphasize, by the way, that resonance works no more automatically in music than it does in the other arts. Resonance is not in the sound but in us. If we're not attentive, if striving hasn't been stilled, if we're not *given over* to the music, then it will be little more than an auditory surface, keeping us company as we go about our business, and offering only a hint of its resonant possibilities. What we hear mirrors precisely the depth it finds in us. There is an awesome difference between mere surface-music and music as aesthetic image, truly heard. And yet we tend to ignore this difference. People will say, "Oh, I don't like jazz," when they've never really heard it.

We've been looking at music to see how resonance arises out of relationships, which range from the most minimal and local to those which are the most complex and encompassing. Resonance, then, is not to be seen as something which happens now and then with particularly evocative musical passages but rather—assuming that we are perceiving aesthetically—as the way we respond to music.

But how much of this can we carry over to other forms of art? It's easy to see how resonance arises from an entire painting, and how symphonic music, jazz, or flamenco can be resonant from beginning to end. But when it comes to a novel or a film, shouldn't we expect resonance to be more of a "special effect" evoked by an occasional fine shot or descriptive passage, while the principal burden is carried by plot and the reactive emotions that it inspires? I don't think so. In fact, I don't think we have a clear view of literature and the dramatic arts until we see how much they have in common with music and painting.

Reaction, resonance, and recognition appear to be three primary kinds of response to art. At any given moment a single one is likely to predominate, though either or both of the others may well be present to some degree (recognition, for instance, can provide a basis for either reaction or resonance, and in the representational arts it is always on hand).

Our response may be mainly reactive—joy and relief, for example, at a timely rescue in a play. I wouldn't expect this kind of reactive emotion to be evoked by absolute music, but it's very common in theatre, film, and fiction, and it may be present, to a lesser extent, in dance, opera, painting, sculpture, song, and so on. Or our response may be more cognitive: recognizing, figuring out, interpreting. A person can respond in this way, of course, to any form of art whatsoever. The third kind of response is a predominantly resonant one. Some forms of art may be more *exclusively* resonant than others, but there is no form where it doesn't play a role.

It should be clear how all of this applies to our experience of an aesthetic image which is actually before us *at a given moment*. But with arts that unfold in time—arts like film, dance, music, and literature—how do we take account of and respond to *larger* segments in time, including the entire work as a whole? Here again we can see the same three primary ways of responding.

First, how does a person respond to the whole work in a *reactive* way? The answer's not hard to find. When Odysseus finally comes home and takes his revenge, or when Macbeth is finally defeated, our response will owe its character and much of its power to tensions that have been building throughout the entire work. If we hadn't had to wait so long for Odysseus' return, or if he hadn't been made to endure insults at the hands of the suitors, our response would be diminished. In the case of Macbeth: suppose he had been ready and willing to shed blood—or suppose, on the other hand, he had been even more reluctant than he actually was, so that his wife had had to kill Duncan. In either case, our reaction to his defeat and death would be substantially altered. Our reactive response takes account of and, in its way, reflects the work as a whole.

A predominantly *cognitive* response is always possible with any work; in fact it's possible even if that work is not at the moment functioning aesthetically. Occasionally, I've traced out the structure of a musical composition by analyzing a score, even though this isn't in itself likely to be an aesthetic experience, since I'm hardly musician enough to "hear" scores as I look at them. But for the purpose of noting orchestration, changes of key, the appearance and reappearance of themes, and so on, the score does fine. I also do this sort of pencil-and-paper analysis of literary works—as do most literature professors, I suppose—picking out patterns of various sorts and fitting them into some overall structure (though almost never on a first reading). When it takes the form of written analysis, this sort of thing can be rather bloodless and abstract—but less so if it happens as you experience a work. In fact, a primarily cognitive response to, at least, segments of the whole, needn't imply any elaborate analysis at all; it may involve nothing more than recognizing and noting the return of some particular motif: "Now that's the third time he's told us he's made 'of finer clay.'" Obviously, some cognitive grasp of the whole may help to provide a foundation for either reactive emotion or for resonance—but, to the extent that this happens, the cognitive element will tend to be dissolved in one or the other of these two kinds of response. In any case, if our aesthetic involvement with a work is strong, we can risk pulling away from the image a bit while extracting analytically a new set of relationships which will then enrich our experience of it. As a matter of fact, the aesthetic field of a great work can be very powerful and may continue to hold us even when we think we're turning away from it.

In considering the third type of response to the whole work, a predominantly *resonant* one, we return to the question I raised earlier: how much do art forms such as film or the novel, which involve plot and reactive emotion, have in common with music?

How does a work that unfolds in time evoke a resonant response to itself as a whole? Here we need to recall what we know about music: resonance derives from relationships, whether these be in a musical phrase or in a large form such as the rondo. A musical phrase, of course, is something we seem to hear all in one piece; with larger forms that's not necessarily the case. You're not constantly aware throughout a symphony of everything that you've heard up to that point. So exactly how *do* we respond resonantly to the entire piece of music? When and in what way are we in touch with the work as a developing whole?

The answer, I think, is that, for most listeners, this kind of response varies from moment to moment—is likely to surge in at certain points in the music and to subside at others. Though our response to what's being played at the *moment* may be resonant continuously, our resonant awareness of the whole or of large segments may be less consistent. When it is present, it will be experienced as an expansion, an enrichment, a deepening of what we're hearing at the moment.

All of this, however, depends greatly on the music and on who is listening to it. Some of us can hear a much longer stretch of music as a unified, immediately present image. But no one, I think, hears an entire movement of a symphony that way. Even so, some listeners may be much more aware than others of what has already been played, at least as a context for what is immediately present, and this awareness is likely to give them a more deeply resonant response, not merely to individual passages but to the whole work. Obviously, when we've heard a work a number of times, we're more likely to have this sense of the whole.

The last movement of Mozart's Violin Concerto in A major (K. 219) is in a rondo form. One central theme, a minuet, appears, then gives way to an episode containing different material; then it comes back, is replaced by still another episode, and so on. Using "A" for the minuet, the overall structure is, roughly:

A - B - A - C - A - D - A - B - A

Now there are moments when many listeners, I think, are likely to get isolated in the music immediately at hand, losing much of their awareness of the whole structure. Particularly during one section, a so-called "Turkish" episode in a different time signature and a minor key, the listener is likely, once having adjusted to this new and exotic atmosphere, to be swept far away from the very courtly minuet. Still, the overall structure *is* the context in which we hear this episode and is likely, if only by effect of contrast, to help shape our resonant response. But then there are other moments during the movement when our sense of the whole is very much heightened: for example, when any new theme first emerges, but most of all when the minuet itself returns, or even when you sense that it is about to do so. As the minuet reappears, this homecoming, often very cleverly, even teasingly, contrived, enhances the theme's native qualities of poignancy, sweetness, and wit. And with each episode and each return, because Mozart does all of this not mechanically but with enormous inventiveness and sensitivity, the resonance deepens and grows richer. The minuet theme, courtly as ever, takes on (for me) a breadth of feeling and a kind of knowledge, to the point that what was lovely in an exclusive and heedless way when it first appeared, becomes, without losing its essential character, more and more *in*clusive, profounder and more mature as the rondo develops. At certain moments, which become more frequent as the movement unfolds, I have a powerfully resonant awareness of the whole, an awareness which is not experienced as anything separate from what I am hearing at the moment—because resonance is never separate from the image—but which is experienced instead *within* the particular passage that I hear, so that this momentary image takes on qualities that are not merely of the moment, acquires a deeper perspective and a richer coloration.

With novels, plays, films, and so on, our resonant response to the entire work or to large-scale relationships within it, happens in much the same way. Jack Kerouac's *On the Road*, for example, is one of the many novels which, for me, demand to be seen as a whole, to be spatialized (particularly so in this case, because the book itself has so much to do with space). The sequential details of the narrative add up to an overall picture, which in turn is reflected in these very details.

Here are Sal and Dean and their friends crossing and recrossing the enormous American continent, compelled repeatedly to leave what they have found at one end and look for something which seems to beckon from the other—bungling relationships, "desirous of everything at the same time," getting high off of travel as they go and yet defeated constantly by the very nature of space, which, like time, exacts a high price for its favors. Every arrival a departure, every gain a loss, every here a not-there, each place in its turn lonely and lost in the night of the vast continent. Separation and isolation travel with the travelers. Nothing to do but stay on the road, going perhaps even faster, to see if, at moments, the road will become home, to see if it will happen that space and time collapse into "the holy void of uncreated emptiness." All this, of course, is one aspect of a more complex structure which the book, like a musical work, unfolds before me and which—now to a greater, now to a lesser degree—brings about a resonant deepening of my response to what I am reading at the moment. Degree is important here. Every resonant image in a work of art tends, to some extent at least, to reach out into the work. And elements that might not be resonant in themselves—a few words of dialogue here, a detail there—may catch the light that comes from the work as a whole, so that for a moment they flare out with this light like tiny mirror-fragments. Much depends on me. With one reading, it might be this detail—on another occasion, that one. But I find many images in *On the Road* which are more reliably and powerfully resonant, images into which the book seems momentarily to condense, or that are, at the very least, orchestrated by large-scale patterns of relationship within it.

We zoomed through another crossroads town, passed another line of tall lanky men in jeans clustered in the dim light like moths on the desert, and returned to the tremendous darkness, and the stars overhead were pure and bright because of the increasingly thin air as we mounted the high hill of the western plateau, about a foot a mile, so they say, and no trees obstructing any low-leveled stars anywhere. And once I saw a moody white-faced cow in the sage by the road as we flitted by.

She sighed in the dark. "What do you want out of life?" I asked, and I used to ask that all the time of girls.

"I don't know," she said. "Just wait on tables and try to get along." She yawned.

Beyond some trees, across the sand, a great neon sign of a roadhouse glowed red. Hingham always went there for a beer when he was tired of writing. He was very lonely, he wanted to get back to New York. It was sad to see his tall figure receding in the dark as we drove away, just like the other figures in New York and New Orleans: they stand uncertainly under immense skies, and everything about them is drowned.

There is a problem in that what I'm trying to illustrate can't *be* illustrated, not without handing someone the entire book to read. The resonant structure of an entire work can in no way be summed up; aspects of it can be vaguely indicated, as I have done here, but even this tends to turn resonance into concept, and the illustrations into "thematic statements."

In order for there to be a resonant response to large-scale relationships, several conditions have to be met. First of all, these relationships must be capable of creating resonance; that is, they must evoke whole areas of experience without reducing these areas to mere identities or concepts. This first condition will not be met if, for example, my sense of a play that I'm watching comes down to merely "a plea for tolerance in these troubled times" or "a paradigm of kinship rituals in the postwar German middle class." A second condition is that our response *at the moment* must not be dominated by reactive emotion. Finally, there must be an image before us that is capable of carrying this larger resonance. As I watch the play, there may not be such an image available at every moment. But if the image before me is sufficiently evocative and if its relationship to the whole is real—not arbitrary, not false—then it may deepen and expand to contain the larger complex of experiential quality that corresponds to the play as a whole.

Of all the arts that involve plot and reactive emotion, it may be that film has the most resources for creating resonance—so much so, in fact, that these resources are often used heavy-handedly or inappropriately. Some movie-makers, determinedly arty, offer us a series of pretty pictures which are not, unfortunately, very well integrated into the whole. Or else you may get efforts to mirror the structure of the film in shots that are so self-conscious or even self-congratulatory as to make you uncomfortably aware of the director alongside of the image itself. I particularly remember responding this way on one occasion during *Julia*. Jane Fonda, as Lillian Hellman, is on her way to keep a dangerous rendezvous with Julia in Berlin on the very eve of World War II. There is a long shot of the train at dawn, as it approaches the German border, plunging into an enormous blood-red sky. A very nice shot really, but I couldn't help smiling to myself just a little, and that was definitely *not* the response the film needed at that point.

Several points need to be made here about the relationship between reaction and resonance. First of all, a powerful reactive emotion can easily trump resonance—at least momentarily. The movie *Repulsion* demonstrates this. It has a number of highly resonant moments. Our sense of the whole film often adds depth to images of Catherine Deneuve's face or of her surroundings: the apartment she lives in, the streets where she walks, the beauty shop she works in. But when it reaches the point where this young woman, who is terrified by sexuality, is going to start using her knife on the landlord—and we *know* she's going to use it; she's already done in the fellow who loves her—then strong reactive emotion is likely to crowd out another kind of response. Seeing a film the second or third time around, incidentally, may change this. One not uncommon result of seeing a good movie repeatedly is that reactive response tends to weaken, and resonant response—if the potential is there—tends to flow back in. Movies that are seriously damaged if you know the plot, and that therefore cannot bear repeated viewing, are as a rule strong on reactive emotion and weak on resonance.

Reaction can jam the circuits momentarily; evolution appears to have assigned it a very high priority, which persists even when real-life self-concern becomes only the projected image of concern. Our developing resonant response to the whole work of art can be seen as something like a starry sky which the bright sun of reactive emotion temporarily washes out of our perception.

Still, it wouldn't be apt to see the two kinds of response as antagonistic. They work together well. Resonance, because it is so fluid and sensitive, is easily influenced—and takes on a special afterglow in the wake of a strong reactive response. Reactive emotion, whether in aesthetic experience or in ordinary life, can feed a later, resonant response. When we read Keats's lines:

> The weariness, the fever, and the fret
>> Here, where men sit and hear each other groan

our response to the verbal image may be resonant, but the quality of feeling necessary to deepen this image would not be there if we hadn't, in real life, already paid our dues in the form of reactive emotion—if life had not, at times, convinced us too that "but to think is to be full of sorrow and leaden-eyed despairs." Reactive emotion in everyday life is a reaction to something specific and causally related to our self-concern. But once the reactive experience is over, some of its quality can be revived and evoked by a resonant object in the absence of self-concern. The particular reactive experience, along with others, has been dissolved into a resonant solution.

It's not unusual for dramatic and literary works to move us from reaction to resonance as a kind of closing cadence. *Repulsion* itself illustrates this. And it's easy to see those final scenes in Shakespeare's tragedies, when the sturdy types come in to survey the wreckage, as a resonant cadence, following the powerful reactive climax when the central figures meet their doom. Our awareness of the whole is very likely to assert itself in these scenes, which offer us a concluding non-reactive image in which to perceive it. To take one example: in the final scene of *Antony and Cleopatra*, conquering Octavius enters the monument at Alexandria to find Cleopatra and her attendants dead. As the scene nears its close, he says:

> Take up her bed;
> And bear her women from the monument.
> She shall be buried by her Antony;
> No grave upon the earth shall clip in it
> A pair so famous.

Relationships between reaction and resonance in a work depend very much on the kind of work in question. We might arrange the arts along a spectrum from the most purely resonant, which would, I suppose, be absolute music, to the art with the greatest potential for reactive response, which would be drama or film. Prose would have more reactive potential than poetry, photography more than painting, representational painting more than abstract painting, and so on. The more an art evokes our response along associational-metaphorical lines, the more resonant it is likely to be. The more an art evokes our response by representing events that we perceive in a causal relationship to a projected self-concern, the more reactive it is likely to be. What happens, then, when we join arts from opposite ends of the spectrum, when we add music to drama and get opera or musical comedy? The reactive possibilities are there but they diminish as music assumes more importance. Compare Verdi's *Otello* and Shakespeare's *Othello*. The libretto is somewhat different from Shakespeare's play, of course, but also the reactive plot situation in Verdi's opera is muted to some degree by the powerful resonant effect of the music. Situations may call for reactive emotion, but the music tends to hold it within a resonant context. Here, instead of using the sun and stars as our analogy, we might do better to picture reaction as the moon—perhaps full, perhaps crescent—in a starry sky.

The kind of effect that is attained by combining music and drama depends very much on the relative importance of each in a particular work of art. When drama has the upper hand, music can actually intensify reactive emotion. This is what happens typically in movies, where we're often scarcely aware of the music as such. Its wider and potentially resonant experiential range is drastically constricted, *defined* in fact by the dramatic situation itself. In this way, music can help to scare the pants off us, to make us cry, to keep us on the edges of our seats. But there are other possibilities in film. Music can make its contribution to an already resonant scene or image. It can also work *against* the action (a Chopin nocturne behind a soccer match), calling attention to itself in the process, and quite possibly creating resonance where none might otherwise exist.

In situations where music clearly dominates, as it does for the most part in songs and in operas, whatever dramatic situation there may be will certainly have its effect on the resonance, but often without compressing it into reactive emotion. This is not to say that, in the hands of some composers, opera cannot achieve a reactive effect: I think immediately of the death of Mimi in *La Bohème*. But in general, opera is a far cry, for me at least, from film, drama, or the novel.

In summary, resonance appears to be—not the only kind of response to the whole work, nor even the "proper" response— but the kind of response which is most faithful to the work in its entirety. There's usually more to a work of art than can be experienced in a wave of reactive feeling, no matter how complex. And the effort to figure out a work—though this may in one way or another prove useful—may tend to schematize it and can take us, at least temporarily, away from aesthetic experience. Resonance, however, is faithful to the work as a whole because it is extraordinarily sensitive and adaptable, is capable of great complexity, and can be as subtle and dynamic as the work itself; because it is not falsified or deformed by a controlling concept; because it is perceived in the work, not apart from it; and because it is necessarily real, personal, and honest.

There's no question of valuing resonance to the exclusion of the other ways of responding to a whole work of art. There is enormous satisfaction to be had experiencing reactive feeling in an aesthetic context. Nothing is more impressive than the power of some art to draw us into an ever-increasing reactive involvement, to lead us toward a climax that resolves the reactive tensions of the entire work. And, as far as an intellectual grasp of art is concerned, I've long believed that paying careful attention to the structure of relationships within a work is more than justified if it provides us with a way of coming to see the work more fully, and therefore of appreciating it more fully.

Also, we need to recognize that individual temperaments may favor any one of these ways of responding. Or an individual may favor one way this time, another the next—even if the same work is involved.

It's hardly my intent to be prescriptive; the whole point is to liberate aesthetic experience, not to set up standards to which perceivers must try to conform. Still, it would be foolish not to recognize that certain notions about art, certain expectations, can close off important areas of aesthetic experience. In particular, a problem occurs when either the reactive or the cognitive mode of responding to art comes to dominate our experience so entirely that the resonance is lost. To look for nothing more in a novel or a film than an emotional roller-coaster ride is to limit radically its aesthetic potential. We end up impatient with anything that doesn't advance the action or give us an emotional jolt—preferably both. And the destruction of resonance by the anxious, obsessive pursuit of significance, the "decoding" approach to art, is a disease of our time, which, like certain other diseases, spreads most rapidly when school is in session. But more of this in a later chapter.

Many years after reading a novel, when I remember very little of the plot and would be even less prepared to offer the sort of philosophical summary that some teachers propose as *the* meaning of the work, I will often remember odd off-to-the-side details: images of people, places, objects—images that have become blurry and yet still retain some echo of resonant feeling. And it may well turn out, if I reread the novel, that these seemingly tangential images become central to a new, richer and more resonant reading of the work. I first read *The Odyssey* in a freshman humanities course. It was my first semester at the university and I was very busy. So I raced through the book, following an essentially reactive course through the plot, making notes on Odysseus' itinerary against a possible quiz. At the same time, my teacher was doing what teachers did: giving me various intellectual reconstructions of what we were reading—"fate and free will in Homer"; "Odysseus as epic hero"; "the journey home as reintegration." You know the sort of thing. Anyway, I wasn't that crazy about the book, but at least I'd done it, the way people do Greece on a European tour. Then, about a dozen years later and very much involved with literature, I found myself remembering some details that gave me a tremendous urge to get back into the book. These were some of the formulaic descriptions that are so common in *The Odyssey* and that were so useful to oral epic poets. The recurring passage, for example, in which a maid pours out water into a silver basin for the guests to wash their hands, and then a "staid housekeeper" brings bread and helps the guests liberally to all they can eat. Images like that *were The Odyssey* for me twelve years after reading it, and, for some reason, they seemed extraordinarily rich and alive. Yet they had scarcely any plot significance, and still less to do with "fate and free will." Then, rereading the work, I found these images to be more centrally situated than I might have thought. There was this recurring sense of coming in out of the storm. A terrifying world out there: monsters, witches, savage tribes, hostile elements. Then to find refuge where something has been won from the terror and chaos—in a civilized enclosure where guests are well treated instead of eaten, where a mere building is a kind of victory, where orchards teem with fruit and pens with swine, where bards sing and stories are told, and where people have at least that hold on time that genealogy allows.

For Odysseus to crawl up naked on the Phaeacian shore, more dead than alive, after days and nights alone in the ocean, and then, not long after, to find himself bathed, oiled, and clothed, an honored guest receiving hospitality at the Phaeacian court: this constituted something like a musical interval for me, a highly resonant one that joined other such intervals

within the work in a profoundly resonant structure of relationships, within which Odysseus' eventual homecoming supplied
not merely a reactive climax but a resonant coda as well. How
much all of this deepened that image of the housekeeper! How
strange that what I retained from an unsatisfying reading of
the book was the resonant germ of far more satisfying readings
to come. Would it have been helpful at the time if my teacher
had lectured on all of this? Well . . . that depends. The
question of teaching is one we'll return to in Chapter Fourteen.

CHAPTER NINE
Beyond Form and Content

"Form" versus "content": this is a distinction I haven't found it necessary to make. Still it might be wise to take some account of these categories, which do, after all, play an important role in the way so many people think and talk about art. The distinction presents itself so naturally, so handily. Not with all of the arts, but with some of them. A particular sonnet is "about" love and death; that's content. But it's written in fourteen lines of iambic pentameter, rhymed according to a certain scheme and arranged with pairs of antithetical images in each quatrain, leading to a general observation in the concluding couplet. That's form. A photograph shows the plight of illegal immigrants awaiting deportation. That's content. It uses dark tones and low contrast. Three figures are visible sitting on a bench, but the depth of field is restricted so that only the left, foremost figure is in tight focus. That's form. Or is it?

Handy as these categories are, people who look closely at art tend to run into problems with them. That despairing mood we see in the photograph of the immigrants may have more than a little to do with "formal" qualities that depend upon framing, aperture, developing time, choice of paper, and so on. So that the "plight" is communicated not merely *in* a certain form, but *by* a certain form. So that form becomes not simply a way of saying something but part of the statement itself. Fine. Now what's interesting is that this point I've just made has been made a million times over. *Without* driving "form" and "content" out of our critical vocabulary.

My purpose here isn't to argue that the terms should be retired, though I could see them go without shedding tears.

What I would like to suggest is a way these terms can be understood and applied without misleading us about art and the way it works.

The form-content distinction at its best, I think, reflects no more than a decision to divide up the aesthetic experience in a certain way for the purpose of description or analysis. What gets us into trouble is talking about form and content as separate parts of the actual work of art itself. Here's a painting: where's the form? where's the content? But it does make sense to understand that "form" is, broadly speaking, a way of talking about art in terms of the medium, and "content" is a way of talking about art in terms of the response. In music, for example, a "sense of sustained longing" is content; a series of unresolved chords is form. In painting, color relationships, composition, and framing are formal elements; chaste and tranquil nudes, glittering fields, and knowing smiles are content. Characters in fiction can go either way, depending. "A sympathetic but ineffectual character, defeated from the start by the harsh realities of ghetto life"—that would be content. But to speak of *characterization* or of the use of contrasting characters to mark certain points of transition in a novel would be to speak of form.

The distinction is rough and a little vague along the borderline, but it has advantages. No longer would we persuade ourselves that, using as a sort of container the *form* of tetrameter couplets arranged in a tripartite structure, Andrew Marvell gives us as *content* a restatement of the *carpe diem* theme. We would have to understand that everything in our response, including the intensification of feeling procured by a structural contrast, and including the complex and delicate contribution that rhythms and rhymes make to resonance, would be "content." And everything in the poetic medium, including whatever thematic statements are to be found, would be "form." Statements, messages, ideas, themes, and such would all turn into form when we pursued them into the terrain of the artistic medium. Camera angles, brush strokes, *pas de chat*, stringcourses, and modulations would all emerge as content when we superimposed upon the images in which they participate the feeling response of an aesthetic perceiver.

But even though I've chosen to offer this particular construction of form and content, I hope the reader will forgive me if I don't use it. There are some intriguing aesthetic issues which are often discussed in terms of form and content, but which I would like to consider, in this chapter, in light of the theory that has been developed.

In Chapter Two we looked at the qualities in an object or a scene that encourage us to detach it from the practical context and perceive it as image. But it's clear that these qualities alone don't account for the attentive interest we give to aesthetic objects. If the object doesn't interest us, if it doesn't speak to our feelings, then its image-making qualities alone won't turn it into art. The object may provide, at a minimum, some sensory gratification; but beyond that, what aesthetic experience requires is the kind of affective-cognitive response we've been looking at in the last five chapters.

Though it's been useful to consider these aspects of aesthetic experience separately—first, the way an image is detached from the practical context, and second, the way a response is evoked—the experience itself is a whole, and our analysis will betray it unless the two processes can be integrated. It would be a mistake, for example, to conclude that when we look at something, we are led first by certain qualities—patterning, framing, etc.—to see it aesthetically, and *then* find other qualities in it that evoke our response. And to suppose a reverse order of events would be just as far from the truth. In fact, the qualities that encourage us to perceive something aesthetically are *also* part of the structure of relationships to which we respond with feeling. Think for a minute about a slow blues, with its repeated AAB pattern:

Ain't got a nickel, baby, ain't got a nickel to my name,
Ain't even got a nickel, not a nickel to my name,
The way you treat me, girl, it's a damn shame.

You spent all my money, left me sleepin' on the floor,
Spent all of my money, left me sleepin' on the floor,
You know, some day you'll want me, I won't be around no more.

This repeated AAB in both the melody and the words is part of the patterning that creates image and encourages us to perceive aesthetically. But stanzas like these are not mere aesthetic containers for something separate called "content." The pattern here clearly plays an evocative role as well. Repetition, as we're well aware, has evocative potential: "I won't! I won't! I won't!" The repeated second line in the blues is an opportunity for expressive variation, but especially, it gives the singer a chance to intensify the feeling, to drive it home the second time around. Also, this continual pattern of statement and intensified restatement contributes to the very slow, obsessive kind of movement we feel in this type of blues; it helps to call forth and embody that fixated, ruminating, wretchedly melancholy condition we all know so well. In a fast blues, needless to say, the same pattern could play a different role.

In other words, aesthetic experience is not divided; there is no boundary in it between what frees us from self-concern and what calls forth our interest. Meter and rhyme are obviously patterning elements that encourage us to perceive a poem as image. But what power they can have as well to evoke experiential quality. Nearly five hundred years ago, John Skelton received a death's head as a gift and, in reply, wrote the poem which begins:

Your ugly token
My mind hath broken
From worldly lust
For I have discust
We are but dust
And die we must.

The short lines with their hammering relentless rhymes strengthen the sense of firm finality (as does the alliteration that links "dust" and "die"). Not that a string of rhyming two-beat lines *has* to evoke such feelings, any more than an ascending musical phrase has to sound aspiring. In fact, Skelton was able to use the same kind of pattern elsewhere with a lighter, more delicate effect. But, given the subject and imagery in this poem, the sound pattern makes an important contribution, fits so tightly into the overall evocative structure that a reader—or better yet, a listener—is unlikely to sense any split between the two.

What happens if we *do* sense such a division? What happens if one set of elements pulls away, becomes "empty" pattern, and competes for our attention with the other elements in the work? Let's suppose a neighbor knocks on the door one day, and wants my opinion of some lines he's written for his girlfriend:

> I have to say I love you, girl
> And yet I don't know what it means,
> I just keep thinkin' of you, girl
> A-walkin' in those tight blue jeans.

Fortunately for him I'm not Alceste; fortunately for me he's not a powerful nobleman. Can I say anything useful? Setting aside any questions I might have about his notion of love, I could point out that what he has written has a split personality. The meter and rhyme have pulled away from the rest and have become a rigidly imposed and empty pattern. My separate awareness of them disunifies what ought to be a unified experience. "Got you," he says, and comes back the next day with:

> I have to say I love you
> But I don't know what it means,
> I just keep thinkin' of you
> In those tight blue jeans.

It's a little better, isn't it? More concise, of course. But also the metrical pattern is a bit more supple, more in harmony with the other elements, less awkwardly obtrusive as a separate aspect. "Tight blue jeans," for example, gets the three strong beats it deserves instead of being forced into an iambic pattern.

Theodore Adorno makes a comparable criticism of the American popular song, which was—at least when he wrote, in the early sixties—standardized to thirty-two bars with a bridge in the middle, and which had standardized "metric and harmonic cornerstones." Unlike what Adorno calls "the higher music," popular music "uses the types as empty cans into which the material is pressed without interacting with the forms." Of course, to be fully meaningful, such criticism would have to address itself to individual songs.

Not only can we talk about the evocative power of specific image-making qualities in a particular work of art, we can also look at the way such qualities *in general* affect our response. Framing in art is not merely a way to detach an image from the practical context; it also encloses certain areas of our own experience and excludes others. Framing creates an inner world where some things count very much and others, which might be important elsewhere, simply don't exist.

Coherent pattern in a work of art gives unity to more than the image; it also tends to unify, in one way or another, the various experiential areas that are called forth. This is saying quite a lot. Philosophy, science, religion struggle endlessly to achieve coherence, whereas it is directly available to art. But at a price: the coherence of each individual work is not transferable. Like the natives of Shangri-La, when it leaves its home it withers and dies. There is much that can be taken out of at least some works of art. But to keep hold of the resonant unity of a novel or a symphony or a play, you would have to disappear inside the work.

Sometimes, particularly with literature, theatre, and film, people try to isolate some aspect of the overall pattern and call it "the meaning" of a work, try even to translate it into a verbal summary. And it is true that in some works of art, one source of pattern and unity is an intellectual schema, either consciously worked out by the artist or else produced without conscious intention but still recoverable by critical analysis. But to see this kind of schema as "the meaning" of a work is to misunderstand art. In fact, from that position it's a very short step to the notion that works of art are merely moving vans that exist principally to convey a meaning from the artist to the perceiver, who then unloads the meaning from the work and finds a place for it among his intellectual furniture. Music, not surprisingly, has been less troubled by this false aesthetic than painting, and painting much less than the arts which use language (though I did once see an ad for a famous art museum's correspondence course; under a reproduction of Van Eyck's *Giovanni Arnolfini and His Bride*, the headline demanded: "HOW MANY PEOPLE KNOW THE REAL MEANING OF THIS PAINTING?"). People who are particularly occupied with literature and who tend to see it as being quite separate from the other arts are the most likely to take this attitude.

I don't want to overstate my point. Of course, it's possible and even worthwhile to extract "philosophy" from some literary works. Literature has an immeasurable amount to teach us about the way things are, the way they've been in the past, and the way they may be in the future—although, if we're looking for instruction in the nature of things, it's by no means a reliable or consistent teacher. But literature, though it may brilliantly and to good purpose play the role for us of psychologist, prophet, metaphysician, or revolutionary, and though it may legitimately be the subject of various kinds of scientific inquiry—anthropological, historical, etc.—still has a very valuable, aesthetic function of its own.

The kind of intellectual schema that we may extract from a work of art can be viewed and evaluated in two ways. We can view it *outside* the work in a context that may be, for example, social, psychological, or ethical. Within any such context, we can ask questions about its significance or validity. Naturally, to the extent that we do this, we've left the art behind, retaining the work only as a social or psychological or philosophical document. *Or* we can view the schema *inside* the work. Here we find ourselves asking not whether it is valid, but how it works. We might, for example, ask how much coherence it provides and to what extent it is integrated into the work as a whole. This doesn't mean that the schema is now locked within a closed system and therefore exempt from any judgment based on our own experience. The system of a work of art is not closed; it opens on the perceiver. But—and this is a crucial point—our response to the "philosophy" of a work when we are perceiving that work aesthetically is very different from the way we might respond to it *merely* as philosophy.

A work of art doesn't have to be true to our experience in any simple-minded sense. Max Ernst can show us two old ladies coming in for a landing in their old-fashioned motorcar. Kafka can put us in the presence of a talking dog. Cocteau can give us a furry beast that changes into a prince. No problem. And yet we may walk out of an utterly "realistic" movie, in which people look and talk as they do in everyday life, and criticize it (legitimately) for not being "true to life." Why? How is it that the most wildly fantastic art may be thoroughly acceptable as an evocation of experiential quality, and will hold us tightly within the image, while a "realistic" film that doesn't quite ring true may drive us out of the image, as we shift in our seats, muttering, "Oh, come on!" A work can be realist, symbolist, surrealist, can be fairy tale or science fiction; it doesn't matter as long as we are capable of letting ourselves believe in the work on its own terms while we're perceiving it. Within the image anything goes—as long as the response that's evoked can be contained and perceived within it as well. However, if we respond not with the image but against it, then the work is aesthetically in trouble.

If all the paintings I had ever seen were careful, realistic renderings and I were for the first time exposed to an expressionistic painting, grossly "distorted" in color and form, I might have some difficulty relating it to my own experience. I would have become used to having my feelings evoked in a certain way. A quiet harbor scene would seem secure and peaceful. A storm and a raging sea might evoke a sense of danger or tumultuous unbridled energy. To each kind of scene its own range of feeling. But here is this expressionist painting of a still harbor, which is nevertheless so turbulent and strange, so distorted and garish, that I don't know what to make of it and respond more or less against it. In time I might come to see that the painting is as much a direct portrayal of a state of mind as it is a painting of a harbor. To appreciate such paintings fully, I would have to allow—in fact would have to open up—a somewhat different mode of relationship between the painting and my own experience. And then, at a still later time, my first view of a nonrepresentational painting might cause the same sort of confusion all over again and make a similar demand for a new way of relating image and experience.

What I'm getting at is that when we perceive a work of art, we adopt, often without being at all aware that we're doing so, an appropriate mode of relationship that gives the work the most direct access to our own experience. "Realism" is one mode, but there are many others, representational and otherwise. This is something that occasionally presents a problem to people when they venture outside their customary range of aesthetic interest. Someone finds heroes like Roland and El Cid "hard to believe"—but of course they are idealized figures, larger than life. Through them the poems can offer us an effective way of perceiving our own values, aspirations, conflicts; but a naturalistic mode of response is likely to close us off to much of what the poems have to offer. Instrumental rock music, working within relatively simple large-scale structures in time, puts its major resources into the dramatic exploitation of the continually moving present moment. Resonance arises partly out of overall structure, but principally from developments in timbre, melody, rhythm, and dynamics from one moment to the next, as they are worked out on the surface of the Big Beat. In a classical symphony or concerto, there is usually more available in the way of large-scale resonant relationships; the present moment typically owes much of its resonance to this "spatialized" structure of unfolding relationships within which it exists. It's possible to listen to a Haydn symphony as though it were rock music, but, with the exception of occasional showy contrasts, the music is likely to seem a little tame on a moment-to-moment basis, particularly in the absence of that overpowering, even coercive, beat. And in the reverse situation—if our expectations are geared for Haydn—any rock music would be likely to sound blaring, boring, and unimaginative. Someone who wanted to travel back and forth successfully would have to bring along a change of modes. Let me quickly add, by the way, that this point I am making about art doesn't add up to a denial of any basis for aesthetic judgments. The best possible mode applied to Work A might give us a far more meager aesthetic experience than would Work B perceived even in an uncertain, fumbling way.

Now, if we take up the question of what causes us to accept or reject a work of art on its own terms, we have at least part of an answer. Our acceptance depends on finding an appropriate mode of response. We won't believe in a work of art if we can't find a mode of responding *within* the image. Maddie and I were sitting in a movie one night; it began with some of those shots of young lovers running on the beach and outlined against the setting sun that you see quite a bit of in poster shops and in commercials for items of personal hygiene. I groaned, reacting against the image—wondering what the hell we had paid four dollars each to see. But Maddie whispered, "No, look! They're making fun of it." And they were. What matters here is that I changed my mode of response. The division between myself and those corny shots became a comic incongruity that could be contained within the image. Or suppose you're reading a novel with a historical setting and your own experience balks, refuses to flow into the image because it's such a foolish misrepresentation of history as you know it. But then perhaps you begin to see the novel less as a representation of life in a certain period than as a representation of myths which have gathered around that period and which invite your response as myths. You click a different lens into place and read on. Talking dogs and fairy tales are no problem.

But we don't, any of us, have an infinite supply of lenses. First of all, we each have personal limitations in this area. But also there may *be* no appropriate mode that keeps our response within a particular work. I could be watching a dance and mutter, "That's bullshit." A friend could whisper, "Look—see it as a dance *about* bullshit." But without some real help from the work itself, it would be very unlikely that I could do that.

Let's return now to the intellectual schema as it appears outside, and inside, the work of art. Let's take an obviously didactic work, the kind that begs to be considered not only as literature but also as true teaching: Pope's *An Essay on Criticism*. It's a poem I have admired for a long time—as poetry and, to no small extent, as literary criticism. But there's this difference: I can swallow it whole as a poem; as literary criticism, it has a lot to say that's worthwhile, and, of course, it has historical interest, but still it's nothing I could endorse unreservedly, nothing I could simply "believe in." *Outside* the poem Pope's ideas are overboard in the perilous seas of literary and aesthetic theory. They don't all stay afloat.

But the poem itself is an ark; inside, everything floats—at least as far as I am concerned. This happens because his theories, in the poem, find a relationship to my own experience which does not rest entirely on their status as true or false statements about literature.

First of all, we need to recognize that his didactic schema is closely integrated into the work and therefore supported by powerful resources of sound and imagery. Pope's critical system emphasizing authority, clarity, balance, good sense, and restraint is reflected in and buttressed by the couplets themselves with their tight, lucid balance and the unarguable conclusiveness of their rhymes. Here, for example, are his lines on wit (used in this context to mean something like "creative imagination") and judgment:

> For wit and judgment often are at strife,
> Though meant each other's aid, like man and wife.
> 'Tis more to guide, than spur the Muse's steed;
> Restrain his fury, than provoke his speed:
> The winged courser, like a generous horse,
> Shows most true mettle when you check his course.
>
> (I, 82-87)

As for the basis on which I can accept Pope's schema, there are several points that need to be made. This whole system of Pope's, with its scriptures and its rules, its Homeric Garden of Eden, its saints and sinners, is a literary religion—and, as with all religions, there's a home for it somewhere in the psyche. There's enough in Pope's system that I like—and what I don't like is historically distant enough to be non-threatening—so that I feel more sympathetic to it than antipathetic. But more than that, it's also part of my own tradition; reading *An Essay on Criticism* is like revisiting a town where you once lived—a town to which you can never actually return but which you have never entirely left either.

Or we could come at it another way. Let's say that *An Essay on Criticism* is a work of fiction and that the speaker is the chief character and narrator. The question, then, is not so much whether I entirely agree with this person but whether he is a character in whom I can believe, and with whom I can empathize within the frame of the poem.

What matters then with this kind of intellectual structure in a work of art is whether we can find an effective relationship between it and our experience, a relationship which allows us to perceive our response within the work. As I said, there are limits. If Pope's system were an oppressive presence in my life—something I'd been trying to free myself from—and if there were no vehicle within the work to carry my hostility, then I'd be likely to react against the poem, and it would function aesthetically no better than it did as literary theory.

What often happens in literature is that the "philosophical" structure of a work offers us a partial truth to which we can relate *some* of our experience but which might be contradicted by other experience were it allowed to step forth. In a sense, this is the rule with all art. Joyous music provides a frame that excludes despair. And that's just what happens, except at times when our own despair is too much on the scene to be chased away by a piece of happy music, no matter how evocative. We can enjoy a poem built on self-assertion and spiteful anger; we can likewise enjoy a poem that evokes feelings of love and altruism. And we may especially value a poem that recognizes *both* possibilities in human experience and somehow mediates between them, because in this last poem there will be room for more of our experience; its resonance may be deeper and richer. But in this poem too, the structure that unifies self-assertion and altruism will have its own limitations, its own *terra incognita* of excluded experience.

The ability of an intellectual structure to sustain itself aesthetically depends in part on the power of the work to evoke certain areas of experience with such intensity that the inappropriate areas are never heard from. A fairly weak intellectual structure might be sustained by other elements—reactive elements, say—which are powerful enough to protect it, just as a mediocre pitcher, who allows one hit after another, can still be handed a win by his teammates who, in the field, keep snatching impossible balls out of the air and, at bat, keep the runs coming in. Movies especially can do this, because of their high reactive potential and the enormous strength of their frame. But not only movies. The structure of ideas in *Man and Superman*, for example, taken in isolation, is, well, OK . . . a little dated. The Life Force, the superman—for some of us at least, a little tiresome. But this structure is so nicely worked out on several levels and so very well integrated into the play, and is supported there by so much persuasive wit, by such vivid characterization, such stagecraft, so sharp an awareness of the difference between drama and philosophizing, that it is only when I'm *away* from the play and considering the ideas in isolation that they can begin to seem dated and tiresome.

Outside of a work of art, an intellectual structure stands or falls by its validity in comparison with competing ideas. Within the work of art, the structure has far greater means at its disposal. We can adopt it temporarily, with the same as-if assumption that we use for fiction itself. We can respond to it not as proposed philosophic or scientific truth but as a myth which, though utterly improbable on the surface, expresses some fundamental truths about human experience. Or we can accept it as expressing *one* basic attitude within the human repertoire. We can even out-and-out accept it, as a comprehensive world view, in a work which is so evocatively powerful and therefore so persuasive that it simply excludes or crushes with the immense weight of its fictive reality any contradictory evidence from our experience.

We need to remember also that art, even art that deals with ideas, is not obliged to seek the kind of intellectual coherence that theorists pursue. The intellectual structure of a work may offer no more than the kind of balance that comes from the dynamic play of opposing principles. The work explores and reflects this counterplay but doesn't attempt to resolve it intellectually. Compare Shaw's play with Peter Weiss's *Marat/ Sade*. *Man and Superman* may give dramatic voice to opposing attitudes but, despite Shaw's own invocation in the Preface of the dramatist's lack of "conscience," there's not much doubt about who the intellectual good guys are. John Tanner's (and Don Juan's) ideas prevail; they include and explain all the others. Tanner may be a comic figure by the end of the play, overtaken by the marriage he had hoped to escape, vanquished by the Life Force, and so on. But it's his own theories that explain all this to us; conquered as a man, he is vindicated as a philosopher. There's confrontation aplenty in this play, but intellectually it's no great contest.

In *Marat/Sade*, however, some of the intellectual conflicts remain open. Marat is in many ways a sympathetic and intellectually appealing figure, but his point of view doesn't include or explain away Sade's—or even Charlotte Corday's, for whom Marat's ideals mean "mountains of dead." Sade may be the writer of the play-within-a-play, but his point of view, though it recognizes Marat's, neither includes it nor triumphs over it. The play is by no means "neutral" politically; in my view, it affirms the revolution, both then and now. But this affirmation hardly disposes of a profound conflict between individually based and socially based values. Weiss uses opposing forces to hold his play together the way an architect uses them to hold a building up, and in this way he arrives at an aesthetic, though not a philosophical synthesis.

Aesthetic "truth," like any kind of truth, has to accord with our experience, but in art there's a much wider range of means by which this accord can be reached than there is in philosophy or the sciences. And this accord, once it has been established, is less vulnerable to time. Aristotle and Aquinas are subject to revision and refutation; Dante is not. Schopenhauer and Einstein are permanently provisional. Proust is permanent.

The "truth" of art is its ability to capture life as we experience it, and to give us that experience back in a coherent aesthetic image. We perceive our own experience not only free of self-concern, but within the context of a harmonized resonant whole. The art that can accomplish this most fully and with the greatest evocative power is the art many of us seem to value most. It is in this context that we need to understand what people call "philosophical content"—a concept, incidentally, which is much more likely to be applied to literature, drama, and so on than to music, painting, or sculpture (though that certainly does happen on occasion). What is regarded as the "philosophy" of a work is at the same time a cognitively-affectively evocative set of relationships and a means toward pattern and coherence, but it is never the "essence" of a work because it is never more than a part, and the only "essence" of a work of art is the work itself as we experience it.

III
CHAPTER TEN
Creating Art

If art is based on a way of perceiving, what can we say about artists? Is their role downgraded in a perceiver-centered theory of art? Do they fit into this kind of theory at all? It might seem that the creation of art—a kind of activity that typically entails so much hard work and such a sense of purpose—has little to do with freedom from striving and self-concern. Will we require separate theories for artist and audience?

In order to pursue these questions, we need first to have some sense of what is involved in creating a work of art. Here, for example, is a painter stretching canvas. Is that part of the creative activity? Now the painter is applying an undercoat. What about that? Are filmmakers creating only when they stare off into space seeking inspiration—or is testing wind machines also part of the creative work? I think it's important to be aware of the entire process involved in creating art—to understand what it is that artists *do*. I picture a choreographer alone, trying out movements, listening to music perhaps, trying out a sequence over and over again—then setting up rehearsal schedules, working with dancers, exploring, seeing what works —then setting lights, discovering new possibilities and new problems, experimenting—worrying over the unexpected awkwardness of a costume, the erratic operation of a slide projector, the growing bad feeling between two dancers. Or we might think about the preparation of an animated film. On the screen, there may be a lovely flow of images, but the animators themselves have to work patiently frame by frame, attending carefully to the mechanical process that this kind of art entails. It may be that on rare occasions a piece of music or a poem is revealed intact to the artist in a flash of inspiration, the way "Kubla Khan" is supposed to have been revealed to Coleridge in a dream. But as a general rule the artistic process is quite a bit grittier than that. Even very good poets are allowed to struggle and curse as they engage the stubborn medium of language.

One way to view the artistic process is to put inspiration first, followed by the effort to realize that inspiration in the particular medium. Croce, I suppose, takes this as far as it will go with his notion that the entire work is present in the artistic intuition. But there are artists who would argue that their own process is exactly opposite to this: you fool around with the medium and, in doing so, *discover* the work you're creating. I think that, for the most part, artists create in a way that is somewhere between these two possibilities. They begin with some notion of what they're after, and, as they encounter the medium, make new discoveries. Of course, the balance here would vary not only from one artist to another but from one art form to another. In music and poetry the initial inspiration, if not for an entire work, then at least for a small part of it, might very well be equal to its finished expression in the medium. In other words, a few lines or a melody can simply "come to you" already fully realized. But arrangements of pigment or clay can never come to you in the same direct way. No matter how fully you visualize them, the medium is still one step removed. And media like theatre, dance, and film are, for the individual artist, perhaps even further removed and more full of surprises.

To look at the creation of art in this way only widens the theoretical gap between artist and audience, and makes it seem even less likely that one notion of aesthetic experience will do for both. How can the artistic process, which is so often tentative and uneven, which so often mixes creative passion with patient tinkering, discoveries with false starts, inspiration with frustration—how can this process be related to what we know of the aesthetic experience? If creation were otherwise, if every artist received her work intact from the muse, effortlessly, then artists would simply be the first percei-vers of works which they had the mysterious power to call forth. And the basis of art, for them as for the rest of us, would remain perception in the absence of self-concern. But artists as a rule don't simply receive their works; they have to make them. And there's the problem. How can you make something without striving?

Still, I think it's possible to reconcile aesthetic perception and the artistic process. We might begin with the very simplest kind of relationship between the two. Let's go back for a moment to "natural" aesthetic experience: the landscapes, flowers, shells, birdsong, waterfalls, sunsets, and so on, which we often find ourselves perceiving for their own sake and in the absence of any self-concern. Isn't there, even here, room for effort and purposefulness—not on the part of any artist, but on the part of the perceiver? I walk up a hill to see the view, or hunt on the beach for the most beautiful shells, or even tend a plant carefully for months in order to enjoy the flowers it will produce. In other words, I strive. True, the moment of aesthetic perception itself will be free of striving, but, having recognized this as a desirable experience, I may spend some effort putting myself in a position to have it, just as I may labor—making the bed, etc.—to put myself in a position to rest.

But we can take this further. I may even find myself tinkering with the "natural" scene in order to make it more satisfying aesthetically. This might be no more than trying out various points of view (there's a haiku about hanging the moon on a pine tree and taking it off again). Or I carry flowers into the house and stick them in a vase. I may even move them around a little until they look right. We've gone from mere perception to the pursuit of perception, and now with these flowers, to rearrangement of the aesthetic image. Where does the creative process begin?

It's not difficult to suppose a world without artists—a world in which there is, to begin with, no art at all outside of natural aesthetic experience—and then to see artistic creation, at least of a fairly simple kind, flowing right back in again as people do no more than pursue a certain kind of satisfaction. They wouldn't have to be aware of what they were doing; they wouldn't have to call it "art." In fact, the particular "out of one's self" quality of aesthetic experience might lead some people in this world-without-artists to pursue it and use it in a religious context. They might, in the choice of a site, or in the collection and arrangement of objects, or in the use of movement or language, be inviting aesthetic experience, but if you asked what they were doing, they might answer in religious terms. In any case, whatever people might think they were doing, it would be very easy for ornamentation to emerge, for decorative traditions to establish themselves. At this simple level, artistic creation would consist of various kinds of manipulation, perhaps even trial and error, in pursuit of a satisfactory aesthetic experience: an interval of perception for its own sake, free, to some degree at least, of self-concern.

There is no contradiction at this level between striving and non-striving. Each has its role to play. If I'm arranging flowers in a vase, there is a constant interplay between manipulation and contemplation. But that two different functions are involved should be obvious to an observer watching me first adjust, then pause to look, then adjust again and pause once more. What would be simply two successive phases when someone climbs a hill to see the view would here give way to each other in fairly rapid alternation, until the flower arrangement was completed to my satisfaction. Still, to speak of an interplay here between manipulation and contemplation is not quite right. There are actually three phases, which may at times succeed each other so rapidly that they're experienced as one continuous process. I adjust, then contemplate, then evaluate the response I've just experienced—perhaps in relation to some intuitively sought-after effect—as a basis for further readjustment.

It's not so difficult, then, to see certain kinds of fairly simple creative activity as a natural outgrowth from aesthetic perception itself. If we're looking for a bridge to take us from perception to the shores at least of artistic creation, then moon-viewing, flower-arranging, and even ornamentation and decoration will do nicely. But is the problem solved? We've made room in our theory for the artist as collector, as decorator, as aesthete, perhaps even as ritualist. But is there a place here that can accommodate that heroic figure, the demiurge who has for some time now been the ideal type of the artist in Western society? You don't hire people like Charlton Heston and Kirk Douglas to play flower arrangers.

It's reasonable to assume that the same elements of striving and aesthetic perception to be found in the pursuit of a "view" or in flower-arranging occur throughout the range of artistic creation, though their interrelationship may, in most cases, be far more complicated. The artist's striving, which in its less successful moments may bring feelings of bitter frustration, is just that—striving. But what the artist strives *toward* is the transcendence of striving and self-concern in an aesthetic image. When some element of this image emerges either in the medium or in the artist's mind, there is—to the extent that the image works—at least a brief instant when striving stops, and the artist disappears, projected into the image that has been created. This may well be only a flash of aesthetic experience; the fragment may even be discarded as the struggle begins again. Or, on the other hand, the artist may be caught up in a strong and steady creative flow—painting or writing or composing unimpeded for hours on end, with striving minimized and the entire experience dominated by aesthetic transcendence in the developing image. But even the product of this sustained inspiration on the part of a writer, let us say, or a composer, may not be exactly right in relation to the work as a whole. It may seem tangential, unintegrated. Sometimes it happens that an artist begins a work which corresponds to a particular experiential complex— then, riding a wave of creative enthusiasm, pursues what turns out to be a quite different experiential area, and is left with either the bases for two separate works of art or else the necessity to create/discover experiential relationships that can bind the two pieces into a coherent and resonant whole.

When does an artist's creative activity become aesthetic experience? This happens at the moment when he is able to perceive, in the absence of striving and self-concern, the image or fragment of an image that he is creating (or even simply choosing). This can happen entirely inside the head. What's necessary in this case is that the mental image be sufficiently detached and framed psychologically so that the artist can momentarily project response into it, in the same way that response is projected into an external object of perception. Perception, after all, does happen *inside* our bodies, and although most of us aren't terribly good at perceiving images without a stimulus "out there," some of us, including some artists, are. Many musicians "hear" a melodic line—and even its instrumental timbre—in the process of creating it, just as they can hear it by reading the notes. The moment when a line of poetry has been created is the moment when you say it to yourself, either aloud or silently. At that moment it is, for aesthetic purposes, a perceptual object. It may be that most artists can't take this purely internal "perception" too far, and need actually to see or hear what they have made in order fully to appreciate it. They put it on paper or canvas or in clay. Or they get up and dance. Or they say it or sing it aloud to themselves. Even Mozart, who could hear and enjoy the most complicated musical structures in his head, would still often hum half aloud when an idea came to him.

What I'm saying then is that, experientially, the aesthetic part of the artistic process is just what we should expect it to be: the part that involves perception in the absence of self-concern. Before a moment of such perception, there may be only effort. After it, there may be critical reconsideration. If the creative work flows effortlessly and freely without any tugging and pushing, as sometimes happens, then the work emerges out of one sustained aesthetic experience. For most artists, it's not necessary to create in this fashion, as long as they have the ability to switch rapidly in and out of aesthetic gear. Particularly in cooperative arts, like theatre, dance, and film, the presiding artist—the director or choreographer—can't expect to create in an effortless, uninterrupted flow, and gear-switching becomes of the greatest importance. An exception would be the cooperative arts which are most truly cooperative: improvisational theatre and improvisational dance.

But where does the work *come* from? Flower arrangement may be easy enough to explain, but what about an opera, a building, a film, or a ballet—works that seem to derive not from any aesthetic tinkering, not from any process of trial and error, but from one massive and coherent vision? Where does such art come from? How does it find its way from the artist to us?

Here we need to tread very carefully. Can we assume that what you or I experience as response, and perceive in the work—can we assume that this was simply "put in" the work by the artist? Certainly this is a very common notion about art: that the creative process is basically a reversal of the relationship between the work and its audience—in other words, that what we get out of a work as a response is what the artist began with and, subsequently, transferred into this perceptual structure.

The more I learn about artists, the more wary I am of any such simple formula, particularly if it claims to explain the way all artists work. It may be that *some* artists do begin with a complex experiential state, for which they then seek perceptual "expression" in the work, or even begin with an exact vision of the work to be created, a vision which embodies something analogous to what the perceiver's response will be. But, as I've pointed out, this is not necessarily the rule. It is very common for artists to begin only with certain intentions, certain feelings, or perhaps certain concrete elements to be developed—musical phrases, color relationships, verbal images, etc.—and *then*, as they encounter the medium, to discover the work in the process of creating it. Novelists often get the feeling at some point that their characters are taking over. The medium itself may have its claims to make. A sculptor may find that the stone or the wood or the metal has its own notions about what is to be done. On one occasion, Rossini even let an accidental ink blot convince him to introduce a modulation. Stravinsky goes so far as to say: "An accident is perhaps the only thing that really inspires us."

Still, could the SENDER → MESSAGE → RECEIVER view of artistic creation, though inappropriate as is to the way many artists actually work, be restated and put in more sophisticated and useful form? Suppose we say that the artist, if he doesn't actually begin with anything comparable to the perceiver's response, does at least discover it in the process of creating the work. A composer may begin with no more than some rhythmic patterns and a sketchy notion of a harmonic structure. But by letting these elements develop and generate new ideas—experimenting to find the direction in which his material seems to "want" to go—the composer may end up with a piece which is not only coherent but even sounds as though it had been there all along, waiting only to be discovered. The composer has discovered more than a piece of music. There is a complex structure of experiential quality that the composition calls forth. The formula could be revised to look like this: SENDER → MESSAGE (discovered in the creative process) → RECEIVER. But even this version, I think, would be enormously misleading.

A painting—the actual canvas and pigment—is one object, the same object for all, no matter who sees it. But the painting *in here*, the inner shape which corresponds to that object—can we say that this is one fixed experiential structure shared by the artist and all perceivers of the work? Obviously not. Two perceivers bring to the work of art two experiential universes, analogous but hardly identical. The work will resonate analogously but differently in each, just as a vibrating string resonates differently in different physical environments. Of course, both the work and the perceiver are far more complicated than this comparison implies. No person can experience a work of art twice in exactly the same way. In fact, it's not at all uncommon for artists to discover new aspects of their own already completed works—new connections, new ways of responding. Our experience of a painting is not a framed and fixed object like the painting itself. The experience is a moment-to-moment process. And, obviously, the process through which the artist experiences a work as it is being created is likely to be substantially different from the process through which someone else will perceive it when it is completed.

Not only that, the aesthetic potential of a work of art may not be fully realized in *any* individual experience, including that of the artist. Many highly valued works seem inexhaustible. No single experience can take account of their entire structure. In fact, one kind of attention may actually crowd out another. We may be so caught up in the reactive plot structure of a movie that we give only peripheral attention to patterns which, on the second or third viewing, may give us considerable satisfaction at a time when the plot has lost some of its reactive power. Successive stagings (or readings) of *The Misanthrope* may, while sustaining something of its essential ambivalence, legitimately shift the point of balance somewhat, since what the play seems to offer is not a single point of balance but a range of points. In my house there is a very rich and lively "nonrepresentational" painting by Bob Paskin, which has been easier to keep on the wall for years than have many other paintings. New patterns of relationship keep emerging—some of them, even, quite incompatible with others. As with many paintings, there is no single perceiving experience that is adequate to it.

But someone could ask: how do works like this get created? Surely the artist's experience creating the work is fully adequate to it—or else how could the work get there? Isn't this asking a great deal of the artist, though? In what way could Shakespeare, when he was writing *King Lear*, experience all of the patterns which, in this century alone, critics of every persuasion have uncovered in the play? Is the next step, then, to say that he experienced them unconsciously? There is a good deal to be said, of course, about the role of the unconscious in creating art. We need to understand, as well, how the untranslatability of resonance makes it impossible for an art work to be exhausted by critical analysis, since the resonance in a particular work, when approached on the level of concepts and analysis, can provide material for an infinite amount of commentary. This resonance is, to borrow Bergson's description of an absolute, "the gold coin for which we never seem able to finish giving small change." But we have to take our understanding of the creative process still farther.

A work of art is not merely the product of an artist's psyche, conscious or unconscious; it is also the product of a human body, which engages the environment with a specific set of senses and motor functions, and which operates rhythmically in accordance with a great number of cycles, ranging from the briefest electrochemical pulses to the overall human life cycle itself. No disembodied mind writes a melody or a line of poetry. Despite the insistence of artists like Leonardo that painting is mental, it is also the entire body that paints. And I'm not referring merely to the physical wielding of a brush. If our eyes were somewhat differently constructed, so would our paintings be. It isn't only dance that celebrates the body. All arts do. If our eyes were lateral, or if we had a bloodhound's sense of smell, if our endocrine system were more, or less, complex, or if our heart beat much faster or slower, then our arts also would be other than they are. And shouldn't individual somatic differences among artists likewise be reflected in their work? We take the body for granted and focus our aesthetic inquiry on the mind, and often not even on all of that.

But we haven't finished zooming out. A work of art is the product not only of a human body but also of a human society, and of a specific time and place. Tiepolo is eighteenth-century Italian. Less narrowly, he is "modern" and "Western." Less narrowly still, Cenozoic and terrestrial. Still less narrowly. . . . ? It's not that the artist disappears when we zoom out but rather that he more obviously becomes part of a larger-scale process out of which the work of art emerges. Tiepolo's ceiling frescoes in Würzburg are the product not only of one painter but of the Roman Empire, the Catholic Church, the Thirty Years' War, the climate of southern Europe, etc. The mere fact that this job was there for Tiepolo to do—in 1750 at the new Residence of the Prince-Bishop in Würzburg—rests on an immensely complex structure of historical events. The very subject matter of these frescoes is an amalgam of classical mythology, medieval political history, Catholic doctrine, and eighteenth-century Enlightenment spirit. And, stylistically, we can see Tiepolo continuing the illusionistic ceiling fresco tradition that has come to him from the preceding century, but investing it with a new clarity and radiant light which, individual and innovative as they may be, also parallel contemporary European developments not only in painting but also in architecture, music, literature, and the other arts.

None of this means that the frescoes are "accounted for" by certain historical and geographical influences, any more than they are accounted for by the earth's placement in the solar system or by the sun's placement in the galaxy. What I'm saying is that the work of art is a part which implies the whole and that, from this point of view, the artist is a medium through which the universe produces works of art, just as the hen is a medium though which the universe produces eggs. The artist is more consciously involved than the hen, but we shouldn't be surprised to see patterns emerge out of this process which the artist neither intended nor was in any sense aware of. I am hardly arguing that the true artist is like the poet in Plato's *Ion*: a medium through whom the god speaks and who creates only when possessed and out of his mind. But we need to understand that there is a dimension in the creation of art that extends far beyond the personal.

Writers, for example, work not only with a language but with more specifically literary forms which are not of their own making. The formulas I enjoy so much in Homer developed through a long tradition of oral poetry. And we often find ourselves appreciating, almost as an independent work of art, a certain style which is the creation of no single artist: we become fans of "white ballet," of musical comedy films, of late eighteenth-century European music, of Gothic architecture, of rock and roll. Obviously, the ability of the individual artist is crucial; you don't get a great ballet by patching together bits and pieces of classical idiom. But, on the other hand, you don't choreograph *Sleeping Beauty* from scratch either, inventing each movement *ex nihilo* as you go.

This suprapersonal dimension comprehends the "internal history" of an art form, but also history in the larger sense. If you want to understand how *The Princess of Clèves* came into being, you need to consider forces that produced, in the midst of vast poverty, a relatively tiny, geographically concentrated, and parasitic class of courtiers who were at once free from and denied a whole range of productive social occupations, and who devoted an extraordinary amount of time to games of social intrigue and romantic love. This "historical background" is not merely subject matter for the novel; it is part of the process that produced it. Like other superb novelists, Madame de La Fayette can be seen as a creator who fashioned a complex and vivid fictional world out of her own experience and imaginative resources (with, in this case, a little help from her friends). But within the context of a larger process, she, like Stendhal or Turgenev, Achebe or Murasaki, can be seen as a unique and high-powered aesthetic medium through which the time and place produce their own image in a work of art. When you look carefully at a good novel, you can often see the larger process projected within it, resolving into concentric rings of increasing scope. In American literature, Ralph Ellison's *Invisible Man* is an obvious example.

We can, if we want, label everything that's suprapersonal either "influence" or "subject matter" and cling to the notion that the artist is the sender of what we receive from a work of art. There is a radical individualism in this view, which may, perhaps, be a legitimate way of seeing things. But it is no less legitimate, and for me it is more productive, to see the artist as part of a process. For one thing, this view helps to maintain the continuity between works of art and natural aesthetic scenes and objects, between the poet and the setting sun. It also helps free us from any compulsion to determine what the artist was "trying to say," since we would consider such intentions as, certainly a significant part of the creative process, but not as the Word from which the created work arises. If art is regarded as communication, with the artist at the beginning, the perceiver at the end, and the work in the middle, then it's hard not to feel a sense of duty when confronted with the work, an obligation to reconstruct the original message. But if we zoom out to include more than the artist in our view of the creative process, then the work becomes something far richer, more suggestive, and more open-ended than any message could be, and our own response is set free: no matter how intense, studious, or analytical, our response is likely to be closer to play than to work. We're less likely to be intimidated by art, since we're not being challenged to decode it. At the same time, we needn't be afraid of touching bottom or "explaining it away"; we can get as deeply into the work as we want because we know that it is inexhaustible in a way that messages are not.

To see the creation of art as involving ultimately a large-scale suprapersonal process is not at all the same thing as that narrow sort of historical criticism which views the work *primarily* as the product of its time. As a student I had more than enough experience with this approach to literature: classes where we would look for the ways in which a particular work was "representative of its age," and, when this was accomplished, would pass on to the next. I remember realizing once, after a four-hour session on *Gulliver's Travels*, that, on the basis of what had been said that day, *Gulliver* could just as easily have been a third-rate literary work. What made it worth reading as something more than a historical document had slipped through our fingers. Ironically, the "historical" approach that was pursued was historical only in a narrow and conventionalized way; for example, nothing that might have sounded "Marxist" was introduced (not that I haven't read Marxist analyses that were equally narrow in their own way). I remain very much attracted to the study of historical context, as a way of perceiving a work of art more fully, and also simply for its own sake, as history. But I know that it can be stultifying if I as a teacher am so occupied with seeing nineteenth-century America in Thomas Eakins that I ignore everything else that his paintings have to offer.

Historical forces don't "account for" a work of art, any more than they account for any single individual. Even if you accept a materialist view of history, it is possible to distinguish, as Marcuse has done, between the "social existence" of individuals and their "inner history," which is "the particular history of their encounters, their passions, joys, and sorrows— experiences which are not necessarily grounded in their class situation, and which are not even comprehensible from this perspective." The individual as artist, though an appropriate object of study for any limited, analytical system—historical or psychoanalytic, semiotic or physiological—is always, also, in flight from such a system, always leading us toward the whole. If you could gather together everything that Mozart's *Marriage of Figaro* owes to its age—and that would be quite a bit—you could never make of it anything more than an immense pile of bits and pieces, a Tower of Babel pointed vainly at the heaven where Cherubino sings *"Voi che sapete."*

What I'm suggesting is that, while we may have good reason to consider a work of art from a particular, even a narrow, point of view, we shouldn't try to delimit the process that culminates in a work of art so that it matches the limits of our own approach. Whatever segment of this process we may concern ourselves with at the moment, we shouldn't be led to deny or undervalue the importance of the rest. In this way, we'll be less likely to place constraints on aesthetic experience —our own or that of others.

It's well known that works of art have often presented a moral threat. But we need to recognize that, by their irreducibility, they may also present us with an intellectual threat. For many of us, the prospect not merely of investigating such works but, as Susan Sontag puts it, of *taming* them—by historical, psychological, semiotic, or other methods—remains irresistibly tempting. All the same, we should learn to resist.

How does a work of art get created? The question invites an endless series of answers. We begin with an artist and a medium. The artist is going to end up with a work in that medium which encourages the aesthetic mode of perception and which is interesting—that is, which corresponds to important aspects of the artist's own inner universe. But exactly how this is managed varies with the temperament and training of the artist, with the medium, and with the nature of the work.

A work, or at least parts of it, can emerge dreamwise, as I said earlier, already embodied in perceptual image, without conscious involvement on the artist's part: a melody, lines of poetry, the image of a painting or building or sculpture, a dance sequence, etc. Particularly in artists who are well accustomed to using a medium, some particular experiential complex can spontaneously generate its perceptual counterpart, can spontaneously find refuge in an aesthetic image. Or the work may begin as an attitude, a feeling, or an intuition *seeking* aesthetic form. This may be an agonizing tragic awareness or no more than a certain intense sensation. Picasso puts it this way, in a fine, indelicate metaphor: "The painter goes through states of fullness and evacuation. That is the whole secret of art. I go for a walk in the forest of Fontainebleau. I get 'green' indigestion. I must get rid of this sensation into a picture. Green rules it. A painter paints to unload himself of feelings and visions."

A work *may* start with the detailed elaboration, in advance, of an overall structure. Don McDonagh tells us that when Paul Taylor, who had been choreographing shorter works, started work on *Orbs*, his first hour-length dance, he began with a detailed verbal outline and "seemingly cumbersome preliminary theorizing." On the other hand, a work can be discovered/created by pursuing the developmental possibilities of a single element, which might be seen in retrospect either as the germ of the work or merely as the irritating grain of sand around which the work began to adhere and take shape. Paul Valéry has said that his poem "Le Cimetière marin" began with "only a rhythmic form . . . which happened to obsess me for a while." And Joyce Cary tells of a story that began when he noticed a girl on a boat: "A nice expression, with a wrinkled forehead, a good many wrinkles." Three weeks later he woke up in the middle of the night with a story. Days later, rewriting the story, he realized that his heroine was the girl on the boat. "Somehow she had gone down into my subconscious, and come up again with a full-sized story."

Some artists are very conscious of the affective shape of their work; others think only of the perceptual relationships. Some seek to express themselves, others to escape themselves. Some artists are highly theoretical about their work; others scorn theory. It is difficult, in other words, to generalize about the way individual artists work. The Hindu tradition of yoga offers different "ways" toward liberation as suitable for differing temperaments. There are "ways" as well in the creation of art, though any culture may emphasize one particular way or another.

What about the satisfaction in creating art? Is it merely the same satisfaction that any perceiver might have? And if not, where does it come from? One thing we should recognize is that for the artist the work is tailor-made art. As an artist, I may not be Bach or Bernini but I may at least be able to create art that corresponds closely to my own situation, my own obsessions, my own physical nature, my own ways of perceiving, and so on. Kafka was in a position to appreciate Dickens and Dostoevsky, but there was no one who had made art out of precisely his own experiential reality. So he had to do it. Borges in turn may have had a passionate appreciation of Kafka, but he needed to hear his own voice, pursue his own obsessions in the context of art.

For many of us, what we lack in artistic effectiveness may cancel out the advantage of concocting art to our personal taste and need. When all's said and done, we prefer to eat out. But even here I'm not convinced that we're not passing up a worthwhile possibility, nor am I convinced that we can so easily know the limits of our artistic potential. And when it comes to artists who obviously do have the talent, the power, the creative ability—then how inviting it must be: the prospect of giving aesthetic form to their very own lives, their own unique and immediate experience.

But why exactly is it inviting? Why would you or I need to make art out of our personal experience? The answer to this is already at hand, isn't it? To rescue ourselves. To encounter our own experiential reality in the absence of self-concern. For a time our lives are no longer something that we undergo, but instead something that we perceive "out there" and free of charge. More than that, this art that we create reveals the shape of our own experience, or gives it shape, so that it becomes a satisfyingly coherent image for our contemplation. At one point near the end of *The Past Recaptured*, Proust's narrator tells us: "The true life, life at last uncovered and illuminated, the only life therefore which is really lived, is literature." Extreme, no doubt. But it tells us a great deal about the satisfaction of creating art.

An individual's aesthetic needs may vary with time. Though we're capable of enjoying a wide range of art, the kind of art we need most may vary from one day or one year to the next. Isn't this because our emotional life, our experiences, and our understanding all keep changing? At any given time, what presses on us the most, emotionally, can affect our aesthetic preferences, sometimes directly, sometimes inversely. Directly when we look for it in art, inversely when we want to escape it in art (although to escape one thing is to pursue something else, another aspect of our experience). So we may well seek out what will be the right art at the right time. But this is precisely what artists can create for themselves. For artists, particularly for those who exert a great deal of control on the medium, there is a special kind of satisfaction to be had. Their needs of the moment, their stresses, their moods, their intellectual and emotional climate—all these create a disequilibrium, as with all of us. But the artist can respond to this disequilibrium by creating her own art, and has the satisfaction not only of enjoying a perfectly appropriate work of art as it is created, but *also* of having made the transition from one state, which involves a complex of tensions, to another, which is their precise resolution in a work of art.

Let me try to clarify this. Let's pretend that I come across a work of art which, though I didn't make it, is by chance exactly tailor-made, not only to my temperament, experience, and so on, but even to my very state of mind at the moment. It is precisely what I need in art. But satisfied as I may be with it, there is still one further satisfaction that only its creator can have felt. Discounting the unlikely possibility that it was revealed intact in a dream, we can assume that the artist had to *work* at it. In other words, for the artist there was not only that complex of psychic tensions which the work, temporarily at least, resolves, but also the additional tension involved in seeking and forming the work itself. Only very rarely does a work materialize without requiring any effort at all. In its very early stages, a work of art may grow unaided, in a sort of fetal darkness and quiet. But for the artist, unlike the mother, labor commonly begins at an early stage. This childbirth analogy, incidentally, may be overused. Perhaps Picasso's notion of "evacuation" is just as apt—and there have been other ways of regarding the artist's work: as seeing, listening, making, finding, and so on. Still, the analogy does point to that additional satisfaction which only the artist can experience in a work, and which is the pleasure of a successful delivery—of bringing forth finally this creature that has been developing not only as a separate identity but also as a part of one's self. Enormous sense of relief and fulfillment (along with, perhaps, some apprehension over the creature's future).

Creation of any sort has its satisfaction. Until the work is complete, it remains no more than a potential within you. You are, at that point, no more than you were. But at the moment of completion, there is not only relief but a sense of expansion.

To create is to multiply yourself. In the specific case of art, there is also the sense of having placed this re-created self in a secure position, within the aesthetic frame and therefore out of jeopardy.

It goes without saying that there are satisfactions to be had by the artist which are entirely apart from a purely aesthetic satisfaction. Even setting aside questions of money, social status, and so on, there may be, during the creative process, moments when the artist feels an enormous pride and perhaps the sense of contact with a possible appreciative audience. But these feelings, to the extent that they are egoistic, can interfere with the process, can even disguise weaknesses in the work by substituting an ego trip for a feeble aesthetic satisfaction. More than one artist has been carried away from the actual work at hand on a flood tide of self-congratulation, which is perhaps just as dangerous in this respect as the ebb tide of despair.

But is the sense of contact with an audience necessarily egoistic? To what extent does the artist need to sense a real or potential audience in order to create? After all, even though the work of art itself is not a message, it may contain some message; in any case, the artist may *regard* the work as a message—and message implies receiver. So obviously any artist who views art as communication will be working to at least a potential audience. But are there artists who *don't* work to an audience?

The question's not so easy to answer. We might find an unpublished novelist or an unperformed composer who claims to create with no thought of any possible audience. But we might be skeptical: "Yeah, I'll bet if an audience were offered to you, you'd jump at the chance." Or we might find an artist *with* an audience who insists, as William Burroughs has done, that he would go on producing even if he were on a desert island with no chance of ever having an audience. But we could still choose to be skeptical, since the artist is speaking not about what he does but about what he *would* do in a hypothetical situation. And there are plenty of artists who would support our skepticism. In the same volume of *Paris Review* interviews where Burroughs tells us he'd go on writing on a desert island, Louis-Ferdinand Céline insists that if he had money, he'd never write at all.

Still another sort of evidence against the necessity of an audience might be those works of art that, in some American Indian societies, for example, have been purposefully and carefully kept secret. But since these works invariably have a religious function, it can be argued that there is an audience after all, though not a human one, or simply that, as religious objects, these paintings, carvings, songs, etc., aren't relevant to the point we're considering. I don't know. It's at least conceivable that a secret art could have some basis in the aesthetic experience itself. An object that someone has carved might well appear to that person, partly because of its aesthetic effectiveness, as a personal source of power. And it might seem that this power would be weakened or diluted if anyone else saw the figure.

Perhaps we can come at this artist-audience question another way. Let's look first at the simplest forms of artistic creation: selecting, arranging, and so on. Even though it may be pleasant to share a garden, the shells one has collected, the room one has decorated, the flower arrangement one has made, we find it easy enough to believe that these things can be done for personal pleasure, without any need of an audience. But as the creative activity becomes more arduous and time-consuming, we find it increasingly difficult to believe that someone has done it solely for personal pleasure. Some people get fairly fancy in preparing a dinner for one. Fine. But at a certain point, if someone has spent the entire day stirring sauces, baking pastry cases, decorating hors d'oeuvres, glazing strawberries—all this with no company coming—at some point we may become less admiring than suspicious: there's something weird going on here. Similarly, we might not be surprised to see someone spend days arranging a bedroom for his or her personal aesthetic pleasure. After all, the room has to be arranged some way in any case, and look at all the time you spend in it. But to put days or weeks on end into a piano sonata or a novel . . .

Maybe we have to consider the type of art involved, not just its difficulty or the time it takes. Novels and symphonies, for example, are traditionally public forms of art. "Symphony" implies performance. A novel is story-telling, and "story" implies audience. Language itself, for that matter, is ordinarily a medium of communication. Architecture is public. Monumental sculpture is public, as are theatre and the kind of dance that involves choreography for a group of dancers. But there is also a kind of dance that's done purely for the pleasure of the dancer. It's not so very uncommon for someone to dance alone at home to records—even for long stretches of time. Nor is it uncommon for someone to improvise on a musical instrument, or even to spend the day doing sketches, without any thought of an audience.

The answer to this question—do artists need an audience, real or potential?—can't be a simple one. We ought to know enough about creating art by now to know that it offers its own satisfactions to the artist, which are more or less independent of any audience. In some of us both the satisfactions and the ability are greater, and we shouldn't be surprised now and then to find some splendid freaks who *do* spend the day cooking their own dinner—or who, to put it more cautiously, would spend the day cooking dinner whether or not anyone else decided to show up. Because this, I think, gets closer to the situation of many artists. They want an audience, want their work to be appreciated by sympathetic perceivers, but are motivated in any case to create. For some people, the hours they spend creating art are, though difficult, even exhausting, still the most satisfying, the most real, the most thoroughly alive hours they know.

Then why the audience? One immediate answer is that the existence of an audience validates this time that the artist spends. It's not just goofing off. Society, not surprisingly, respects artists who satisfy a social need; relatively little value is attached to sketching or improvised dancing done privately, and purely for its own sake: "Well, when do we get to *see* some of what you're doing?" Sharing art makes it a less masturbatory pleasure. The audience, moreover, validates more than an artist's use of time. It assigns him a position within the society. Merely as a doodler on the piano or a whittler of wood, you have no social existence; as an artist you do. Still, an audience offers even more substantial rewards: money, acceptance, fame—even, according to the prevailing mythology, immortality, if you manage to make the Big List.

But there remains more to be said for an audience. It is, after all, an audience for the very art that you have created. Which means that these people accept your art, that it works for them. And this in turn means that the experiential structure which you perceive in your work is, to some degree at least, shared and accepted. To have an appreciative audience means to establish contact with others on a profound level. True, the audience may confer social rewards, but it is *beneath* the everyday social reality that this contact with others is made, that this experiential community is achieved. "Yes," they seem to be saying, "on this level, too, I can see you; furthermore, I accept you on this level, and even more, I share your experience." In our society particularly, our "lonely crowd," to achieve that sense of community through a work of art is no small thing.

It can also be very useful to have an audience in mind when you create art. The existence of even an imaginary audience can keep you aware of your work as a framed and coherent perceptual image, can keep you from getting lost in it (which is not the same thing as losing yourself in it) in a way that leads toward what critics sometimes call "self-indulgence."

I've done a fair amount of theatrical improvising, sometimes with and sometimes without an audience, and have become aware of differences between the two situations. When a group improvises without any audience at all, when everyone present is in the scene—what I call a "closed" improv—a number of things are likely to happen. Some of the people at least are likely to dissolve into their characters, to reach that depth of identification that children sometimes reach in make-believe games when they come very close to forgetting that they are not in fact superheroes or explorers or mommies and daddies. This kind of improv resembles play or fantasy in another way: there is often a more blatant element of wish fulfillment, not merely acting but acting out. Closed improvs tend to be very loose structurally; the scene may divide into several points of focus; it may sag for a while; then new developments may sweep it off into another kind of scene altogether. Furthermore, these closed improvs can go on and on, if no limit is set. In fact they're damn hard to get out of.

Sometimes when I've ended a workshop with a closed improv, there really is no end. People just leave when they have to, still in character. The improv separates into smaller scenes moving out into streets, parking lots, God knows where.

But an improv with an audience—even if this audience consists of only one person—presents the players with a special set of problems. You have to worry about sight lines, about voice projection, about character projection. You have to keep a point of focus within the scene so that the audience isn't forced continually to deal with several centers of action at the same time. And this in turn means that you have to cooperate carefully and attentively with the other actors. You have to worry about pace, about development from beginning to end. You need to cooperate in giving the scene a clear shape and sense of direction. Interminable, floppy group fantasies are not nearly as much fun to watch as to be in; as a result, actors in an audience improv tend to be much more aware of the scene as a theatrical image, and aware of the *whole* scene in space and time, rather than only their part of it. This movement toward a coherently shaped whole sets limits on the extent to which any individual player can simply disappear into his or her part, or act out a personal fantasy.

Now this contrast in improvisational situations has something to teach us about the effect of an audience on the artist. If you're an artist, the existence of a potential audience helps to bind you to your craft—not necessarily because you are afraid of their criticism or eager for their praise, but because the sense of working to an audience keeps you aware not merely of what you feel or intend but of what it is you are actually making: the aesthetic image, which will have to function on its own without any assistance from your good intentions and your creative fervor. In one sense, the theatre is an excellent metaphor for the arts in general. A novel is a stage trick. You have to keep checking to see how it looks from out front. What is so obviously true of fiction or of film is also true of the other arts. There is a work area, a backstage where you put things together, and an "out front," where only the image itself exists.

As a general rule, artists need to be able to move between backstage and out front with relative ease. But there are forces that sometimes work to keep an artist ignorant of how the developing work looks from sixth row center. It's easy to become wrapped up in a sudden surge of feeling or a new idea, in the application of a technique, or in following out the logic of one particular element. Here, awareness of a potential audience can provide a healthy counterbalance.

This awareness also strengthens the artist's own aesthetic perception. A work that you are creating may be almost too close, too personal, may lie dangerously near the domain of self-concern. Awareness of an audience can strengthen the aesthetic frame. Perhaps it seems more reasonable to assume that the existence of an audience, of onlookers, might intimidate the artist and discourage a determined self-exploration. But I think the opposite possibility is at least as likely. Without any audience, you may be tempted to see the work merely as your own behavior, and therefore vulnerable to the self-concern that attends behavior. With a potential audience, the work becomes an artifact, becomes distanced. There's the sense that anything embarrassing in it won't be charged to your account.

Finally, it may be worth mentioning some ways in which an audience may *not* be helpful in the creation of art. The obvious social rewards it offers may be more useful to an artist in potential—that is, more useful *before* they're conferred than after. Rilke describes fame as a sort of ultimate weapon against those whom persecution has only fortified in their solitude: "And at this clamor almost everyone has looked up and been distracted." It's probably not necessary to go at any length into the various kinds of danger that audiences have presented and still present to the artist, since these are fairly well known. The clamor of fame may include a clamor for consistency or novelty, for conformity or outrageousness, for omniscient wisdom or a sort of autistic genius, for relevance or escape, for prudery or pornography. This kind of pressure may seem particularly strong today, but so has it been in other times. In *The Odyssey*, Penelope interrupts her bard, telling him to choose a less sorrowful subject, and Telemachus has to defend the bard's right to entertain "as the spirit moves him." In any case, these demands of the audience seem less menacing when you compare them with the out-and-out political oppression—including imprisonment, torture, and execution —which artists continue to suffer in various parts of the world today. Over 250 years ago, because of a satire he had written, the young Voltaire was beaten up on the streets of Paris by the Chevalier de Rohan's lackeys, and then imprisoned. Today in Russia, he might be in a "mental institution" or in Siberia. In the United States, he'd probably be all right, might even make a few bucks; but in Pinochet's Chile, which the United States brought into existence, he would most likely be long dead, and all his Chilean Candides, Zadigs, and Hurons dead with him.

CHAPTER ELEVEN
The Art of Performance

Is performing an aesthetic experience? How? And to what extent?

Let's recognize at the outset that "performer" is a wide category. A concert violinist is a performer, but so are the extras in a crowd scene. I recall my own debut in opera (it was also my farewell performance, for that matter). I was a super—which is the same as an extra—in *La Bohème*. And though I prided myself on having an important function (as a waiter in the Café Momus, I had to pick up the pieces of a plate after Musetta hurled it onto the stage floor) and even a difficult role (since I couldn't wear my glasses on stage); still, I'm not sure that any of this required aesthetic involvement on my part. I *did* like the music very much, and the lights and the costumes. *Maybe* I moved better as a result, but I wouldn't want to have to argue the point. The main thing was to find the broken pieces of plate without my glasses on.

Looking at performance in relation to aesthetic perception, we can begin to make some distinctions among types of performers. To what extent can the performer perceive the image that's being created from a perspective approaching that of the audience toward whom it's oriented? If it's my job to fall from an upstairs window in a movie, I'm not likely to perceive much of this image—not until I see it on film. However, if I'm giving a solo violin concert, though I won't see what the audience sees, and though even the sound will be rather different for me, still, my image of the music that's being played isn't going to differ radically from theirs. But for someone playing in an orchestra, say in the brass section, this divergence increases; the sound will be balanced not with that particular musician in mind but for the folks out front. In my late teens I saw *Coppélia* once from the first row, off to the side, just a few feet from the trombones. I was shocked at what I heard; I must have come in with the assumption that orchestral sound was some kind of absolute like the speed of light—the same everywhere. I'd always liked the trombones in *Coppélia* but this was too much of a good thing. But then a dancer with a small part in a ballet might have a perception even *more* divergent from that of the audience. He wouldn't see the entire piece (except, perhaps, from the wings); and even during his time on stage he might have a very limited view of what was going on. During someone's solo, for example, he might have to hold an *attitude* which directed his gaze toward the unpainted backside of a cardboard tree.

None of this says that performing, even in a walk-on or in the back row of a crowded dance number, can't be exciting, electric, and, on its own terms, an aesthetic experience. But it does discourage any generalization we might want to make in this area. When I was three, according to family legend, I performed in my first radio drama—on a local station in Tucson. I was supposed to cry, so they pinched me. I doubt that this was an aesthetic experience.

Still, we can't evade the issue that easily. Someone could insist: "I'm not concerned with babies crying and walk-on parts; we're talking about performing *artists.*" All right, then, suppose we take another look at the concert violinist. Here is someone who is in a position to perceive more or less the audience image—at least of the music. But if aesthetic experience is based on perception free of self-concern, how is the violinist to manage it? In one way, this performer is under even more pressure than the composer, who is at least free to play with various possibilities, free to stop, revise, rearrange, wait for inspiration, and so on. Imagine yourself playing the violin in front of two thousand discerning music lovers, and approaching a very fast, long, and difficult passage which is close to the limits of even a virtuoso technique. *Self-concern?* I feel the early warnings of panic just thinking about it. But of course I'm not a concert violinist. And here we get to the matter of technique.

When you're first learning to drive, it's difficult to attend to anything but the mechanical operations themselves: steering, braking, working the clutch and gearshift, giving signals; it's as though you haven't enough hands and feet. There's too much to do—especially when you must at the same time stay aware of the road, traffic signals, other cars, and so on. As you get better at the mechanics of driving, your attention is sufficiently liberated so that you can take in the less obvious, less immediate aspects of your driving environment. Finally, you can do *all* of this and also converse or sing, listen to the news or solve a math problem (though there's always a danger that this can make you less alert as a driver). With musicians and dancers, the same sort of development takes place, except that, once the basics have been acquired, their attention generally stays with the music or dance itself. It is technique that frees a performer to perceive, aesthetically, his own performance.

Let's say you acquire the technique that enables you to undertake a particular piano piece. Then you practice it, mastering the fingering, the dynamics, the phrasing—so that your body learns the piece, just as your body learns how to drive. During this process—particularly after the earliest stages—you engage in a trial-and-error process. You perceive in the written music a certain structure of relationships. Preparing the piece consists partly of investigating *in yourself,* through playing, the resonant potential of this written structure. Your own relationship to the work is, not surprisingly, somewhere in between that of the composer and that of the audience. Like the perceiver, you're confronted with a given structure; like the composer, you're constructing a perceptual image. The transition from artifact to event is not mechanical, and requires an additional set of artistic decisions superimposed upon those of the person who created the original artifact. Out of this situation springs the performer's dynamic: the artifact and the self come in contact and produce the event. You and I may both be performing Debussy's *La Cathédrale engloutie,* and we may both want to realize as fully as possible the resonant potential of the music as it is written. No tricks, no gimmicks. It's not Chopin, nor is it Gershwin. Still, we're separate individuals. Like you, I will be obliged to discover, through playing, my own resonant inner structure embodied in my own translation of the artifact. To look for a single "ideal" interpretation would be to forget both the inexhaustible richness of art works and the individuality of aesthetic experience.

Let's say then that your body has learned the piano piece, that you have made a host of conscious and unconscious decisions about translating the artifact, that you have developed a way of playing the music that seems to realize its own unique potential and at the same time authentically evokes and embodies your own individual experiential quality. At this point, when you play the piece, you may find yourself freed from striving—for most of the time at least—and in a position to enjoy the music (and the kinesthetic and tactile image as well) in the absence of self-concern. But this doesn't imply that, having reached this point, the pianist is a perceiver in the same way that someone in the audience is. No matter how thoroughly she may have learned the piece, and no matter how little conscious attention she need give the physical movements involved, merely watching a pianist perform should convince us that she is consciously, even intently, shaping the music as it emerges.

From a mechanistic point of view, we could divide performance into the intention, the act, and the perception. The performer (a) intends to strike the keys in a certain way, (b) strikes them, and (c) hears the sound. But this kind of analysis distorts the nature of musical performance, which is not experienced as a series of intentions followed by actions which produce sound but as a continuing movement, in which the feeling, the thought, and the will that shape performance tend to fuse with the act of playing and with the music which is created. Actually, the mechanistic breakdown is a more accurate description of what beginners do: "Let's see now, I've got to do *this*—there we go—oh, so that's what it sounds like." But development as a performer, it seems to me, leads toward a unified experience. Instead of striving to achieve a certain effect, to create a certain resonance, accomplished performers have so thoroughly identified purpose, execution, and image that what they want to achieve and the physical action this entails are likely to be dissolved in the music itself. From the mechanistic point of view, there is neural activity, followed by muscular activity which is perceived kinesthetically; then the sound is produced and perceived. But I suspect that for an accomplished performer the causal connection is likely to be experienced in reverse— the sound image plays itself through the performer—or even to vanish altogether in the image.

That's why it's not difficult to see the aesthetic aspect of at least musical performance in essentially the same way we've been looking at aesthetic experience up to this point. It is based on perception—here including kinesthetic perception— in the absence of self-concern. Naturally, the performer, like a mere perceiver, may not be at the aesthetic maximum throughout a performance. Art as experience isn't simply "off" or "on," and performers are well aware of the extent to which they are or are not cut loose aesthetically, of the varying degrees to which they may be absorbed in the image during a performance.

Actors and dancers present a somewhat different situation. To a considerable extent they are alienated from the image which they offer the audience. They may perceive an image, but it's a different one. Actors are somewhat closer to the audience's point of view because they can at least hear their own voices. Dancers, however, though there may be music to hear and a performing environment which they perceive from within—perceive their own dancing kinesthetically, and this may or may not serve as the basis for some "secondary" visual image of themselves dancing. This divergence from the audience image may raise special problems of technique and training in certain types of dance, but it doesn't by any means prevent dancers from experiencing their own dancing aesthetically. Kinesthetic image can be detached from the practical context just as visual or auditory image can. In fact, dancing as a source of aesthetic experience undoubtedly has a longer history than does dance as performance. Dancing rescues one's own bodily movement the way literature rescues one's language. I've heard Alwin Nikolais describe dance as "movement for its own sake." That goes right to the point. And movement for its own sake turns out to have enormous resonant potential for the dancer as well as for the audience. Aesthetic experience begins for the dancer, as it does for the instrumentalist, when the image takes over. I think many dancers would agree that, not just as personal experience but also as performance, dance doesn't realize its full potential until, as self-concern fades, the image absorbs the dancer.

Actors raise another aesthetic question. Acting is not exactly movement for its own sake, nor is it speaking for its own sake. The aesthetic image—to the extent that an actor perceives one—isn't dominated by kinesthetic perception as a dancer's is. The actor participates in the representation of a dramatic scene, and this dramatic scene—not simply movement, not simply language—is the actor's music. Striding across the playing space, I approach someone, my fists clenched, my upper body thrust out aggressively. He sits in a chair and crosses his legs, and as I reach him and stand menacingly over him, he lights a cigarette. This human encounter in which I participate, free of self-concern, and which I perceive from the participant's point of view, provides a complex multi-sensory aesthetic image. This is theatre perceived from within —an aesthetic possibility that is, incidentally, constantly available to us in ordinary life, although we rarely take advantage of it. All of these things that I ordinarily perceive instrumentally or else disregard—the way we place ourselves, move, and speak; these eloquent spatial relationships we create; the feelings and thoughts that animate us; the constant dynamic of our adopted roles in mutual confrontation—all these together can become aesthetic image, which, as with dancing, may be no less satisfying to the actor than to the audience. However, to the extent that I have to strive, have to separate the intention, the act, and the image from each other, then to that extent I, like the dancer or musician, will be perceiving not aesthetically but in the light of self-concern. It is also true of the actor and the dancer that, however intense their aesthetic experience may be when performing, they are likely to be cut off to some extent from the entire work as a coherent aesthetic unity. *Macbeth* is one thing to the audience, another to the actor who plays the title role, and quite another to the actor who plays Macduff.

Musicians create a perceptual image which they have in common, more or less, with their audience. But we see that, for actors and dancers, there is considerably more discrepancy between the performer's image and the audience's image. We can also see how the tension between those two images is reflected in the history of both of these performing arts. There is, for example, the centuries-old debate as to whether the actor should actually *be* the character and, as much as possible, feel the feelings that are portrayed, or whether the actor should be a cool-headed simulator whose technique creates an illusion for the audience which the performer doesn't share. This debate is much older than Stanislavsky and his method. Over two centuries ago, Diderot demanded that actors be cold and calm, without participating in the illusion which they created for the audience. He cited various actors of his time as models. But there have also been theorists, and actors aplenty (Sarah Bernhardt, for example), who strongly disagree. When you encounter a deeply rooted and persistent debate of this kind, you suspect that there is a good deal to be said for both sides. For an actor, the choice of a point of balance between the extremes may rest in great part on individual temperament. Aesthetically, it appears that there are possibilities for actors in both approaches. It may be that "cool" actors and "warm" actors experience quite different kinds of perceptual images, more resonant in one case, more reactive in the other.

In dance, the tension between audience's image and performer's image has been especially important in shaping the history of the art in this century. Classical ballet, particularly as it was at the turn of the century, began with the audience's image; technique and training were clearly oriented toward this end. Dancers' bodies were forced, like bentwood, into a vocabulary of visually pleasing, and mostly frontal, shapes. But while classical ballet was reaching spectacular heights in the early part of the century, new developments were emphasizing the *dancer's* image of dance. Isadora Duncan came running and skipping into the dance world of St. Petersburg in 1904, a self-proclaimed "enemy of ballet," calling the dancers "mere puppets in motion, not people." And Martha Graham, a generation later, developed a technique, an approach to dance training, which starts not with an audience image to be achieved, but rather within the body, with breathing and with the basic bodily experience of contraction and release. Still, it would be simplistic to assume that dance abandoned one orientation for the other. What Duncan, Wigman, Graham, and others did was to open (or re-open) the dialectic. Duncan herself was a great admirer of Loie Fuller, whose dances with enormous billowing scarves and shifting patterns of colored light were highly theatrical and audience-oriented. Nor do I want to imply that classical ballet can't be experienced aesthetically by the dancer, only that classical ballet training *begins* with audience image while modern dance training is likely to emphasize the dancer's image as well.

A careful look at the aesthetics of performing would require a book in itself. What I've tried to do here with performers—as in the previous chapter with composers, painters, writers, and so on—is to suggest how their experience relates to aesthetic experience in general. Without minimizing the differences that separate composition, performance, and mere perception, I want to point out the continuity that exists.

On the one hand, there is a highly individual and creative element in any person's aesthetic experience. To experience a drawing or a song or a building doesn't consist merely of *receiving* it. Each of us translates it, recreates it with the materials provided by an individual body, an individual consciousness, a universe of experience acquired in the course of an individual life. The performer shares some of the work of the composer, writer, or choreographer—and we are all, in one sense, performers. Naturally, we're not all obliged to create an image for others, so we may not be performers with respect to the audience. But with respect to the artifact, we are. On the other hand, it is as perceivers that painters and pianists, architects and dancers are able to experience their own work aesthetically. This mode of perception, for the artist as well as the audience, announces the presence of art, and therefore validates what the artist is doing. I'm not saying that artists are only artists when they're perceiving aesthetically. They may spend a great deal of time looking at the developing work instrumentally as a task to be completed, puzzling over questions: "How do I get behind the chair before she enters?" "This wavy blue thing doesn't work. What do we need here?" "What rhymes with 'Alps' besides 'scalps'?" "Does the phrase end with the two-beat rest or does it want to go on?" But the solution is likely to make itself known *as* a solution, or at least as a possible one, by appearing in the aesthetic mode. Someone might ask how the artist is able to perceive a developing work critically and aesthetically at the same time. How do you perceive something in the absence of self-concern and yet with the intention of making a judgment about it, of deciding if it belongs, if it should be modified, if it can be developed and in what way? But of course we all do this sort of thing, even as perceivers only. Sometimes our aesthetic involvement is not complete or is intermittent, and we make judgments or raise critical questions while we're perceiving. But even when we're totally within the image, our memory, afterward, will provide a basis for judgment and comparison.

Perceivers, creative artists, performers: the emphasis changes from one category to another, but there is clearly continuity as well. Have we anything to gain from emphasizing this continuity? Book Four will suggest that we do.

IV
CHAPTER TWELVE
Art and Society

If I have failed, except in passing, to deal with art in its social context, this certainly doesn't represent any attempt to de-emphasize that context. In part, what I've hoped to accomplish up to this point has been to *complement* social theory, which, despite its enormous contribution to our understanding of the way works of art are created and received, has not, it seems to me, been able to account for the essential nature of aesthetic experience. If I haven't so far given more attention to the social aspect of art, it's simply because I thought I could make myself more useful in another area.

But there are some questions about art and society that I'd like to take up, in a very limited way, in this chapter and the next. First of all, granting that art is to a considerable extent shaped by society, we can ask to what extent it may, in return, exert a social effect. Is art capable of changing society? This is quite an important question; now as in the past, a good deal rests on how it is answered.

To say that an aesthetic image is detached from the practical context means that we don't have to *do* anything about it: just perceive it—that's all. What does this tell us about art and social change? Does this mean that aesthetic effect and social effect are entirely incompatible, so that a work can produce either one or the other but not both? The theory that has been developed in this book might seem to point to an essentially conservative role for art. If we perceive something aesthetically, doesn't that mean that for the moment at least, we accept it? Not accept it as good, necessarily. Just accept it: "That's the way life is." As I pointed out earlier, to see my back yard aesthetically is to let it be. As is. This view of art would make it the bosom friend of the status quo. Art and social change might be seen as *alternative* ways of coming to terms with an unsatisfactory world.

We find ourselves confronting what has become a familiar division. On one side: the people who look at the world, find it wanting, and try to change it. On the other side: the people who, skeptical of social change, disengage from this unsatisfactory world, but allow it to redeem itself as spectacle. I think of Schopenhauer, one of the great theorists of disinterestedness in art, who found it "a diversion" when, during the unsuccessful revolution of 1848, soldiers came to fire at the "*canaille*" from his windows. I think of Flaubert, who came to Paris that same year with a friend to look at the revolution "from an artistic point of view."

Perhaps, however, we ought to be wary of letting this division dominate our understanding of art and society. If art really does arise out of perception in the absence of self-concern, then can't it be seen as a complement, not merely an alternative, to social engagement, allowing people to realize *both* kinds of relationships with the world? Just as we can undergo romantic love in our ordinary lives and also contemplate it aesthetically in a work of art, so we can concern ourselves with changing society but also, at times, look at that society, and even at our struggle itself, detached within the aesthetic frame. Granted, there may be an *aestheticism* which truly does seek refuge from ordinary life within aesthetic experience and which disdainfully turns its back on the "practical" world. Oscar Wilde, for example, the quintessential aesthete, describes action as "the last resource of those who know not how to dream." But this aestheticism is hardly an inevitable expression of the fundamental nature of art. The view of life and art which Wilde proposes is the product of a particular social setting. The aestheticism that emerged in nineteenth-century Europe and that has altered somewhat but by no means disappeared in this century arose in great part out of an alienation from the new social structure dominated by a finally triumphant bourgeoisie. Moreover, this aestheticism tends to be much too flamboyant and aggressive to be considered a "retreat" from society; it has, in fact, been loosely allied with an anti-bourgeois "counterculture" that is far from unpolitical, no matter how much it may sometimes claim to be or want to be.

I don't think there is anything *essential* in art that leads people away from social concern. We would all agree, I suspect, that just because for a period of time you experience an aesthetic image detached from the practical context, this doesn't lead you, when the experience is over, to ignore the demands of self-concern. You continue to feed yourself, protect yourself, care for your loved ones, and so on. And isn't social involvement simply an extension of these self-preserving, self-enhancing activities? Some of us allow ourselves to be mystified with respect to social concerns, to see them as a fundamentally separate kind of activity. The real world includes family, friends, work, recreation, etc., and then stops. What lies beyond is unreal, or it's "politics," a "fool's game," "the same old bullshit," what have you. But why is this? That larger social world impinges on us, like it or not. To be out of work is a jarring revelation of the public foundation on which "private life" rests. Between the concern that makes us cautious as we cross a busy street and the concern that involves us in social action to keep toxic wastes from being dumped into our water, air, and land, there is no break whatsoever, only a continuum. You can be struck down by a car; you can be poisoned by a local factory; you can be sent to die in a war you never chose to fight. What pulls us back from this larger social sphere is confusion, alienation, a sense of helplessness, even fear of reprisal—but hardly the mere fact of aesthetic experience.

But to say that there is nothing essential in art that discourages social engagement—though the point may well need to be made—doesn't take us very far. The question remains: in what way can art exert an effect on society? Does the sense of contradiction persist? Does it seem that to perceive an art work as something detached from the practical context would rule out the possibility of any social effect whatsoever? Actually there is no contradiction. Art may be a special form of experience, perceived in the image and free of self-concern. But it *is* experience, not oblivion, and as such it can affect the way we perceive, the way we feel, the way we think, and the way we act. It's true that aesthetic response is contained in the image and doesn't lead out of it. But even if our aesthetic involvement is complete while we're perceiving a work, *afterward* the remembered experience may be associated in various ways with the practical context—or this may happen intermittently while we're still in the presence of the art work, as a momentary break in our aesthetic involvement comparable to the kind of break that professional critics and artists themselves are likely to experience.

I've said that art can affect the way we function. In this respect it is both weak and strong. Weak because it's only an image and therefore doesn't demand to be dealt with in the same way that ordinary experience does. To see a painting of a battle, no matter how considerable its emotional impact, is not likely to affect me the way seeing the battle itself would. But art has its own strengths as well; in shaping our attitudes —if only for a short time—it can call upon very powerful resources. To take a vulgar example: haven't you been irritated to find yourself responding quite involuntarily with warm feelings to some soft-drink or fast-food commercial on TV, a cynical hype skillfully exploiting the evocative potential of music and film? And what the commercial can do is trivial compared to what can be achieved by a great playwright or composer or film director. Art has still another advantage. Precisely *because* it's only an image, we may be more tolerant of certain subjects and certain attitudes in a work of art than we would be in ordinary life. This has limits of course; people do stalk out of movies from time to time. Still, someone who's not terribly keen on labor unions may "go along" with *The Organizer* or *Norma Rae*, when he would resist a more direct appeal. Of course, this tendency to go along with art, while it may open us up to a wider range of experience than we would otherwise accept, goes hand in hand with a tendency to pull away when we're done. The magician leaves the stage; the bubble bursts, and we're back in the real world. This "magic spell" aspect of art, theatre in particular, led Bertolt Brecht to search for ways to make his audience *less* likely to go along unthinkingly with a play; he wanted them not to lose themselves in the work but to remain conscious and critical. It has been debated: did Brecht succeed in this or did he become an "illusionist" in spite of himself?

In any case, we're not amnesiac about art. To some extent, we remember it. We may learn from it; we may, even in very subtle ways, be changed by it. Art, as I've pointed out, doesn't merely evoke experiential quality but composes it as well; within each person's universe of experience, a work of art can establish new relationships which may lead that person to look at things in a new way. To what extent do these new relationships continue to be of importance when we've turned away from the work? That depends. We're more likely to assimilate them if they're not *entirely* new, if they accord well with what is already in us. I picture two tourists walking out of Chartres Cathedral on a quiet winter afternoon, still under the spell of that vast reverent gloom pierced by the unearthly brilliance of the stained glass. One of them experiences a poignant but fast-fading urge to enter the world of Catholicism. The other, whether aware of it or not, has been moving for some time along the path to conversion and needed no more than this to take him the rest of the way. Sudden conversions are rarely sudden.

But to talk of conversion can lead us away from the subtle effects of aesthetic experience, which more commonly instigates delicate shifts in sensibility, gradual expansions of awareness, tentative readjustments of understanding, slow bolstering or undermining of commitments. I would expect a work of art to make noticeable changes in a person's behavior or outlook only if it were part of a much larger process of change in that person's life. Often, of course, when this process approaches a decisive point, one single experience may get the credit; this could be—why not?—an aesthetic experience.

Moving from individual cases to the overall social picture, we can make the same sort of point. *The Exorcist* may have sent a few people back to the Church, and *Norma Rae* may have led a few people into union organizing, but we wouldn't expect any large-scale social change unless the situation were already ripe for it. What we *might* expect would be for such films simply to exert a pressure which other social developments—including, perhaps, other films—would either counter or support.

I don't want to discount the potential importance of individual works of art, not only as scarcely visible elements in a cumulative development, but also occasionally as dramatic catalysts that can help to precipitate some substantial social effect. It happens occasionally that a work of art acquires, over and above its aesthetic function, the status of a symbol or rallying point for a social movement. Not only did Beaumarchais's *Marriage of Figaro* contain within it an attack on aristocratic privilege, but also, because of the opposition it met at the hands of Louis XVI and a faction at court, the play became, even extrinsically, an instrument of social struggle. With admirable prescience, the king declared that in order for the performance of Beaumarchais's play not to be a "dangerous inconsistency," the Bastille would have to be destroyed. "This man laughs," he said, "at everything that ought to be respected in a government." *The Marriage of Figaro* was banned. Beaumarchais in turn told people: "He doesn't want the play performed; I say it will be played, should it be at Notre-Dame."

This battle over the play was given an interesting turn because of an old French tune which had early in the century acquired anti-English words and, therefore, nationalistic associations, and which Beaumarchais had used as the melody for one of his songs in the play. By a complicated chain of events, this song, *"Malbrough s'en va-t-en guerre,"* became a sort of popular anthem which people could whistle in defiance on the streets. Georges Lemaître, in his biography of the playwright, says that "for about two years 'Malbrough' became the war song of the French crowds fighting along with Beaumarchais in his 'war of nerves' against the king." The play's eventual public performance was a victory indeed. When it opened, on April 27, 1784, there were enormous crowds trying to get in and continual applause throughout the show, which, under those circumstances, took five hours to play. And people were singing "Malbrough" all over Paris.

We mustn't forget that the social effectiveness of the play was in great part extrinsic: what would *Figaro* have been if there had been no royal condemnation? On the other hand, the condemnation was no accident but a response to what was, in fact, subversive in the play. In any case, it would be silly to say that *Figaro* brought the Bastille down. Nor was Beaumarchais himself a revolutionary. But that this play had a meaningful social effect would be hard, I think, to deny. Napoleon certainly wasn't inclined to deny it. He remarked that the play was already "the revolution in action," declaring that under his own reign a man like Beaumarchais would have been locked up in the asylum. "People would have called it despotic," he added, "but what a service it would have rendered society."

Arlo Guthrie clearly aimed at this kind of social effect in his monologue *Alice's Restaurant* (recorded in 1967). To some extent he succeeded. The record, with its brilliant folksy satire of the war, the draft, and the police, and its catchy little tune, which was sung on the streets in demonstrations all over the country, made no negligible contribution to the anti-war movement. But on the other hand there were no king and courtiers, not even a mayor, trying to suppress it. So its contribution remained essentially intrinsic.

These examples come from what is, for me at least, the positive side; I'm well aware that art can have another sort of social effect as well. A standard example is *Triumph of the Will*, Leni Riefenstahl's propaganda film glorifying Hitler and the Third Reich. And Hitler himself more or less appropriated the music of Wagner. As an adolescent, he had been inspired by a performance of *Rienzi* to believe that he could become a leader who would make the German people great. He had the *Rienzi* overture played at the opening of every party congress, while Bayreuth itself, William Carr tells us, "from the early 1920's . . . became a Nazi shrine." Literally a shrine. One German wartime film had a shell-shocked flier experience a sudden cure at Bayreuth during a performance of *Siegfried* (and wounded soldiers were, in fact, sent to Bayreuth for a sort of musical therapy and re-inspiration). Obviously, there is nothing in Wagner's music—heroic and nationalistic though it may be—that simply turns people into Nazis (though his poisonous anti-semitic writing is not so easily exonerated). But in that social setting, utilized in the way that they were, these works of art were able to lend powerful support to the Nazi ideology. In a very rough way, and with some misgiving, I could say that Wagner's music did for the Third Reich what "freedom songs" did for the civil–rights movement of the 1960's. To the real virtues of art, how much I would like to add this one more: that art, like some sort of moral compass needle, always, no matter where we find it, points toward the good. But I can't.

Would we agree (a) that art can have an effect on the individual's relationship to society, and therefore on society itself, and (b) that works of art may differ in their social effect? If so, then we stand on the brink of an important and contro-versial aesthetic doctrine, which holds that art works are to be judged not merely according to the aesthetic satisfaction they may afford individuals, but especially according to their effect or potential effect on society. This doctrine has been ad-vanced, since Plato, in connection with a variety of positions; it was advanced on behalf of a religious ethic in Tolstoy's *What is Art*, and in this century it has been explored most deeply by Marxist theorists.

If art could never be anything more than a respite, there might be no problem. But since it *can* have a social effect, is the artist justified in turning away from the most urgent social imperatives to pursue a so-called "neutral" art, which, in fact, can never be neutral? It is not only Marxist critics who have raised the question: why can't art be art *and* be socially responsible as well?

It's interesting that when you apply this question to the individual artist, you can come up with two very different answers, both of which need to be taken seriously.

First of all, I think it's easy to demonstrate that artists have to work from what they are, not from what you or I would like them to be, or even from what they would like themselves to be. Here is a sculptor. Let's assume that she's a serious artist, which means simply that she wants to produce the best art she can. It may be that she has a genuine social commitment which is incorporated successfully in her creative work. No problem. But suppose that's not the case. Suppose instead that she feels some obligation, either external or internal, to introduce into her work a social commitment which she doesn't actually have or which is no more than superficial. Is it possible to do this? To create art means to produce an image which evokes, *in the artist* first of all, a complex of experiential quality that is perceived in the image itself. Doesn't this mean that, as an artist, the sculptor has to be what she is? Has to be somewhere within her own range of experiential possibilities?

To fake it as an artist is to seek an image that will evoke qualities which in fact you don't have but would perhaps like to think you have. If art were made solely of ideas, that would be possible. In ordinary life we can sometimes establish ourselves in a social or intellectual group by learning and repeating catch-phrases. But experiential quality can't be willed or pretended into existence. When "would be" substitutes for "is," you get concepts and conventionalized images instead of experiential reality—a "travel-folder" version of the real thing. The wooden thud of pretense replaces the delicate vibrations of resonance.

I remember watching *All in the Family* some years back, admiring the acting very much, but growing weary of the liberal issues which were imposed, one a week, on characters and situations they did not fit. I'm not in a position to say whether the writers and directors believed or didn't believe in this liberal-democrat ideology. But as artists they didn't believe; it was all forced into existence—"brotherhood" one week, "women's lib" another—perhaps in compensation for cashing in on the idea of the heartwarming racist as TV hero. Next to the real evocative power of Archie and Edith, these dutiful manipulations had about as much authenticity as a wedding gift thank-you letter. Did *All in the Family* do some social good? Perhaps, but it seemed to me that the artificial incorporation of these liberal causes implied a subtle negation; or perhaps it exposed a certain inauthenticity in the liberal position itself, which wanted "brotherhood" and "women's lib" added on as ornaments to an essentially unaltered social structure, and which softened racism to no more than a personal foible, like Lucy Ricardo's celebrity mania. In any case, I couldn't help thinking that Archie Bunker's many colleagues in the audience would have no difficulty in making off with the redemptive cheese (see Chapter Seven), while easily escaping the cumbersome aggressive trap that would spring so predictably each week.

What I'm saying is that our sculptor, if her art is to be authentic, has to work within the limits of her own experiential universe. If she were to be changed as an artist—in the direction of social commitment—this change would have to be a real one and a profound one, extending below the level of concepts. But even if she were genuinely engaged, there might still be problems. Some experiential areas exert more pressure than do others toward realization in an aesthetic context. There might be obsessive patterns trying to liberate themselves within the image of her sculpture, patterns not in any obvious way political. Or she might actually be seeking a psychological balance in her art, concerning herself with certain inner areas, certain needs which her social involvement ignores or denies. Finally, it might be that she would *like* to incorporate this social involvement in her sculpture, but has not yet found the aesthetic means, the authentic link between the two.

Obviously, there is always the possibility that a person will change. But I think we have to understand also that *authentic* politically engaged art is not simply a voluntary matter, subject to the artist's will. Still less is it subject to the will of a political group or of the state itself. What do we have then? A vindication of the disengaged artist? Yes, we do have that. But, as I said, we can apply the question of social responsibility to the individual artist and come up with two different answers.

The notion that artists should be free agents, bound to no social goals or values but only to the imperative of the art work itself, emerged clearly as an aesthetic ideology only about one hundred and fifty years ago. It remains attractive, particularly so when we recall the pressures that have been put on artists by the various totalitarian regimes of this century. But this notion has a mystifying aspect as well. It tends not merely to say "Hands off!" to society, but to encourage our belief that the social context actually is *not* involved in the creative process. It tells us that artists should be free, but also implies that, unless "interfered with," they *are* free.

Art, however, is not at all "neutral," whatever that would mean. As I've already stressed (in Chapter Ten), art is in part the product of a society. The "artist as free agent" ideology, in its mystifying aspect, reminds me of the days when campuses were becoming centers of social action, and some administrators and faculty used to warn us that the university should not be "politicized." The answer, of course, was: "Are you *serious*? Don't politicize this university which has war-research contracts, ties to the CIA, an ROTC curriculum and a preponderantly white male faculty, and whose trustees are political appointees chosen from the business elite of the state? *That's* what you're telling us not to politicize?" Art may not be a mere reflection of social forces, as in some simple-minded application of Marxist theory, but neither is it floating free in a "neutral" aesthetic space.

We cannot assume that our hypothetical sculptor is, as a creative artist, socially neutral to start with, so that the only question facing us is whether or not a social orientation should be "added" to the creative process. Artist, art work, and audience exist in and are defined by a network of social relationships. We should not be surprised if the kind of art this sculptor creates is affected by her sense of a possible audience, by her understanding of her own social role as sculptor, and also by the kind of success she may aspire to. Does she have the clear sense of working toward a particular audience, as might a carver of funeral sticks in an African tribe, a stonemason carving figures on a medieval cathedral, a sculptor patronized by the court of Louis XIV? Or is she uncertain about a possible audience and therefore more reflexive, self-oriented as an artist? To the extent that she *is* conscious of an audience, what kind is it? Other sculptors? A circle of friends? Wealthy patrons? Working-class people? Critics? The sense of audience is one force that helps to narrow the enormous range of aesthetic possibilities in an artist. Another such force is the artist's understanding of the role that will be played by the work itself. Does she see it as part of the public life of the community? As an offering to friends? As a competitive entry submitted for evaluation to persons in a position of power or authority? As a feature of galleries and private collections? At this point in her career, what would success be? A favorable write-up in *Artforum*? A tenured teaching position? Popular acceptance? Commissions from businesses or public agencies? Political effectiveness? A foundation grant for foreign study?

I don't want to be simplistic; an art work doesn't carry the answers to such questions inscribed on it. But wouldn't it be naive to deny the influence of these relationships, to exclude from the creative process the social context in which this sculptor creates? If so, then we need a two-part answer to our question about the artist and social responsibility. The possibilities for some kind of social engagement in an artist's work are not merely a function of individual temperament, but are themselves linked to the social structure. In fact, a general tendency to see the artist as being "free" from the social process is itself part of this structure. The doctrine of art-as-propaganda offers one kind of support to those who hold power; the more subtle doctrine of "neutral" art offers another.

The myth of the solitary artist pursuing an aesthetic vision while the world rushes by unnoticed may be a flattering one and it may also help to make alienation more endurable; it may even, as myths tend to do, reveal some basic truth—in this case about artists' singlemindedness: the way they are likely to be entirely given over to the work at hand. But having said this, I have to add that it gives a tremendously distorted and limited picture of artistic creation. The myth may be liberating—and good P.R.—at a time when social demands are oppressive to the artist. But the myth itself can become a form of oppression: "Hey, you artists are too good, too lofty for these sordid realities. Pursue your lonely vision and keep your nose out of the political process."

If our sculptor finds, after all, that her art remains uncongenial to political commitment, then even those who might prefer to see her work take on this political dimension will have to accept things the way they are. An artist has to play the hand she's dealt. But we also may want to see if the deck has been stacked. There are excellent reasons—and not just aesthetic ones—to respect the freedom of artists. But since this very freedom has its deceptive aspect, we should also recognize that the system of social relationships within which art is produced must be looked at critically. We know, for example, that during the period of aristocratic ascendency in Europe, painters, playwrights, architects, composers, and so on who came from the lower classes had good reason, generally speaking, to direct their efforts, not to their peers, but to the aristocratic class or to the hierarchy of the church. The aristocratic class has effectively disappeared. Artists no longer look to courts for patronage. Some—including many film-makers—pursue a mass audience through media dominated by commercial interest. Some seek acceptance primarily from other artists (this is common among poets, for example). Some, particularly in the fine arts, resemble their counterparts of centuries past: alienated as artists from the people among whom they've lived, they are impelled to look upward socially for recognition and reward.

If, incidentally, I have given the impression that I believe all art should be "activist" art, I certainly haven't meant to do so. That is one position. Another is arrogant disdain, in the name of aesthetic autonomy, for social concern in art. What we need, and what I think we're beginning to move toward, is a synthesis that strives to understand and do justice to both the individual creative process and the overall social process. There is nothing to gain and a great deal to lose from bullying artists in the name of the state or in the name of the revolution. Art doesn't respond well to this kind of bullying, not because it's isolated and otherworldly, but because its truth is experiential rather than conceptual; its truth is the cognitive-affective truth of resonance—too deep and too elusive to be forced into compliance, either by the artist or by anyone else. On the other hand, the social existence of artists is not separated from their creative work. In every epoch art is socially defined and integrated; it is not to be seen *merely* as the result of social forces but neither does it pursue an independent course. The political-economic processes that created Lincoln Center, that send modern dance companies on lecture-demonstration tours to universities around the country, that put authors on TV talk shows, that give certain rock stars annual incomes in the millions of dollars, that determine network TV programming, that lead the art department of a high-prestige university to style itself "conceptualist" —all of these *matter*; all of these ultimately exert their effect within the "privileged" frame of the work of art.

Artists are not to be bullied, but there is no question of leaving them alone—how could that be possible? What we need to ask is not whether there should be an economic structure around the arts, whether there should be public policy, but simply: what kind? For now, let me merely register the questions. I'll return to them in Chapter Thirteen. At present I'd like to pursue the question of art and its social effect.

We may recognize that works of art vary from one to another in their social effect. But a very interesting question remains. Does *art itself*—not merely this song or that painting, but the very aesthetic experience itself—have a social effect? And if so, of what sort? Perhaps we may not come up with an answer which is universally applicable, but we may at least be able to recognize tendencies.

For example, art tends, doesn't it, to exert a socially cohesive effect? To the extent that aesthetic situations are participated in by a group, there can be the sense of a shared, even a communal subjectivity. Other social institutions may establish *objective* relationships between individuals, but art can establish a *subjective* bond, a sense of experiential unity. Singing and dancing in a tribal society may have a magical function; they may provide an aesthetic release, may even induce an extraordinary, religious state of consciousness; but they also constitute a sort of experiential bath in which the individuals are immersed together, a sacrament which celebrates and fosters the merging of the individual into the tribe.

In a huge and complex industrial society, this cohesive force may not always be as obvious, but we shouldn't discount it. It's certainly possible for someone isolated in a large city to sit alone reading poetry and sense some experiential contact with a social unit that might be of any scope, from a relatively small clique united by taste and temperament up to the human race itself.

Most obvious today in the United States is the cohesive function of art with respect to sub-groups within the larger society. *Nashville. Motown. Woodstock.* These three place-names invoke not only aesthetic categories but social group-ings as well, which have had more in common than aesthetic preference, but in which art has played an impressively cohes-ive role. The art of a ruling class *or* of a revolution has a social effect that derives not merely from the particular form which that art takes, but also from the fact that those who share in it sense a subjective community with each other: "These people are my kind of people."

This cohesive function is not universal in art. It would seem to play a less important role in natural aesthetic experience. (There is, though, a very old Japanese tradition of group excursions to see flowering trees, to go moon-viewing, etc. Also some kinds of natural scenes may acquire sub-cultural reference; in fact, the very ability to appreciate what we call "nature" helped to identify an aristocracy of feeling in late eighteenth-century Europe. And here in San Diego, I know that there has been, from time to time, a bit of a sunset cult among beach dwellers.) Even with art works—which are much more likely than natural scenes to imply an audience—I doubt that a cohesive function is *necessarily* present in our aesthetic experience. But that it is a tendency rooted not in any partic-ular kind of art but in the nature of art itself, seems a reasonable conclusion.

Closely related is the tendency of art to act as a cultural transmitter. A building or a song, a play or a folk tale can provide the most effective kind of schooling, can define our past, present, and future, tell us how we are expected to feel and behave, tell us what is of value and what is not. But since there is, perhaps, nothing about art which is better understood than this function, I won't dwell on it, except to emphasize that this transmission is, also, cohesive in its effect.

So far we've come across nothing to imply that art, essen-tially, is critical of society. Obviously, *individual* works of art can encourage social criticism, but is there anything in the very nature of art that would give rise to such criticism? I would like to think there is, since this would go a long way toward resolving the whole troubling question of art and social responsibility. But what I'd like to think isn't necessarily what's so. We want to resist getting sloppy, taking that testimonial-dinner approach which finds in art every conceivable virtue.

Even though we recognize that certain individual art works, because of their particular subject matter and political perspective, may constitute a criticism of society, it's hard to see how there could be any such critical element in the very nature of art itself. Once again: perception in the absence of self-concern would seem to imply acceptance, not criticism. I *accept* my back yard when I see it aesthetically; for me to view it *critically* is to view it in the light of self-concern.

Still, there is a possibility, I think, that art—all art—may provide, not social criticism necessarily, but a possible basis for such criticism. We need to remember that art involves more than merely perception in the absence of self-concern. When I perceive aesthetically, I perceive my own response *out there* in the image. When art is working, there is no antagonism between what is in here and what is out there; the art work not only evokes my own subjective response but accepts it as well. Now, a work of art may be detached from the network of practical relationships, but that it exists in the objective world is clear. The painting, the poem, the song are clearly out there. So that, when I perceive my own subjectivity, my own experiential quality in the work, that very work constitutes a validation of this subjectivity in the objective world. The art work demonstrates that our subjectivity *exists* beyond the individual self. The art work is, on the experiential level, an ally in the world out there.

Now consider, by way of contrast, the kind of relationship which can exist between individual subjectivity and social institutions (not which necessarily must exist but which *can* exist). To the extent that institutions are based solely upon the *objective* existence of individuals, an antagonism can develop between the institution and the individual as subject.

In this society particularly, as our institutions grow more and more powerful and all-embracing, the individual becomes more and more rationalized in objective, institutional terms.

The individual as IBM card is the reigning cliché of our time—and the very truth. Increasingly, what we *are* can be punched onto a computer card for the use of schools, banks, legislators, marketing departments, social scientists, TV producers, law enforcement agencies. The card is all they know of us and all they need to know. More and more, what we actually experience as process—fluid, whole, unfathomably deep—is redefined into hard-edged categories, sorted out into shallow compartments. And, most important of all, this redefinition is not merely external to us; we tend to accept it and to see ourselves according to its terms. Every aspect of subjectivity can be, in the real-estate sense of the word, "developed," parceled out for institutional definition and exploitation. Even social misery and rebelliousness are defined, exploited, recycled by institutions—the ideal goal being a closed system that consumes its own waste products. Misery feeds the therapeutic institutions and the "self-help" industry, and is also channeled by advertising into consumption. Rebelliousness is merchandised. And sexuality is defined, processed and packaged until, as they say in the pork business, nothing is left but the squeal.

In such a situation, unreconstructed subjectivity becomes a possible basis for social criticism. This subjectivity doesn't simply *equal* social criticism, since such criticism to be meaningful requires analysis. But without subjectivity which remains far enough outside the institutions to be critical of them, there is no basis for a challenge to society.

Can it be that art, which instead of defining and rationalizing subjectivity, evokes it, accepts it, and validates it in all of its irreducible dynamism and abundance, can it be that art—all art, not merely political art—to the extent that it works, has an effect which is potentially political?

Herbert Marcuse, though his aesthetic categories are rather different from the ones I have been using, is led toward the same kind of conclusion in *The Aesthetic Dimension*: "I see the political potential of art in art itself, in the aesthetic form as such." Marcuse's emphasis here is not so much on the validation of subjectivity as on the "promise of liberation," deriving from aesthetic "form," "which gives the familiar content and the familiar experience the power of estrangement—and which leads to the emergence of a new consciousness and a new perception." What Marcuse establishes is a basis for criticizing the traditional distinction in Marxist aesthetics between "progressive" and "decadent" art. In response to that Marxist criticism which scorns "inwardness" and individualism in bourgeois literature, Marcuse points out: "The 'flight into inwardness' and the insistence on a private sphere may well serve as bulwarks against a society which administers all dimensions of human existence. Inwardness and subjectivity may well become the inner and outer space for the subversion of experience, for the emergence of another universe."

Here in this point of Marcuse's is, I believe, the very nub of the matter; we need only extend it from the particular types of literature in question to cover art itself: there is in aesthetic inwardness and subjectivity what can be seen as a political dimension. Sánchez Vásquez makes a comparable point: "Creation comes to mean rebellion." He is particularly concerned to justify the same sort of art that Marcuse defends:

> The "accursed" (*maudit*) artist of the late nineteenth and early twentieth century is accursed because of his insistence, expressed through his creative activity, on resisting the inert and abstract universe of the bourgeoisie. By objectifying himself, by making human or humanized objects—works of art—the artist assures a human presence in things and thus helps prevent the reification of humanity.

How attached we can become to particular works of art! I think of a teen-ager in the 1950's, never tiring of hearing the Everly Brothers sing "Cathy's Clown," of myself at nine reading *Boy Scouts to the Rescue* over and over again, and now having a similar relationship with *Felix Krull* or *A la recherche*. I think of Maddie seeing *Beauty and the Beast* for the sixth time, of Catharine and *Amarcord*, of myself again and *Playtime*. There is a family feeling that people can develop toward works of art, an almost protective affection, which is not to be confused with the contentious posturing that "art lovers" sometimes fall into. These works know us and participate with us as we are experientially; they provide sustenance at the core. We feel the truest kinship with them. The works to which we feel most allied may give way to others as we change, though there may be some which manage to grow with us, greeting us anew at successive stages. This sense of alliance, which is so obvious in the case of a person's favorite art works, exists to some degree in any aesthetic experience. The work validates our subjective existence, and has the potential at least, to strengthen our hand vis-à-vis institutions that seek to objectify us. The work of art, an object itself, is like a friend at court. It suggests that the objective world, though it may well seem so at times, is not irremediably hostile to our inner self. Even more, the moment of aesthetic perception, detached though it is from the practical context, still, because it allows this temporary reconciliation of subject and object, leaves behind at least some cause for wondering if it might indeed be possible to remake things "nearer to the heart's desire."

I should add that this essentially individual experience can easily take on a group character. In conjunction with the cohesive tendency I've already described, it can contribute to the development of a bohemian counterculture, of a somewhat defiant adolescent subculture, or of a revolutionary movement. For bohemia, Rimbaud. For the adolescents, "Cathy's Clown." For the revolutionary movement, *"Malbrough s'en va-t-en guerre."* Still, I want to emphasize: whether or not it's identified with a movement or subculture, any song can be a freedom song. Any art can be "subversive." For me, once, it was John Coltrane playing "My Favorite Things."

But I earlier insisted that Wagner's music became a Nazi "freedom song." Does this contradict the notion that there is inherently in art the basis for a challenge to social institutions? Not at all. The *Rienzi* overture appears to have done for the young Hitler the very kind of thing I've been talking about. Later in life, he described the annual Bayreuth festival as "the most blessed time of my existence." Wagner's music, a friend of Hitler's observed, "became an integral part of his personality." *Social criticism* is a very inclusive term; everything depends on what kind of criticism it is. Again, we don't want to claim more for art than it can deliver. I've said that art can strengthen the hand of the individual—as it apparently did Hitler's—vis-à-vis the prevailing institutions. But as I've also pointed out, it offers no moral compass needle (particularly since perceivers can interpret a work as they see fit). I suspect that *The Sorrows of Young Werther* provided Napoleon, who read the novel seven times, with an experiential ally. If Napoleon found the inner strength to challenge the political structure of Europe and spend hundreds of thousands of European lives in his pursuit of an empire, there may well have been works of art that helped him find it. The point I've tried to establish is a limited one: insofar as social institutions are antagonistic to the subjective existence of individuals, art plays what is potentially a political role by validating and supporting subjectivity, and, also, perhaps, by suggesting the possibility of a more congenial objective world. But what all this means specifically depends on the particular situation.

"Still, can't we hope, at least, that art will make people more humane, more accepting of each other?"

Humane and accepting toward members of a particular community, perhaps, because of art's cohesive tendency, but this community might have the most bloodthirsty attitude toward outsiders.

"But then as the world becomes more aware of itself and as communities come into closer aesthetic contact, as we move toward Goethe's notion of a *Weltliteratur*, which, for our purposes, would be a world art, isn't there some hope that art can make its cohesive contribution to a sense of *human* community?"

Perhaps. Shall we say that the jury is still out? Has the enormous presence of black music in the United States done anything to mitigate racism? Perhaps. Perhaps without it, things would be far worse still. It may even be that if you're going to hate black people or gypsies or Jews, you will feel the need to close yourself off to their art. As a teacher of comparative literature, I have certainly observed that art can expand the sense of community. But this expansion, if it does take place, is a fragile thing—as art is a fragile thing—in a selfish, fearful world. If the material base of society is ever altered so that it does less to incite our selfishness and fear, then perhaps we will have reached the epoch of fragile things, and art may come into its own as a social force.

To the extent that art does have some social effect, isn't there a possible contradiction between the two tendencies I've described: one cohesive, the other critical? That may be. Let's look more closely at this.

The aesthetic image objectifies and validates subjectivity. This can help to maintain a strong base outside thoroughly rationalized and institutionalized areas of consciousness—a base which may become, insofar as institutions are felt to be unnecessarily antagonistic to the self, a political base. Now if, in addition, the individual senses that his subjectivity, embodied in the work of art, is shared by a sub-group or social class which also shares his criticism of institutions, then the work of art, becoming more overtly political, exerts an effect which is critical in one direction and cohesive in the other. It's not necessary that the work be politically explicit. When I was an undergraduate, "folk songs" in general had this effect: not just obviously political songs like "Union Maid" and "Los Cuatro Generales," but also, let's say, "Sweet Betsy from Pike" or "The Longest Train."

Isn't there art, though, which tends to bind individuals not to a critical clique or revolutionary movement but to the overall society or the dominant institutions themselves? Clearly there is. We might think of the singing, dancing, and costume at a tribal wedding. Or of the great cathedrals of the European Middle Ages. Or of movies like *Alexander Nevsky*. Or of "Rule Britannia" or "Deütschland uber alles" or "The Star-Spangled Banner." With, of course, the proviso in each case that the work *is* actually functioning aesthetically and cohesively for the individuals who perceive it. The proviso is crucial. "The Star-Spangled Banner" may have a ritual function, like the Pledge of Allegiance. But the particular kind of cohesive effect that art exerts requires more than ritual. What makes art cohesive is the sense that one's own experiential quality, perceived in the image, is shared by others in the group. This resonant response that we seem to share is not a concept, not a value, not an obligation or a profession of faith, but rather a living portion of the experiential self. For "The Star-Spangled Banner" to work as patriotic art, it has to work as art. Aesthetic response is assent freely given to the image; it can't be forced, faked, or willed into being. There needs to be some experiential area which can be perceived entirely in the image, without any sense of division between the image and the perceiver. Now this kind of response is certainly possible even if, in other areas, the perceiver may have reservations. Just as I can find a basis for assenting aesthetically to Alexander Pope's

Essay on Criticism "even though," so I may, as a medieval Catholic, assent to Reims Cathedral, even though I have reservations about the archbishop; and so a great many people in this country may assent on one level to the national anthem with its brassy splendor, its sometimes exciting imagery, its defiant assertion of national pride, even though they may be ready to insist on another occasion that the country "is going to the dogs." But there are limits. One work of art by its success, another work of art by its failure can raise questions about the appropriateness of institutions to the inner life. As the experiential basis for assent dwindles, patriotic art loses its ability to bind people together in the context of a society or institution. Patriotic art can live for a time on promises, but it begins to die with promises broken. For some people, "We Shall Overcome" and "Light My Fire," between them, cut the experiential ground out from under "The Star-Spangled Banner," which Jimi Hendrix did manage for a moment spectacularly to redeem—but only by narrowing its vast cohesive scope and turning it (again) into a revolutionary anthem. For the anthem to regain some of its old evocative power, there might have to be either a new revolutionary commitment to the future or a new enemy (which latter, as of this writing, seems the more likely, I'm afraid).

Ultimately, I think, art is subversive of social structures which fail to win or keep any substantial assent on the immediate unconceptualized level of subjective experience. Not just "political art" (which retains, of course, its own particular value) but art itself. Any art which evokes and validates subjectivity can undermine patriotic and institutional art works to the extent that these lose their ability to do the same. Small wonder then that rulers and ruling classes are so often tempted to control the arts, since even "neutral" art may not be entirely safe. Small wonder that revolutions, which have tended since 1789 to seek not merely a restructured society but a refashioned human image, are similarly tempted. What this tells me is that we need, in all seasons, to demand that the arts have fresh air and plenty of room to grow, so that we can deny one further instrument of coercion to those who rule, and so that we can protect revolutions from their own self-constricting tendencies.

CHAPTER THIRTEEN
Society and Art

The most decisive feature of capitalist society, then, is that economic life ceased to be a means to social life: it placed itself at the center, became an end in itself, the goal of all social activity. The first and most important result was that the life of society was transformed into a grand exchange relationship; society itself became a huge market. In the individual life experiences this condition expresses itself in the commodity form which clothes every product of the capitalist epoch as well as all the energies of the producers and creators. Everything ceases to be valuable for itself or by virtue of its inner (e.g., artistic, ethical) value; a thing has value only as a ware bought and sold on the market.

—Georg Lukács

Whereas objects establish relations with human beings, and thus have human significance through their use values, their exchange values appear as attributes of the objects themselves, without relationship to human beings. Objects lose their human meaning, their quality, their relationship to man. The commodity, we might say, is a human object, but in a dehumanized form; that is, it is no longer appreciated for its use value, for its relationship to a specific human need.

—Adolfo Sánchez Vásquez

What a pity if we were to consider art as a *means* to social change and say nothing about it as a possible *beneficiary* of social change.

Art may have its basis in individual experience, but society has surrounded this experience with a system of social arrangements that sponsor it, define it, and help to shape it. Obviously, these arrangements include theatres, galleries, recording studios, high-speed color presses, and so on. But they also include legislatures, ad agencies, gossip columns, corporate-earnings reports, art-appreciation classes, disc jockeys, swap meets . . . it makes a fascinating list. This entire system of arrangements is likely to have its effect on works of art, just as it will affect the way you as a perceiver respond to them. In other words, aesthetic experience, personal as it is, can also be seen as a social product.

Art may be universal, but these arrangements that surround it are not. If we don't like them, we don't *have* to live with them. The way society provides for art is just as legitimate a subject for criticism as any other aspect of society. Though food plays an important role in all human life, the way it is produced, distributed, and consumed will vary from one society to another; and we are willing to make judgments in this area, to say that one system of food distribution is fairer or uses resources more effectively than another. Few of us, however, look at art in this way. Even more with art than with, say, agriculture, education, or politics, we tend to assume that the way things are at present is simply "natural." After all, art is not linked in any essential way to our notions about economic, political, or technological progress; and so, though most people know very well that there is *stylistic* change in the arts, they tend to take the social context for granted, to see it ahistorically: no past, no future. And yet, even our very categories of *art* and *artist* belong to this time and this place, though we have very little awareness that this is so.

Have we learned anything, then, about aesthetic experience which could lead us to question the appropriateness of its present social context? I think we have.

To understand the full extent to which art has become the kind of commodity that Lukács and Sánchez Vásquez describe, we need to be aware not merely of the role of the marketplace but also of the role that *knowledge* has come to play in our attitude toward works of art. Knowledge, though it is not capital, strictly speaking, is analogous to capital in some ways. In personal or corporate terms, knowledge is a key resource, often directly translatable into hard cash. There is, moreover, a marked tendency for knowledge to accumulate where wealth and power are, and to be allotted on very unequal terms to the rest of society (attempts, for example, to bring the poor—especially the minority poor—into higher education are half-hearted and short-lived). If you like, knowledge itself can be seen as a commodity which is defined by its exchange value and which can be used to acquire other commodities. This brings us back to art.

Art, as commodity, can be acquired with money or with accumulated knowledge. After I started teaching, it took me a while to understand that many students enrolled in a poetry course were not after the *experience* of poetry so much as they wanted to *acquire* the poems, which would then, in one way or another, increase each student's own personal assets. And this acquisition would take place at the moment when I, a retailer licensed by the State of California, handed over to them the "real meaning" behind the words. Occasionally in class when I cast some doubt on my ability to do that very thing, I would sense, in a student's response, the feeling of "Ah, cunning devil! They probably save that for their graduate students."

I'm not sure that many people, deep down, really believe that the art in a public museum is free to all (or available at least to everyone who can pay the entrance fee). Either you are a millionaire and can afford actually to own a great work of art, or you devote years to study and become an expert who knows what these works are all about. Everyone else is no more than a windowshopper, or at best has only some token share in a great work, like the person with one share of General Motors. I hardly mean to deny that aesthetic experience occurs in these situations—only to reveal the kind of mystification it has to contend with.

The dominance of exchange value over use value tends to keep people on the *outside* of art works. It emphasizes the value of these works as objects rather than as experience. This is not a superficial misunderstanding, easily remedied by the application of aesthetic theory. It is very much part of the way of seeing that is inculcated by a capitalist society. It doesn't universally prevent aesthetic experience, of course, but, in overall social terms, it exerts a steady counter-aesthetic force, which will affect people in different ways depending on their own background, the art form involved, and so on.

"Popular art" carries its own mystification, and is even more blatantly a commodity than "high art" is. Generally speaking, it's an unashamed commercial undertaking, whose products are packaged, merchandised, and consumed, with the remnants either discarded to make room for new items or, sometimes, re-launched on the second-hand market. The emphasis on exchange value could scarcely be more obvious. Enormous interest and excitement attaches to the marketplace itself: the finagling, the competition, the charts and rankings. Movie grosses, rock stars' incomes, best-seller lists, network schedule-jockeying—all this is big news. Performers too are commodities, and their packaging, overnight sales-promotion, consumer acceptance, and rapid obsolescence all constitute news which *itself* becomes a commodity and which may even attain wider circulation than the performer's records or films. Popular art, especially, is dominated by fashion. As Lukács points out: "the novel, the sensational and the conspicuous elements assume an importance irrespective of whether they enhance or detract from the true, inner value of the product. . . . *It is of the essence of the market that new things must be produced within definite periods of time*, things which must differ radically from those which preceded."

Popular art is accepted as mass-market merchandise: widely available, relatively standardized, and inexpensive in every way. One needn't be a millionaire, and only a very modest amount of expertise is called for.

What's ironic is that this last point is not nearly as true as it seems to be. Someone who's been a moviegoer since childhood has developed, effortlessly, a considerable knowledge of the form. Not much backstage knowledge to be sure. No talk of camera angles and jump cuts. But this person is likely to have become relatively perceptive and discriminating all the same. In the same fashion, I have no analytical system for dealing with people's faces—at least no *conscious* system—nor even a set of categories that I could readily label. But like everyone else, I have the keenest sensitivity to slight differences in the shape of a jaw or the curve of an eyebrow; my response to faces is acute, complex, rich, and subtle; after all these years I am, in other words, a terrific audience for faces. There are people who have been listening to symphonic music for many years, who may know little of music theory, but who have a sense of structure, who are familiar with a wide range of styles and who listen to music with discernment and enjoyment. Mere exposure to an art won't produce this kind of knowledge. But a combination of exposure, enjoyment, and genuine interest is likely to do so. Still, the person who has developed this kind of knowledge of, say, detective fiction might be awed and intimidated by what he considers "literature," and unwilling to pay the price he thinks it exacts. Yet it seems to me ever so much easier to tell Bach, Mozart, Brahms, and Prokofiev apart than to make the discriminations that people I know are able to make among a multitude of rock groups, lead guitarists, and such.

My point is simply this: any real distinction that we could make between "high" art and "popular" art is exaggerated by mystification. The one is seen as a high-ticket commodity produced for an elite, inaccessible to plain folk, in one way or another too costly, "too much trouble"; the other is mass-market merchandise, ready to use right off the shelf. You could suspect that these categories aren't as neat as they appear, if only from the way some art forms can change their social coefficient. Fairy tales and folk ballads turn into "literature." African tribal sculpture is not only elevated to museum and gallery status but becomes an important influence on European artists. The Strauss family become staples on classical-music stations. "Serious" composers discover folk music. Jazz first appears at the very bottom of the socio-economic scale, acquires an absolutely terrible reputation, and then works its way up, drawing erudition and connoisseurship toward it as it rises. And what are we ever going to do with movies? For a while it looked as if there might be a two-track system possible, with plain "popular" movies on one side and fancy foreign movies—"art" movies—on the other. A whole generation of critics helped to dismantle that distinction.

But please understand. I'm not "leveling"—just questioning the prevailing aesthetic class system, which contains and pre-forms much of our understanding of art. No question of making Edith Wharton knuckle under to Barbara Cartland. On the contrary. The supermarket romances to which so many people are addicted these days, which do for the psyche very much what candy does for the metabolism, are not only sugary and tempting; these books are protected by steep attitudinal tariffs which greatly exaggerate the cost of novels such as Wharton's: Cartland is "easy reading"; Wharton is literature, i.e., "homework." I'm not sure these formula romances—though they have their own charm—would hold up quite so well in a "free trade" situation.

In "high" art and "popular" art alike, the importance of the perceiver and of his experience tends to be downgraded in favor of something approaching idolatry toward the work and the creative artist or performer. Shakespeare, Mozart, and Rembrandt are regarded with awe and reverence; we are encouraged to approach them on our knees. Similarly, singing stars, movie stars, the top rock groups not only become famous, and wealthy as maharajas, but also can acquire a magical, almost godlike status.

It could be argued that this is inherent in the nature of art and that, aesthetically, it does no harm and may even enhance the experience. But I think there are reasons to believe otherwise.

What can happen with star performers is that the status, personality, and charisma of the artist take away from or even replace the aesthetic experience itself. I don't mean to be priggish. I'm sure that to have been a screaming fifteen-year-old at a Beatles concert, to have been part of the "red sweatered ecstasy" that Allen Ginsberg describes in "Portland Coliseum," is to have had a very substantial experience in its own right. But in more general terms, as a way of approaching art, this sort of idolatry, whether of Rod Stewart or Baryshnikov, tends at best to restrict the resonant range of aesthetic experience, and can even lead out of it or deny it altogether. It's also possible for this over-concern with the artist to compensate for and to distract us from deficiencies in the art itself. When a singer makes eight million dollars a year, when you can name his wives in order, when he's been on the cover of fifteen magazines, all of this creates a froth, an excitement which you may be able to project into and perceive in the image of his singing. All well and good. But what if, when the froth dies down, there's not that much there, and, instead of looking for better singing or a better song, you're led to look for more froth somewhere else? In other words, this disproportionate emphasis on the externals—on celebrity excitement and market value—amounts to a misdirection which can lead us toward an engagement with art that is off-center. It is *very* good for business, however.

With painters, composers, novelists, and so on, we encounter a somewhat different, though parallel, situation. Here the artists are only rarely invested with any glittering jet-set celebrity, ephemeral but heart-throbbing. What they acquire, gradually, is the lofty grandeur associated with our highest and most enduring values. They become part of our "precious heritage" and so on. They are monumentalized. Fine. They deserve it. But unfortunately, as artists they also deserve better than that, which is for their works to be encountered aesthetically. And here there's some contradiction. To establish an author or work as a cultural monument can introduce a counter-aesthetic distance between the perceiver and the image. And not just a distance but also a sense that the work is above one's reach. This enshrinement of an artist can also introduce inappropriate elements into the perceiver's experience, elements which may even, like the idolatry of pop stars, take the place of a genuine aesthetic response. We enter the Rembrandt room with respect, awe, reverence. There's considerable excitement at being in the presence of paintings which are not only masterpieces of Western civilization, but also, in this case, worth big bucks on the art market. This excitement may substitute for any substantial aesthetic experience. And *that*, somehow, will be what Rembrandt is all about. Now the more experienced "art lover" may not be so totally mystified. But there are degrees. Monumentalization can encourage a falsified response even in more sophisticated perceivers. There is the sense that in the presence of a masterpiece *you* are being judged. So, unless you choose to play the equally mystified role of anti-snob, it may be difficult to avoid a rigged conclusion: your response *must* be worthy of the masterpiece. And so you make sure that it is. What happens is that perceivers can become used to being alienated from their own response. They don't want to think of themselves as faking it. But neither do they want to risk failing the test. So they learn to accept a *willed* response as the real thing. Needless to say, this too is counter-aesthetic. Moreover, it tends to become a habit; there are people who, unwilling to trust their immediate response and equally unwilling to admit that this is the case, lose their ability to respond directly and spontaneously to "great art." If they are lucky, there will be detective stories or space movies or show tunes to fall back on.

Finally, idolatry, whether of a long-dead novelist or a nineteen-year-old rock star, goes hand in hand with systems of mediation. For the rock star, it is magazines, talk shows, posters, T-shirts, etc., that serve this function. This kind of hoopla maintains an enormous exploitation industry around the popular arts. For the novelist, as for "great art" in general, a priestly caste of teachers, experts, and critics exists as mediator between the perceiver and the masterpiece. This isn't to deny that teachers and others can be aesthetically useful. But what happens is that this caste, like all priestly castes, tends to make its presence indispensable. You see the painting *through* the teacher or critic or guide; without them you feel helpless.

In more general terms, the danger of overemphasizing the lofty status of the artist or the work of art is that this encourages a false understanding of the aesthetic experience. Aesthetically too, the kingdom of heaven is *within*. We need to trust our own response—cultivate it and inform it, of course— but trust it and, above all, value it, because individual perception and response form the true center of art. Without this self-trust and self-respect, we are thrown off balance aesthetically, our experience is less authentic, we have allowed ourselves to be mystified. Our experience of art—or of some particular art form—remains off-center and not entirely satisfying.

Socially, what all this suggests is the need for art to exist in a context which does not grotesquely exaggerate the status of certain performers, which does not turn art works of the past into official monuments guarded by a caste of haughty priests, and which recognizes the essential importance and the legitimacy of individual aesthetic experience. Above all, what we need is for art to exist within a system which is not dominated by the marketplace, with its emphasis on exchange value, and therefore on the *outside* of art works. (It should go without saying that there would be no benefit at all in substituting for the marketplace the judgments of a ruling clique. I'd certainly rather keep the marketplace than have one of those juntas our government loves so well or some ham-handed Kremlin running the show.) Maximization of profits should not be the motivating force behind the presentation and distribution of what we refer to as "popular art." Rock groups should not be encouraged to give concerts on the scale of and with all the mystique of papal appearances. The money that now goes to a small elite of superstars in films and music, TV and book publishing, would be enough to reward these individuals generously relative to the median income (if this were thought necessary) and still support a vast number of other worthy actors and musicians and writers.

Massive centralization should give way to a system of many centers, managerially less efficient but aesthetically more productive, and it should become more feasible, both economically and psychologically, for artists to seek a local or a regional audience. Decentralization of theatre, dance, opera, symphonies, TV, even film, would help to demystify these arts; and it would provide much wider opportunity for composers, playwrights, directors, choreographers, and so on.

As for schooling in the arts, since education is the subject of the chapter that follows, I won't pursue it here, except to say that schools need to find ways of teaching the arts and of preserving and transmitting the art of the past without doing so at the expense of the aesthetic experience itself.

But if we're going to talk about change in the social arrangements that surround art, there is still another feature of the present system that needs to be challenged. It is not only as aesthetic audience that most of us are intimidated but also as artists or potential artists. In the chapter on performance, I stressed the continuity that binds creative artist, performer, and audience. But this idea of continuity doesn't go far enough. From a theoretical point of view, I can see no reason why people in general should not be capable of fulfilling all three of these aesthetic functions. To be a great painter or a great actor may require a very special combination of temperament, aptitude, and commitment. Precisely—and therefore many of us have the attitude: "If not great, why bother?" I know, however, first-hand the considerable aesthetic satisfaction to be had as a fair actor, a mediocre though enthusiastic folk dancer, an ignorant composer. I also know that this kind of experience has made me a more receptive and sensitive perceiver. Just as we accept an exaggerated and to some extent artificial distinction between high and low art, so we also accept unjustifiably sharp divisions between artist and non-artist, and between amateur and professional. We tend to accept the idea that most people are not artists—never can be, never will be. And among artists, amateurs scarcely count; we may appreciate that they cultivate the piano or like to write, but obviously if they were any good they would be in the big time. As a result of this kind of attitude, we get the amateurism we deserve.

It's worth reminding ourselves that among human societies there are other possible arrangements. This is Charles Mountford's description of Australian aboriginal society:

> There is no special artist class in an aboriginal community. Every member of it, young or old, will sometimes be an artist . . . All aborigines are natural artists. I have yet to meet one who would not or did not want to paint. Naturally, some are more skilled than others and take more care; yet anyone who has watched these people at work, totally absorbed and oblivious to the world around them, will be convinced that these artists are experiencing the same pleasure in their efforts as creative artists do in any community.

I've had the opportunity to teach both creative writing and improvisational theatre to people with absolutely no experience in these arts. In the case of creative writing (an odd term),

I've taught people whose negative attitudes and false notions made them worse off than beginners. And I've been struck by the amount of satisfaction that these "non-artists" can find as artists, and, in a number of cases, by how much their work has to offer from a perceiver's point of view. Creative writing admittedly is a problem. By the time students reach college, there is much to overcome: anxiety and a stubborn self-distrust in the area of writing. Still, even here a certain amount of unteaching and unblocking, along with some technique and a look at effective writing, can help them develop rapidly.

It's the theatre classes, however, which have taught me the most. When I began teaching improvisation to beginners I was flabbergasted at how good "ordinary" people can be. Naturally, it takes massive technique, acquired during years of training and apprenticeship, to become a competent, versatile, reliable actor. And that's the choice people confront. Either run off and become an actor—a full-on life commitment—or resign yourself to staying forever in the audience. The third possibility has been "amateur" theatre, which can often turn out to be more of a social than an aesthetic involvement. But here in my classes were people beginning in a matter of months to produce honest-to-goodness theatre, which at its best left any notion of amateurism out of the aesthetic picture. I asked myself: where does all this come from? My initial answer was that, because of dreaming, which is a sort of built-in theatre, because of the constant role-playing that people do, and because of enormous exposure to dramatic art in films and on TV, people have much greater latent talent for theatre than they do for other forms of art. Since then, I've revised my opinion. Perhaps theatrical ability is developed more quickly; still, I suspect that there may be as many potential musicians as theatrical improvisers, as many painters as musicians, as many dancers as painters, as many poets as dancers.

It's easy to imagine a society in which each city would have not only various local symphonies, dance companies, theatrical repertory companies, and so on, but also *neighborhood* chamber groups, jazz bands, folk ensembles, theatre groups, folk-dance clubs, art exhibits, film projects, TV productions. It's easy to imagine such a society but not so easy to say how we might get there from here. At present, economic forces in the arts, with some very important exceptions, tend to converge at the top and at the center. The money spent on pharaonic jumbo art-centers could pay for a number of more modest buildings spread out to cover a wider geographical range. Local television, if it weren't crushed, by networks, beneath the combined weight of New York and Los Angeles, could develop and keep talented writers, actors, directors, and producers; could serve its community well, and could also make an individualized contribution to the diversity of programming available for exchange with stations elsewhere. At present, rock, jazz, and country radio-stations, with their attention fixed either on the charts or on tried-and-true "oldies," are inhospitable to local talent. Painters and sculptors, if they want to make it, have to go where the important critics and the important galleries are, where art history is made, where the money is; the alternative is to remain "provincial" and therefore of no importance. This means New York, or just possibly one of a few other cities. And a would-be modern dancer who's never been to New York is like a would-be cardinal who's never been to Rome.

But how do we get there from here? Most people not only don't regard themselves as artists, but are quite sure they could never become artists. They may play a little piano; they may have been good at drawing in school or have enjoyed a drama class and thought they might like to do more of it some time; they may sing a little or write poems, or do stained glass, or have a knack for taking striking photographs; they may be storytellers or marvelous dancers, but none of this counts. None of this is worth *really* cultivating. Once the point of decision is passed, once you have decided not to run away and join the circus, which is more or less the way we see a professional commitment to art, once you've made that decision, you can forget it. You may play the piano, but you're no artist. Art is up there and we're down here. That's not only what the schools teach. That's what the record companies and TV networks, and museums and jumbo art-centers teach.

What am I saying? That we should stop putting our resources behind the best art and settle for a vast mediocrity, that we should stop "striving for excellence?" Trade the excitement and ferment of New York, Tokyo, Amsterdam, and Paris for a vast Kansas of Sunday painters? Isn't one New York City Ballet, housed appropriately in Lincoln Center, worth a hundred lackluster regional ballets in sweaty little local auditoriums?

But does it really come down to a trade-off? I would suggest that a thriving "amateurism," if we have to call it that, *promotes* high quality in art: not merely because it provides a seed-bed out of which occasional great artists may grow, but because it provides an aesthetic atmosphere that's alive and exciting, because it provides an audience with genuine interest and with some knowledge and taste as well.

Another set of arrangements for art is indeed possible. But it would come only if there were fundamental changes in the society as a whole. Decentralized art—a thriving amateurism —art works appreciated neither as commodities nor as mere ideological tools, but rather for their aesthetic use value; all of this, I think, would require (and contribute to) a truly democratic and decentralized socialism: that is, a society which at this point exists nowhere on the face of the earth. But good sense and a vestigial humility bid me stop at this point. The sociology of art in a decentralized socialist society: this book has bitten off more than enough already without adding in that little morsel.

CHAPTER FOURTEEN
"Intro to Lit, MWF 9"

To know the plum tree:
your own heart
your own nose

— *Onitsura*

If aesthetic experience happens in the absence of self-concern, then just what are we going to say about "Intro to Lit" (Required), 3 units, MWF 9? Students are reading *Moby Dick* in preparation for a final exam in two weeks. One is applying for financial aid next semester and needs at least a B, but preferably an A in the course, which means an A on the final. One of his friends in the course is pre-med and is trying desperately to push her average up as close to a 3.5 as she can; she also needs an A on the final. Another friend is pledging a sorority. Without a C average, she can't be initiated alongside her pledge sisters. She's been managing a C in the lit course so far, but, unfortunately, she needs a B to offset the D she's likely to make in Biology. But the thought of not getting initiated is so depressing that she finds it hard to study.

Now for *Moby Dick.* More than seven hundred pages long. And what is Professor X going to ask on the final? That's the big question.

Sound familiar? This is art in school. Out of school, these students would probably never read *Moby Dick.* In school, they're not only going to read it, they stand an excellent chance of learning to dislike it. Or, at the very least, to respect it and avoid it ever after. And, I should add, by virtue of what is described in "Intro to Psych" as "stimulus generalization," to respect and avoid ever after anything that even resembles *Moby Dick,* that is to say, all "great literature."

School giveth and school taketh away. It teaches the arts, but in a counter-aesthetic fashion. That's actually funny, if you're in a laughing mood.

In school the practical context closes in on the work of art. Noninstrumental patterns turn into instrumental ones. Resonance is an immediate casualty. Resonance won't get you through a final exam. It can't be evaluated, or coerced into being. It's individual, it's nonconceptual, and, worst of all, it fades in the presence of self-concern.

Resonance deepens as we open wide to a work, as, within our own universe of experience, we allow it to be what it is. But the "art appreciation" student confronted with a painting knows he will be expected to say something appropriate and acceptably knowledgeable about it. He can't afford to relax and encounter the painting on its own (and his own) terms; he can't afford to play with it. He has to encounter it in a way that will satisfy the teacher. The *lasciate ogni speranza*—"abandon all hope"—inscribed over every test in music, art, or literature is: *"I want you to demonstrate to me . . ."* So the student confronts a painting, blinded by his own purpose (that is, the teacher's purpose). In return, the painting elicits a mild anxiety. It's just . . . *there*. What does it mean? What do you say about it? "Art Appreciation" will be the course where he learns something to say about it. And that is precisely what we expect from such courses: one ends up with something knowledgeable to say about various works of art. What else is there? Not, by the way, that there's any necessary conflict between knowledge and aesthetic experience. On the contrary: why not knowledge *and* aesthetic experience?

The resonance that poetry can evoke is reserved for those who trust themselves. But it's a rare literature class that encourages self-trust. Just the opposite: the student is a cringing neophyte being led by the hand through the World's Great Poetry Museum, interrogated and judged at every turn. Do well, learn to instrumentalize the poems to your teacher's satisfaction, and you're a "good student"; authority smiles on you. Do poorly and you're a cockroach in the palace of art.

Art is there to set us free. But what happens when a teacher intervenes, as coercive authority, between the perceiver and the work? (Not that teachers necessarily choose to be coercive; the institution assigns us that role.)

If students are forced into music, literature, and art-appreciation classes which expose them to great art and turn them off to it at the same time, exactly what is gained? In universities, we're used to thinking of required courses in the arts as a way to *protect* these subjects. But we should make some distinctions. These requirements may protect the departments involved. They may even help to protect the arts as cultural institutions. But it's by no means clear that they protect the arts as arts.

One thing we need to recognize is that the effect of such courses will depend on each student's own aesthetic history. The typical class in the arts is a contradiction: it offers both learning and alienation. Students who come in with a strong, aesthetically satisfying relationship to one or more of the arts are, of all, the least likely to be turned off and the most likely to recover, should any damage be done. They will choose either to play or not to play the classroom game, but in either case, their own aesthetic experience will be around to remind them of how things really are. Often such students have established their relationship to an art fairly early, before the academic stakes get raised, at an age when the various arts are still more or less "recreational" and the teacher's demands minimal. Ilya, who has now entered junior high school (and whom a few readers may remember from *The University of Tomorrowland* when he was much younger), is a good example. Starting in late infancy he was read to a lot. He had his own picture books, and we were always bringing home huge stacks of books from the library. When he learned to read, it was on Hergé's series of *Tintin* comics. By ten or eleven he had read hundreds of books—all of Madeleine L'Engle, all of Hugh Lofting, all of Tove Jansson, all of Arthur Ransome—at a time when reading such novels was still a pure pleasure and freely chosen. School by and large had little to do with literature, which was something to pursue at home (or in school when other work was finished). Now as he gets to classes where literature is turned into homework, he'll be much less vulnerable than someone who hasn't had that kind of reading experience.

Students who are able to resist the academic turn-off may well have an aesthetic background that owes little to schooling: parents who read literature or are eager concertgoers, friends who do theatre or are dancers. More than a few middle to upper-class children are loaded with art experience entirely outside of the school system: music lessons, young people's concerts, junior theatre, sketching classes at the art museum, folk-dance camps, origami workshops—and on and on and on. So, to a considerable extent, the ability of students to withstand the negative aspects of academic education in the arts is a matter of social class.

In any case, most of the students in an average state university "Intro to Lit" class do *not*—as I well know—have a strong personal relationship with the art. And what most of us who teach literature do for these people is to frost any such relationship in the bud before it has a chance to flower. In fact, the job may well have been done in high school before they come to us.

The stronger a person's aesthetic involvement is, the more weight it can bear. If someone's relationship with an art is sufficiently developed, even an occasional intolerant, authoritarian teacher may present no serious problem as long as he or she has something useful to offer. But the involvement of most students with literature or classical music or fine arts is undeveloped, very slender at best; and it can bear little weight. What purpose is served then by making their "introduction" an anxiety-filled, intimidating, judgmental experience? (Then am I advocating "lightweight," unstructured, lowest-common-denominator courses? No. More of that later.) What students commonly end up with is a force-fed and fast-fading collection of terms, historical information, critical principles, and so on; "exposure" to a certain number of works; and a requisite attitude: a mystified, rote respect for the art and its great practitioners through the ages (along with a quite genuine respect for their teacher, who is able to "understand" it). The student herself may even feel, afterward, that she "got a lot out of it"—or then again she may not. But in aesthetic terms, the real test of the course is in the kind of relationship the student has to the art *after* the course is over. Does she seek it out?

Does she delight in it? Has the art opened up for her? Do the works she studied in the course continue to draw her? Is she able to perceive new works that she encounters more fully and in greater depth? Is her response to the art authentic and self-confident?

Art–appreciation courses in high school and college would appear to be emphatically democratic; they take arts that were once the preserve of the upper classes and make them available to all. Actually, I think they serve as a kind of gate. Very many children of the educated, affluent elite pass through; they are, as I've said, likely to have developed early in life a substantial relationship with one or more of the "high arts." And they have examples to follow all around them among those who traditionally have had the privilege of patronizing these arts. Much of this may also apply to children of families on their way up, whose parents recognize the importance of the arts in certifying social attainment. Children of lower social position *may* pass through the gate, to the extent that they—because of temperament, opportunity, family tradition —have their own close involvement with art. The rest—the majority by far—though they may well learn to *respect* the amusements of their "betters," are in fact turned off by courses where intimidation, dullness, and alienation constitute too heavy a load for their fragile involvement to bear, and are thrown back on *Laverne and Shirley* and furniture-store kitsch, on the "popular" arts that are rightfully theirs.

Someone could counter that the people who don't get through this gate are obviously the ones who aren't, under any circumstances, *capable* of appreciating serious art. In fact, I suppose this is what a great many teachers, and others, actually think. But this would require us to believe that the correlation between social class and aesthetic preference has —what?—some genetic basis? The lower-middle class is bio-logically predestined to prefer sad clowns to Jackson Pollock and Marc Chagall? What nonsense that is. Besides, many years of teaching have demonstrated to my own complete satis-faction that this simply isn't so. Students who were turned back at the gate in high school or college do have the potential to read literature with satisfaction (though one doesn't begin with Pound's *Cantos* or *Ulysses*).

What does this mean, then? That everyone will end up loving Bach if given half a chance? I'm not so sure that everyone *needs* to love Bach. It's not a question of "raising" the world up to European high culture. What I continue to question is the aesthetic class system. I question the assumption that the masses really do deserve greeting-card verse instead of poetry, that in architecture they will instinctively prefer McDonald's to Gaudi. That's crazy. I honestly do believe that if jazz, mountain folk music, and American Indian decorative art had not so obviously come *from* the people, the elite would be able to convince itself that these arts are too good for ordinary types.

What service do we render the arts by making them appear difficult, intimidating, out of reach? If you wanted to turn people on to poetry, would you start out by handing them a three-page list of technical terms and announcing that there would be a test next week to determine whether they were able to apply the terms to the poems? Would there be a test at all? "Dear Class: I want to invite you to appreciate poetry. And if you don't do it right, I'm going to flunk you."

I dread seeing film establish itself in the schools. How wonderful that for half a century the academic world virtually ignored movies. A golden age. When you went to the movies, there was no question about motives; they were absolutely pure. None of this going because it was good for you or because you wanted to be the kind of person who appreciated movies. Who would waste a Saturday evening on that? Good movies and bad movies got made, but an audience emerged that was, on its own terms, reasonably sophisticated. People who wanted to get intellectual or erudite about movies did; people who didn't, didn't. But both for the kids at the Saturday matinee and for the film buff who could tell you who the assistant cameraman was on *Lady from Shanghai*, it was pure satisfaction all the way. Still is, perhaps, but there are ominous signs.

A couple of years ago, a student handed me some information he'd jotted down that happened to be on the back of a dittoed test for his film course, a course offered for general students. I glanced at the test: *Choose four of the following six*

. . . use evidence to support your thesis [about what the film "says," please note] *. . . demonstrate that you are aware . . .* A typical test in other words. Grim.

The *movies*! God, I hate to see it happen. Once, a film I wanted to see was playing in a film class. So I thought I'd catch it. But the atmosphere was awful. Never mind that there were no Good & Plenty's in the lobby, nor even a lobby. I could feel the whole grade-and-coerce miasma around me in the room; it was a week before mid-terms. I had to get up and go. A great teacher could probably overcome this kind of environment. But why give yourself such a handicap? Occasionally, in a piece of intellectually fashionable writing, I see a film referred to as "text," and I get faint.

We *could* teach film appreciation in the university. It would be fine. But we'd have to change the university to make it work.

In describing the effect of teaching on students who have little involvement with the arts, I may have implied that the rest of us are entirely unscathed by the process. But that's not true. Should we assume that someone who has chosen to major in literature or art history is immune to educational damage? I don't think so. First of all, the decision to major in such a subject is not necessarily a sign of aesthetic involvement. And even students who do have genuine interest in a particular art may find that a more dutiful and less satisfying response to the art is the price they have to pay for increased knowledge and sophistication. But it is not knowledge and sophistication in themselves that exact such a price. The problem lies in the way the art is taught.

From the age of twelve or thirteen, I read poetry with great pleasure, as much outside of school as in. For a while it was Poe and Kipling, Vachel Lindsay and Alfred Noyes. Do you remember Alfred Noyes?

> There's a barrel-organ carolling across a golden street
> In the City as the sun sinks low

Then Frost and Burns and Wordsworth. When I got to UCLA, my favorite poets were Wordsworth and Dylan Thomas (I was scandalized, when Thomas died, that his death didn't make headlines in the newspapers). I had had one literature teacher all through high school. She was enthusiastic, encouraged us to read aloud; if she tested at all, it was on names and dates— that sort of thing. She did me no harm. Then, in the course of four years at the university, my knowledge of English poetry expanded enormously. At the time, I believed in the grading system; tests were an exciting but also extremely tense business, and there was a lot of insecurity and anxiety getting mixed with the satisfaction I got from poetry. In fact, my orientation to literature was changing. Literature, though I wouldn't have put it this way at the time, was becoming more of a testing and proving ground for intellectuals. It was also becoming something that I would not turn to purely for my own satisfaction. We did *Victory* in my freshman general-education literature class. The experience was so unpleasant that to this day I can't read Conrad.

Let me tell you about that class. I have the clearest memory of this one particular day. We've been assigned a poem by Emily Dickinson. The professor walks in and, getting right to business, asks us what we think the poem "means." His manner isn't particularly encouraging; no one, you understand, *wants* to answer. But we get graded for "participation," so, slowly, the feeble attempts are made. After each student's effort, he just sort of stares at the person for a moment and then says: "Anyone else?" When the answers finally peter out, there's one of those awkward low-tide moments. Confession made, we wait to hear our penance. Finally he says, "All right, now let's look at the poem and find out what's really going on," turns toward the blackboard, and begins to diagram what I would later learn to recognize as one of those ultrasophisticated postgraduate explications. You know the kind. They make you realize that for the last hundred years every reading of the poem has been trash. It's the English department's answer to scientific discovery. Academic high-fashion. I learned to do it myself. You read the poem. You read *everything* that has been written about the poem—*all* the critics. Then you ask yourself: "OK, now how can I make those bastards bite the dust?" It's not necessarily a harmful activity in itself—keeps the wheel turning, opens up new aspects of a work, gets people promoted. But what happened, of course, was that this umpteenth explication of the Dickinson poem became an instrument of oppression used on us poor fresh-persons. The general feeling was a sort of dull awe at how clever Emily Dickinson was and a feeling of relief that there were people around like our professor who could understand her. But the whole process clearly left us out.

Within the traditional academic framework I had a few extraordinarily good teachers, but none who challenged the framework itself. By the time I graduated and went to work, I had stopped reading on my own. Some psychology perhaps, but no fiction, no poetry, no plays. I'd made no decision to stop; in fact, I would have found it difficult to admit that I had stopped. But there it was. One can go to graduate school in this frame of mind; in fact, that's part of the problem. In my case, I took a healing five-year break. But the full return trip to literature as an art was delayed still longer. There were three or four fine teachers in graduate school to whom I owe a great deal, but it was especially when I started teaching, and began trying to provide my students with a freer context in which to read literature, that I myself began substantially to regain the aesthetic freedom I had had at sixteen.

It's interesting that, right in the middle of that time as an undergraduate, when I was losing the aesthetic immediacy of literature, I found myself going back again and again to the old Los Angeles County Art Museum, which was still in Exposition Park, near the Coliseum. Up to that time I had paid little attention to museums and galleries. But now I'd keep getting this urge to head over there and look one more time at the ancient pottery, jewelry, and glassware, the Roman busts and sarcophagi, the medieval wood sculpture—and especially at the paintings: martyred, haloed saints; Holy Families; portraits of aristocrats, knowing, dressed to the teeth; dark Dutch interiors with their loaves and jugs; landscapes you could get lost in with feathery trees, somber skies, and a river where one or two human figures would have led their cattle to drink. And I kept going back, without particularly telling anyone because it seemed so strange and self-indulgent to be driving clear across L.A. to the museum when I'd been there only the day before. Like getting on some kick where you just *have* to eat cantaloupe every day, or play ping-pong. But more so. I adored the museum.

Trying to understand what I kept coming back for, the best answer I could find was that the experience was "King's X"— what you used to call out during tag at recess to suspend the rules. If you'd tripped and banged your knee or had dropped something out of your pocket that had to be retrieved, you crossed your fingers and shouted "King's X!" While it was in effect, they couldn't get you. That was, I guess, the beginning of an aesthetic theory. But, with respect to education, what's significant is that the King's X of fine arts appears to have come in (along with that of music, I should add) to replace the no-longer-reliable King's X of literature. It was my good fortune —and still is—never to have studied the fine arts in school.

If the history of my alienation from literature were no more than a personal anecdote, I wouldn't have told it here. But I've talked to colleagues who have shared this kind of experience. And I continue to see around me teaching methods and attitudes which suggest that literature has been displaced from its aesthetic center. In fact, things may be getting worse. Roger Shattuck speaks of "a literal usurpation . . . which would depose literature and grant sovereign authority to one or more of several competing disciplines." He lists some of the "pretend-ers": structuralism, communication and information theory, speech-act theory, reader-response theory, and Marxist and Freudian criticism. We're not talking now merely about intro-ductory courses in art appreciation. We're talking about an academic curriculum that extends as far as the Ph.D. and that is supposed to prepare the very people who will be teaching these arts to others.

There's no question of legislating how the arts should be taught. As a teacher, your approach to the subject will depend on what you're after. If you're a physicist, it may be solely in relation to acoustics that music enters your course. The ques-tion I want to raise here is: what can be done by teachers who are concerned (or ought to be) with a particular art *as* an art?

In what way can teaching serve aesthetic experience? Have I implied that it cannot? I hope not. Good teaching—and there are many teachers around who are *very* good, insofar as their institutional role will allow them to be—can not only enhance our appreciation of individual works but can make us more perceptive, more sensitive, more open to an art in general. It may be that I've encouraged some readers of this book in their belief that one person's experience of a work is just as satisfactory as another's, that in art "everything is relative," and that, therefore, each of us should mind his own aesthetic business. This kind of attitude is often, as I suggest in the Introduction, not so much free as it is defensive: the scar tissue left by academic intimidation. I've found, talking with students, that when I maintain that the aesthetic center is in the individual perceiver, when I question the relevance of coercive authority, when I deny that art works can be reduced to a conceptual meaning, and so on, there will often be those who assume that I'm saying just what they want to hear: "It's all relative." "Don't pick things apart." "Just leave everyone to enjoy it in their own way." But these things are not at all what I'm saying. They represent an attitude (antithetical to the teacher's claim to authority) which does its own kind of injustice to the aesthetic experience.

In fact, we learn from each other all the time. After a movie, we may trade observations: —Didn't you love X? —Oh, you know, I never noticed that! Merely to describe your own response is to suggest a point of view from which the work can be perceived.

Whatever helps someone perceive a work more clearly or fully can enhance the aesthetic experience. Whatever helps a person establish a connection between the work and resonant areas of response can likewise enhance aesthetic experience. Obviously, to judge each person's experience of a work according to some absolute standard would be oppressive and deadening. But it would be equally oppressive to insist that we have nothing to learn from each other. Picking a work apart as an end in itself may well be counter-aesthetic. But picking a work apart—to use that loaded term for "analysis"—in the interest of a more satisfying perception and response is not only legitimate but something we all do to some extent entirely outside of the academic context. Your ability to distinguish the separate instrumental voices in a piece of chamber music or jazz is something you may take for granted. But this is analysis of a very basic sort, and without it, your ability to perceive what's going on in the music is radically diminished.

We mustn't assume that analysis is bound to have a deadening effect on resonance. As a matter of fact, analysis can help to liberate it. This week I've been teaching the first volume of *The Tale of Genji* in an introductory class; today we were talking about the importance of seasons in Japanese literature, and about the relationship between Genji's love affairs and the various seasons of the year. Recognizing this structural pattern is not a way of "decoding" the work but rather of unfolding it. In this particular case, analysis helps to uncover potentially resonant relationships, analogous to musical relationships— the enormously evocative transition, for example, from Genji's "winter" princess with the red nose to his "springtime" beloved, little Murasaki—which a more purely reactive and unanalytical concern with plot is likely to obscure.

Nor is there any reason to deny ourselves the satisfaction to be had from the varied insights and connections—psychological, political, historical, and so on—that analysis of art works can produce. We can study "ideas" in art. We may even find ourselves pursuing these ideas outside of the art work and purely for their own intrinsic interest. We're not obliged to be singlemindedly "aesthetic," even when dealing with art for its own sake.

There are no aesthetic grounds for rejecting analysis, provided that it is not done in a coercive framework, that it is not reductive, and that it does no great violence to the resonant potential of the work—which, admittedly, is a big "provided." What one hopes for in the teaching of the arts is analysis done with some sense of play, some grace, some respect for the quality of aesthetic experience, and not in a grim, eye-bugging, formula-mongering fashion. (Since the nineteenth century, some of us who teach and write about literature have sought to "legitimize" literary study by remedying its embarrassing deficiencies as a science. One looks at the scientists, so obviously useful, so obviously important with their cold clean Method, their spectacular results, their abundance of diagrams and formulas. One looks at the scientists and starts scheming:

"Now if there were just some way to do that with the arts . . ."
I've heard this described as "blackboard envy." But we have
our own function, which the preeminence of science renders
not less important but more important than ever.)

I'm not insisting that more analysis *necessarily* enhances
aesthetic experience. This is a crucial point. Let's say that I am
about to listen to Brahms' First Symphony. Should you insist
on analyzing its thematic structure for me in advance? Perhaps
it will be more important for me to establish a relationship
with the work first on my own aesthetic terms. Then should
you hand me the analysis afterwards, explaining that this is
what I may have missed? Will my enjoyment of the first
movement be enhanced if I carefully follow the various themes
through the exposition, development, and recapitulation,
noting their changes of key and so on? Perhaps it won't,
perhaps it will. This will depend on me and on how your
analysis is presented. Art is delicate. How easily the symphony
can be transformed into a task to be performed. To the extent
that I feel coerced or threatened, or feel I am being asked to
substitute the map for the territory, I may recoil from this
attempt to "pick things apart." We're being led toward a
conclusion: the question concerning analysis is not *whether*,
so much as *how* and *under what circumstances*.

It is essential in teaching (the appreciation of) an art that
each student be able to respond to the art freely. What does
this mean? On the one hand of course: the most conscientious,
high-quality teaching one's own limitations will allow. But on
the other hand: respect for the aesthetic freedom of everyone
in the class. To make no contribution or to give them watered-
down teaching would be an insult. But it would be a greater
insult still to try to coerce them into some desired response to
the art they're studying, or to maneuver them into seeing art
works primarily as the means to an end: some future exam.

But that's preposterous. Taken seriously, it might mean,
among other things, no tests. What are Doctors for if not to
give examinations? No *tests*? In a *university*?

Precisely. I myself haven't given any for about twelve years.
Journals, projects of various kinds, papers—these can be very
productive and aren't so likely to be damaging, because they

allow individual students to go their own way. Obviously, there remains an element of coercion in any course that has a required body of reading, listening, or viewing, along with required projects of some sort. But this kind of pressure (without which, in the coercive context of a university, any single course may well collapse as a submarine would that had no internal pressure to counter that of the ocean around it) has nothing even approaching the counter-aesthetic potential of the testing and grading system. To be required to read a book or listen to some music is not an *ideal* context for appreciating the art, but this requirement doesn't interfere with the student's response. Even to be required to keep a reading or listening journal, or to do any comparable open-ended and ungraded project is not likely to take away from a student's aesthetic autonomy (unless the requirement is set out in a narrow and heavy-handed way). But when it is established that students will be judged and rewarded or punished according to how they perceive a work of art, then the chances that this work will function effectively as art are substantially reduced.

I should emphasize that I don't grade journals and other such projects (though I may well comment on them extensively). They're either done or they're not. People choose grades in a course according to the amount of work they want to do, the extent to which they want to involve themselves. The higher grades are likely to require a very substantial commitment. If many students choose to work for a high grade, so much the better. Obviously this kind of system is an outrage to what passes for academic tradition, but that's another story. Nor do I want to write at length here about my own teaching methods, or set them up as some kind of model. Teaching is personal. One's methods have to match one's temperament. And I recognize that a particular "non-coercive" teacher may teach poorly, while another, more or less traditional teacher may teach very well.

My point is simply that it's possible to teach courses in the arts, courses with a high degree of content—including the traditional elements of analysis, history, and theory—without seriously interfering with the aesthetic function of the material studied. (Needless to say, in such a course, a teacher may still have to confront damage which has been done to the students elsewhere.)

The absence of tests and grading forces a teacher into closer contact with the class. If what you are doing is inappropriate, boring, and alienating, the students, not occupied taking feverish notes for the final, will surely let you know it one way or another. On the other hand, in a course of this type, "heavy" content is less likely to be intimidating, and may even stand a better chance of being received with interest. A fairly sophisticated and complex analysis, when it's offered in a spirit of discovery and free play, is much less deadening and intimidating than when it is put forth in the voice of authority as the official reading of a work, with ominous overtones of future inquisition. Even my teacher with the high-fashion Dickinson analysis could have pulled it off in that very class of gaping novices, if he had not pronounced it *ex cathedra* and if he had established the right kind of learning environment.

Consider the difference between, on the one hand, a concern with *not missing* what is in a work, which implies not only a dutiful attitude but also the belief that the work can somehow be emptied of its significant content, and, on the other hand, an interest in *discovering* new aspects of the work, which leaves the work permanently open and the perceiver free.

A good deal of what teachers experience as resistance derives from the grading system. Without it, if I put forward some reading of a work, students can test this reading and accept it or dispute it as they choose. If this leads us to consider the theoretical questions underlying interpretation and judgment, that's fine too. But the atmosphere is more cooperative than disputatious. And my own contribution to the course, because I'm not insisting on respect, is likely to be respected. But when grades are at issue, such discussions can take on an entirely inappropriate tone, somber and judicial. The less intimidated student may demand: "How do we know your interpretation is right? How can you say that mine was wrong?" The teacher gathers his robes around him: "It's not necessary that you agree with me. I ask only that you support your thesis with appropriate evidence." Evidence which the teacher, lofty, even-handed, incorruptible, will weigh before pronouncing sentence: "B minus." Fine, fine. But what does this have to do with art? I find also that, in the absence of grading, my written comments about a student's reading of a work have a better chance of being considered seriously. Because they're offered in a cooperative, rather than an antagonistic or judgmental spirit, they are less likely to be read defensively or, what is worse, heeded automatically in submission to authority.

A course can be demanding, intelligent, and full of content, without recourse to traditional testing and grading, which, where the arts are concerned, interpose a necessarily coercive authority between the perceiver and the work, and weaken the aesthetic experience by introducing into it a basis for self-concern. Moreover, such a course, if it's competently done, seems likely to teach more to more students than a comparable, well-taught traditional course. This claim is, of course, hardly based on any sort of controlled study. But I've taught both ways and, if the less coercive and intimidating way didn't produce obviously better results, I would give it up immediately, because, I have to admit, it's more difficult. Tests, grades, an authoritarian role, canned fifty-minute lectures—these are all wonderfully supportive, and enable you to ignore more than a few teaching problems. In fact, once or twice, talking to a newcomer who was unusually anxious about beginning teaching, I've actually encouraged starting with the classic format of midterm, final, quizzes, and term paper. Because there is nothing easier, it seems to me, than to teach that way.

What about standards, though? Any departure from the traditional coercive and authoritarian structure of education is said to invite a "lowering of standards." But what standard is it that countenances in students and teachers alike the erosion of the aesthetic base of an art? The grading system creates "standards" in its own image; what is testable becomes all-important, while aesthetic experience, untestable and unstandardized (though eminently teachable) becomes irrelevant. One of the most interesting and artful aspects of a literature class, or any art class, can be an exploration of the experiential basis for a resonant response, and the development of connections between the work on one hand and the individual universe of experience on the other. But this kind of approach encourages, in all of us who are there, a cognitive-affective, associative, play-full and open-ended way of discussing a work of art, a way, obviously, which assumes considerable respect for the individual response. It is as appropriate in graduate courses as in introductory ones. It's usually a very productive approach, and an energizing one. It can augment and vivify structural analysis, historical investigation, and so on. There is, however, nothing less suitable to grading than this approach, nothing more incompatible with the notion of testable standards. Therefore, by the weird logic of the academy, it is this approach which seems out of place, while tests and grades are enshrined at the very center of the educational process.

I can hear someone protesting—perhaps with a certain iritation that has been building during the reading of this entire chapter:

"All of this is well and good, but may I remind you that the study of any art is also an *intellectual discipline*—which means that it's going to involve facts, theories, and careful analysis. What a student needs to learn is not how to play with facts and theories or tell you how he feels about them. What he needs to learn is how to think about them critically and with intellectual rigor. If you really want to do your students a favor, you'll be tough on them. You'll keep your standards up and not just let everyone 'do his own thing.'"

Actually, this not-so-hypothetical reader and I are more in agreement than it might seem. But there are problem areas. Which students are we talking about? General students in an introductory course in music or literature or fine arts have much less need of scholarly rigor than they do of aesthetic discovery. Facts, theories, and analysis, of course—but only as a means. What these students need above all is to have the art open up for them, and to establish the basis for a long-term relationship with that art. Advanced students, however, are in a different position. They need teaching that keeps the art alive aesthetically but that also establishes them within an intellectual discipline such as art history, music theory, or comparative literature. Someone might ask: is it possible to do both? Is it possible to engage seriously in the advanced study of an art without betraying its essential, aesthetic function? I think many of my colleagues have proved that this *is* possible. But it is something one needs to work at, something which in an academic environment is a bit like swimming upstream.

Another problem area: what do we mean by "standards?" Should "standards" mean simply "grades?" I don't think so: in meat inspection, perhaps, but not in intellectual activity. One teaches and maintains intellectual standards by practicing them. And the history and critical theory of an art can be taught very well without the traditional grading system. Advanced students, who may have a professional orientation toward the art, will have enough occasion to be evaluated (when they write research papers, for example, or take a foreign-language exam, or request recommendations). Other students don't really need to be evaluated—at least not in the customary fashion (the Notes and Comments contain a further consideration of evaluation). As far as the discipline itself in a general sense is concerned—the critical and scholarly study of an art as carried out in books, journals, and so on—I find it hard to believe that standards here are kept up by A's, B's, and C's. I would suggest that such standards are maintained by free encounter—competition, if you like—in intellectual activity, within a society that values and supports this activity. In school, it is advanced students who are most concerned with theory, history, and so on. These advanced students, particularly as they approach some sort of professional involvement with the subject, tend to have a more authentic motivation, a motivation next to which the grading system seems trivial and demeaning.

There are other problems in teaching the arts. Merely knowing that one is going to have to deal with a particular work in class can have an effect on teachers comparable to the effect that tests have on students. Generally speaking, we find ourselves in that aesthetic category—which also includes creative artists, performers, and critics—of persons who need to be adept at switching in and out of aesthetic gear. Artists and performers who can't do this don't stand much of a chance. Critics, unfortunately, and especially teachers may simply bypass the aesthetic mode without thinking twice about it. If this happens—and it happens all the time—what shall we expect the critic to discuss and the teacher to teach?

Am I leading to an absurd point? Is the art teacher supposed to stop when each slide is shown, gasp "Isn't that marvelous?" and then continue: "Note the use of atmospheric perspective and diagonal composition?" Ridiculous, of course. But, though there's no formulaic solution to this problem, it is nonetheless a real problem. It's not at all uncommon for an art-history class, even an art-appreciation class, or a music or literature class, to admit the aesthetic status of its subject, even to discuss it using aesthetic terminology, and yet, at the same time, to reduce these works of art to nothing more than dry collections of points dutifully made and dutifully recorded.

Art can be threatening, not only morally and politically by its subversively experiential character, not only existentially, when it knocks over the comfortable stage-settings we like to surround ourselves with, but also intellectually, as I've already suggested in Chapter Ten, by virtue of its stubborn irreducibility. We spend our lives learning to abstract, reduce, categorize —to the point that a work of art may be profoundly frustrating. In school, this reductionist tendency, when it encounters art, is playing in its own stadium, so to speak. I'm reminded again of what Susan Sontag says about interpretation (which she calls "the revenge of the intellect upon art"): "Real art has a capacity to make us nervous. By reducing the work of art to its content and then interpreting *that*, one tames the work of art. Interpretation makes art manageable, comformable." But even the decision to pay more attention to "form" in art, which is what Sontag suggests toward the end of her essay, can leave us, in an educational context at least, substituting a comfortable intellectual wrap-up for the work itself.

Part of the solution to this problem has to do with the structure of the course. But part also has to do with the teacher's own relationship to the works of art that are being studied. How easy it is for us to replace the work of art itself with a more or less fixed commentary, which may be joined, in the case of literature or music, to a fixed collection of illustrative excerpts. *Paradise Lost* becomes a series of topic-phrases, such as "Cosmology," "Puritanism and Free Will," "Latinate Diction," "Baroque Composition," along with a bundle of underlined passages to match. Understand, I'm not rejecting this as a teaching method. But how is the problem to be solved? How are we to avoid the "tour guide syndrome?"

What I propose is what some teachers do already. Teachers in the arts need to re-open themselves to the works they teach, setting aside temporarily, as much as possible, any pre-existing pedagogical apparatus, and relaxing, as much as possible, any tensely instrumental sense of purpose. In other words they need to re-invite—or perhaps invite for the first time—an aesthetic relationship with the work. There's no question of seeing the work innocently, as if that were possible, but, rather, openly, accepting the possibility of a fresh response, which, though it may not do justice to the "official" features of a work, may bring its own revelations, and, most important, may re-establish this work on its foundation of aesthetic experience. I find that most of what I teach can be re-experienced many times over without losing its freshness and abundant possibility—and if not, then I'm likely to wonder if it isn't time to change courses, or at least reading lists (even the best art can, in time, be eroded by habituation).

Teachers and students need the freedom to encounter—and re-encounter—a work on its own ground. I know that with a work I've never taught before there's going to be an urge to get the show on the road: "Now what exactly am I going to *do* with this thing?" Nevertheless, if I hope eventually to be able to say something real and useful about a work, I need a preparatory period during which I'm not obliged to say anything about it at all, during which the work is not forced to be anything other than what it is, in me. A time of attentive silence.

It should go without saying that a teacher needs to be open not only to the work but to the class. Here there's a dialectical process involved. On the one hand: the very legitimate obligation to be thoroughly prepared, and the accumulation of a body of technique with which one approaches a class. On the other hand: acceptance of the presentness, individuality, and spontaneous potential of the class itself, a convergence in time and space. The dialectic remains constant. Each class meeting establishes its own synthesis.

What about that teaching which has as its goal not merely the appreciation but the creation of art? Can we simply transfer over whatever we've learned so far about teaching? Not entirely, because there are some separate problems involved.

Freedom is not always as important for the would-be artist as it is for the perceiver. For perceivers the work itself is at hand to focus their energies and provide a structure within which to respond. Beyond this, the most that a teacher needs to do, directly or through discussion, is suggest patterns of relationship in the work, establish a referential context (which may be historical, for example, or philosophical), help the perceiver to open up appropriate experiential areas, and so on, but always carefully respecting the individual's aesthetic autonomy. Artists, however, have no such pre-existing image that will focus and structure their activity; they have to discover their own work of art. For this reason, artists can suffer from an overabundance of freedom. Stravinsky speaks of his "terror" starting out to work and confronting "the infinitude of possibilities that present themselves." It is the limits he sets that deliver him: "My freedom thus consists in my moving about within the narrow frame that I have assigned myself for each one of my undertakings. I shall go even further: my freedom will be so much the greater and more meaningful the more narrowly I limit my field of action and the more I surround myself with obstacles."

Mature artists have usually found their own ways of passing from the world of infinite possibility to that other world of absolute necessity which is the work itself. Less mature artists tend to flounder. And here teachers must strike their own balance. On the one hand, it may be productive to limit a student's freedom, that is, to stipulate ways of making the transition from possibility to necessity. On the other hand, this kind of limitation, if overdone, can deaden the student and encourage a non-self-reliant and therefore imitative kind of art. The balance depends so much on specifics of art form, situation, temperament, and so on that little can be said about it in a general way.

The balance between freedom and direction is a central problem in the teaching of artists and performers; this is one reason why teaching approaches are, and should be, so various. We can note opposing pedagogical types. One teacher imposes a rigid program of highly structured exercises and assignments, expects a particular result, and tends to be dogmatic and intolerant in aesthetic matters. Another stresses discovery and "creativity," gives open-ended assignments and tends to be accepting and inclusive. Both may be very good artists themselves. These are types, of course: real teachers are more complex. But what I'm getting at is that some students may feel the need for one approach and some for the other. A developing artist may well feel that it will be productive at a certain point to go from one kind of teacher to another.

Those who teach artists are artists themselves, or ought to be. And sometimes that entails a certain narrowmindedness. The psychological arrangements that enable a person to do sustained work as an artist are not always compatible with a broad, accepting attitude where aesthetic matters are concerned. Often, to study with an artist is to use that person's intense and limited focus as a temporary basis for one's own development.

The teaching of artists or performers never fits comfortably into an orthodox academic institution. Nothing is more alien to the assumption that education can be meted out in standardized packages of uniform content, quantitatively measurable in relation to specific testable goals. Here again, the grading system provides the point of focus for a more general problem. We might be willing to accept a somewhat more coercive atmosphere in at least some classes, a bit more of the knuckle-rapping approach from artists who are good enough and basically sympathetic and concerned enough to pull it off. But A's, B's, C's? How insulting they are, not merely to the student but to the art itself. It's a rare creative attempt that doesn't raise complex questions of evaluation. How gratuitous, how essentially empty a grade is, stamped on a painting, or a dance or poem. I've seen a number of student poems which were far *beneath* grading. And I've seen some so far above it as to be demeaned by that little schoolteacher's "A." Most student poems need to be addressed as such, not as though they were sides of beef. And, of course, viewed as *motivation* for artists and performers, grades make no sense at all. There are real reasons to make art and real satisfactions to be had in doing it well. Do we want to hide them?

EPILOGUE
On Value Judgment

"That was a great movie!"

"It was a piece of trash."

"How can you say that? I thought it was really exciting from start to finish."

"So is a root canal. Look, it takes more than fake blood to make a good movie."

"There you go again. You're missing the whole point. Can't you see that the violence in this movie is *saying* something?"

"That's for sure. It's saying, 'I want to be one rich movie director.'"

"You're ridiculous! I hope you realize you would have hated *Hamlet* when it first came out."

"*Hamlet* didn't die in a trash compactor."

"They didn't *have* trash compactors. Why did you come tonight anyway? You could have been home watching *Mary Poppins*."

Judging art may pose no problem to the individual, but as soon as we begin to discuss and compare our judgments, or even merely to express them, it's another story. In fact, the question of aesthetic value-judgment has been a perpetually difficult one. Here are a few reasons why:

1. These judgments, even when they take objective form, depend at least in part on subjective experience. If I say that a film comedy is inventive, or that a guitarist plays with great clarity, or that a short story makes brilliant use of metaphor, these may be statements about the work of art (or performance), but it is my own experience that validates them and makes them relevant. Someone else might reply that she

doesn't find the film inventive at all, that what I call "clarity" she calls "coldness," and that the story's metaphors may well be brilliant but are also self-conscious and unintegrated.

2. There is no single criterion according to which all art is to be judged. Or rather we could say, yes, there is a single criterion: "Do I like it?" But as soon as we want to get beyond "I like it," and consider what there is about a work of art that *causes* us to like it, we can end up with a number of criteria which—and here's the real problem—exist in no fixed order of importance that very many of us would agree on. I remember once when a local music critic argued in one of his reviews that there were "objective" criteria for judging music and that he could list them. His list included, I believe, "inventiveness," "imagination," "expressive range," "subtlety," and so on. Now, setting aside the question of their objectivity, and even assuming that other experienced listeners would come up with precisely the same criteria, there's still the question of their order of importance, which is something I don't think we could get agreement on, but which becomes crucial when we make comparative judgments. That is: do we prefer an imaginative concerto with no subtlety to a subtle concerto with no imagination?

3. At least part of the difference in the way two works of art will affect us is *purely* subjective and can't be taken very far at all beyond "I like it" or "I don't like it." It's easy to say you prefer purples to greens, a trumpet to a sax, detective novels to science fiction. You may even be able to explain yourself a little, but we're still pretty well stuck at the level where lemon custard ice cream contends with fudge almond. It's at this level that there is no disputing tastes.

There are approaches that seek to avoid some of these problems; perhaps the most attractive one makes its judgments more or less objectively on a historical basis. We attach greatest value to art which has shown that it can, in Samuel Johnson's words, "please many and please long." And I would certainly not be alone in saying that, more than any friend, more than any critic or artist, it is history whose aesthetic taste I most respect and whose recommendations I'm most likely to follow.

The succession of generations is a screening process. It doesn't screen out what is topical, only what is *merely* topical. Art may represent its age; but in works that please far beyond their time, this representation can be expected to have depth: that is, it reaches past that conventional surface—all too easily accessible, and changing from year to year—which falsifies our actual perceptions, thoughts, feelings, and motives, and which is so commonly mistaken for life itself. The average writer of a daily or weekly TV drama, pressed for time and intent upon immediate acceptance, turns instinctively toward this surface the way engineers turn toward their tables and charts. The writer tells his audience what it wants to hear—as do the director and the actors. This continually changing surface is an "image" of life in the same sense that one speaks of "corporate image." Art that fails to get past it in any way is unlikely to be cherished as art by future generations, for whom it will be outmoded, though it may survive as a historical document.

Even a historical approach to evaluation, however, presents serious problems. For one thing, history may not help us judge contemporary art, and in fact may even hinder us. If we try to extract standards from the art of the past and use them to judge new art, we risk blinding ourselves to its unique contributions, and, like many a critic over the centuries, may miss the boat entirely. *After* the fact—when the new art has gained acceptance and when its novelty is less overwhelming —we may have no difficulty in recognizing the traditional virtues in it. But historically based criteria, at that point, do no more than certify a judgment which has already been made.

Another problem is that even the judgment of history is subject to revision. A work may please many and please long— for a century or even longer—and then begin to lose its audience. Another may have to wait to gain an audience. J. S. Bach's music languished in relative neglect for almost a century, John Donne's poetry for almost two centuries.

Furthermore, the historical approach has a certain bias built in. It tends to be dominated by the needs and styles of custodial institutions such as museums and universities, and may somewhat overemphasize the aesthetic artifact at the expense of the aesthetic experience. A touch (sometimes more than a touch) of the mausoleum. Also, historical judgment tends to screen out (and therefore de-emphasize) the kind of art that can't adequately be preserved. For example: dance of the past (before the advent of moving pictures) needs to be reconstructed before we can experience it, and as we go back in time, that becomes increasingly difficult. It's not really possible for us now to experience the art of Noverre (even Isadora Duncan's is beyond our reach). This might mean that dance, having left behind it in past centuries no impressive and enduring wake of masterpieces such as we associate with painting, literature, music, and architecture, risks being taken somewhat less seriously as an art. On the other hand—who knows?—perhaps dance, like film, has been liberated by this relative freedom.

Historical criteria may be useful in a prescriptive way to publishers, curators, teachers, and so on, but for the individual they can be no more than gently suggestive. That is, to the individual they say, "X, Y, and Z have been appreciated over a span of time and may well be worth your attention." But they should never be taken to mean, "You *must* appreciate X, Y, and Z, or be found wanting." What we call "the classics" represents an averaging out and a synthesis of individual tastes. Why should anyone's own aesthetic predilections have to match some official list of "greats?" In this connection, I remember the erudite and enthusiastic host of a classical-music program that I used to listen to many years ago—a man for whom the nineteenth and twentieth centuries simply didn't exist. He played what he liked: Josquin, Palestrina, Dowland. "Modern" to him meant Telemann. Why not? Does one *have* to like Berlioz? We teachers may try to help people widen their range of appreciation, but this should be done in the students' own aesthetic interest and without any implication that they have to "measure up" to the Big List.

To be aware of the problems surrounding evaluation doesn't mean that we're stuck with a mere relativism that would deny the possibility of any common ground in aesthetic judgment. I've tried to show in this book that art, as experience, *has* an identity, that there is a particular area, which can be roughly traced out by aesthetic theory, within which the satisfactions of art are to be found. The better we understand how art affects us, the better able we will be to see why one work of art may be more or less effective than another (in this book Chapters Five through Nine, I would say, are particularly relevant to the question of value judgment).

When we talk about value in art, we're not talking about anything so mysterious. The value of art is what it can do for us. And here there is the possibility of finding common ground. This common ground means that we can talk to each other about aesthetic value meaningfully and productively. But it doesn't mean that we can hope to "settle" questions of value on the basis of standards that are universally valid. One reason why we can't is that within the area of what we can legitimately expect art to do for us, there can be, as I've said, an equally legitimate difference of emphasis from one individual or one culture to another.

Let's look briefly at some of the forms this difference can take. To simplify, let's discount all of the individual differences that could be said to involve mere incapacity of one kind or another: prejudices, blind spots, ignorance of a work's referential context, or the kind of unfamiliarity with a particular type of art that can turn complex aesthetic structure into an undifferentiated blur.

Again, to simplify, we can pass quickly over the question of how habituation affects aesthetic judgment. Some works of art—often the ones that are most respected—resist habituation because they continue to open up new patterns, new resonance, new empathic possibilities. But even this resistance may have its limits. There have been music reviewers who, after years at the mercy of the local maestro and his audience, have seriously overdosed on Beethoven's Fifth and Tchaikovsky's Sixth. Less dramatically, we can see in anyone a certain natural movement of taste, pulled by new aesthetic possibilities and pushed to some degree by habituation. This natural movement is accelerated, of course, by fashion and snobbery. Thus the familiar scene of sophisticates pulling up stakes just as the latecomers troop in, looking around in wonder and delight. But we'll set this question aside, along with that of unfamiliarity (the very opposite of habituation), prejudice, and so on. Let's look at some of the ways in which individuals may, quite legitimately, differ in their aesthetic emphasis.

For one thing: it seems clear that we don't all seek (or tolerate) the same levels of sensory stimulation. Such differences may have little or no effect on literature, but they may well contribute to someone's preference in a choice between Matisse and Braque, between pop ballads and amped-up rock music, or between *Pelléas et Mélisande* and *Boris Godunov.*

One person may get the most satisfaction from art that evokes the greatest breadth of experience, while another may particularly relish the kind of art that offers great evocative intensity held in a narrow range. A novel might be expected to cover a wider range than a lyric poem, but it isn't the size of a work that necessarily makes the difference. I don't think Truffaut's *The Story of Adèle H.* is a shorter film than Altman's *Nashville.* But *Adèle H.* holds an amazingly, almost painfully, steady focus on romantic passion, whereas *Nashville* pulls in everything it can, is in fact stretched way out with incongruities and contrasting perspectives. Setting aside the films themselves, are we able to say that one approach is universally preferable to the other? I don't think so.

One person may be drawn to more exclusively resonant art; another may particularly appreciate reactive power. One person may enjoy aesthetic experience that is more cognitive and meditative; another may want to be swept away. One person may want art that evokes what is ordinarily closest to self-concern; another may respond better to art that treads on safer ground. Many of us have areas where self-concern is not easily suspended, fears (or desires) which, when they are evoked, threaten to break through the aesthetic image. Or we may have particular obsessions which tend to seek themselves in art just as they manifest themselves in dreams.

Even assuming that we are all open to the full range of possible aesthetic satisfactions, still each of us will present an individual pattern of emphasis, an individual profile that will help to determine not only which works we prefer but which arts as well.

To what extent are *values* a legitimate basis for aesthetic judgment? Someone says, "I like stories that teach tolerance and understanding." Another says, "I don't go to movies that condone sexual permissiveness." Still another condemns abstract art as "elitist" and "escapist." On the one hand, I would be the first to discourage someone from establishing his personal values as a sort of ideological filter between the work of art and his inner self. This kind of filter can intercept much of what is perceived before it is able to reach those experiential depths that are the source not only of resonance but of our ability to respond empathically as well. Someone doesn't let himself respond resonantly to a religious painting "because it's all superstitious nonsense"; he doesn't let himself feel what it's like to be Emma Bovary, "because she's just a foolish woman." Only what is approved gets through, and even that is likely to have lost some of its evocative power in passage.

On the other hand, we can hardly say that a person's values ought to have *no* effect on aesthetic preference. Authentic values have their own depth; they're rooted in the way we see the world, in the way we feel, in the very structure of our experience. For this reason, even if we open up to all art as fully as we can, our response is likely to be more complete and more wholehearted to works that correspond to these deep-rooted values. I have friends who are as enthusiastic about Lawrence's *Women in Love* as I am about Huxley's *Island*. I would gladly concede that *Women in Love* is a more skillfully done piece of fiction than *Island*, which frequently sags and creaks under the weight of its ideas. No matter. Though I like Lawrence's book very much, *Island* is written in my native tongue, as it were, and I love it. Each of us experiences a different universe; little wonder if we favor the works of art that come closest to reflecting that universe.

What about values which are *not* well grounded in a person's experience—or which even contradict it? Someone who is holding tightly to such values may be especially likely to react defensively against "unorthodox" works of art, works which in his case will be truly subversive. Conversely, someone whose values have great experiential depth and breadth may be much more willing to open up to art which evokes "the other side"; it will be refreshing but not necessarily threatening.

Finally, our values also come into play when we evaluate aesthetic experience retrospectively. Let's say that I've read two very different novels this week and have given myself without reservation to both—and have enjoyed both very much. Still, I may well give the edge to the novel that called forth what I most value in myself. With one person (or generation) this might be compassion, reasonableness, a sense of balance. With another (or even with the same person in another phase) it might be wildness, passion, the sense of breaking free from all restraints.

What all of this suggests is that since it is not possible to place the various elements of aesthetic satisfaction in some generally accepted ranked order, nor to entirely ignore individual psychological differences, nor to adjudicate individual differences in values, then the question of aesthetic value judgment stays permanently open.

As natural and as useful as it may be to make value judgments on art, I would like to suggest that this tendency is itself something we can look at critically. There is no question that evaluation at its best can help us see art more clearly, that it can expand our aesthetic range and sensitivity, that it can make us aware of worthwhile art, and that it can instruct and inspire artists by identifying strengths as well as weaknesses in works of art. Unfortunately, aesthetic value-judgment does much more than this as well. It's a weapon in the hands of elitists, who call their art "Art" and offer it up as one more proof that they are in fact an elite. Value judgment can be a kind of mystification which, as I've pointed out, may alienate people from their own experience of art. In the hands of coercive teachers, value judgment can be a disaster: the *imposition* of taste by edict under a sort of aesthetic martial law. Quite often, this does no more than drive people back to the "popular" arts, which they can henceforward enjoy with that added pleasure that comes from a guilty conscience.

But I've already written about art in school, as I have about the transformation of art into a commodity, a transformation which tends to exaggerate the importance of evaluation and which surrounds us not only with sales figures, pop-music charts, box-office reports, auction prices, and best-seller lists, but also with "shopping guide"-style critics armed with their rankings and little sets of stars.

Newspaper and magazine reviewers have an important role to play in bringing artist and audience together. Even more, these reviewers can help people find an appropriate mode of perceiving new works that might otherwise merely have disappointed their expectations; reviewers in this way serve as a complement to schools, which are not ordinarily at their best with current art. There are reviewers, however, who show us evaluation in its least favorable light—evaluation as a form of self-aggrandizement practiced by would-be aesthetic Overseers. Their brutal assaults exciting the blood-lust of the crowd are passed off as "maintaining standards"; their quirks and prejudices are transformed into aesthetic principles. Denying the complexity of the art work and its audience in favor of simplistic "verdicts" and vain posturing, these "critics" are no more than the aphids of art (though they may well like to think of themselves as its gardeners).

But even for those of us who have no such official status, evaluation can be an ego ploy. A preference for one singer or one composer over another becomes "who we are" (even if in some cases this preference is as arbitrary as our allegiance to a particular football team). Like those defiantly loyal creatures in beer and cigarette advertising, we define ourselves by our tastes—to the point that defense of those tastes becomes simple self-defense. Evaluation moves toward the center of our experience of art. Everything has to be sorted out; creating our selves with our judgments, we have little room for uncertainty: "*Well* . . . ? What did you think of it?"

With two people this becomes a familiar kind of ego game. Not that I mean to be unduly solemn or disapproving here. Who hasn't enjoyed this particular game? Besides, without the overheated discussions, without the festive post-mortems among folk who shriek, gesticulate, call each other names, and wax clever over endless cups of coffee, art itself might almost seem diminished. But perhaps if we can only recognize what we are doing *as* a game, it may leave us at once less confused and less dogmatic about the arts; and in the long run, discussions may be more enlightening, less belligerent, and maybe even as much fun.

Evaluation is hardly to be condemned in itself. It's implied in the very act of aesthetic choice. Your choice of what movie to see. A gallery's choice of paintings. A producer's choice of plays. A teacher's choice of texts. And then, *after* we've experienced a work of art, evaluation seems like a very natural part of the way we integrate that experience. Fine. Now—having said all this, let me add that I've found enormous satisfaction in *suspending* value judgments about art. Walking out of a movie and *not* deciding how good it was. Turning away from the peremptory "Well, what did you think of it?" that tends to pop up, whether from within or without, as soon as the lights come on or the book is closed. This absence of judgment is a certain kind of silence—possible even while you're having a lively discussion—which can be very nourishing. Deep satisfaction in contemplating art of all sorts without having to remind myself where to place it. Not because there's anything wicked about evaluation. As a matter of fact, judgments that really want to get made will rise to the surface sooner or later, more informed and more authentic for not having been forced. I should add that all of this applies to art that has at least something going for it. The suspension of judgment gives that "something" a little air to breathe and room to move in. Works that have nothing much going for them more or less force judgment on us. Particularly when we're confronted by a work that's not what it tries to be or claims to be, value judgment is actually a part of our immediate response: "Baloney!" Our response pulls away from the image and becomes a judgmen' on it rather than a participation in it. But when our response is fully absorbed in the image, there will be no place in it, at that moment, for judgment.

With a hopelessly unappealing work, then, nothing is lost by judgment. With a work that has at least some interest, we may benefit by leaving ourselves open. Value judgments—positive or negative—tend to be restrictive, to set limits on our relationship with a work and to rigidify that relationship. The more quickly they come, the more limiting they tend to be. I've seen this illustrated over and over again in students' reading journals. I find myself urging: "Look—make a deal with yourself. *Tomorrow* you can judge the hell out of this book. But for now, why not just pay attention? And open up."

It's also possible to see evaluation as a way of disowning or at least of distancing ourselves from what we have just experienced. We may be uncomfortable feeling ourselves touched by a work of art, or even changed by it—so that the act of evaluation becomes a way of putting the work back in its place. The house lights come on. We get up to leave, making that almost embarrassing transition back to the "real" world: "Now that was a well-acted film!"

Again, I don't mean to make a moral point out of this. Let's judge all we want and have a good time doing it. Why not? We'll stay up one night arguing about movies, books, composers, whatever we like. Alexander Pope will be there sipping coffee and talking, taking it all in. Late in the night he'll put his cup down, look around with a wicked smile on his face, and say to the room at large:

> 'Tis with our judgments as our watches, none
> Go just alike, yet each believes his own.

We'll find this very funny at two a.m. Before long everyone in the room will be laughing like crazy. Inside our laughter will be silence. And inside the silence we'll hear the music of that night.

Notes and Comments

Chapter One

p. 10   **a way of perceiving:** A recent *New Yorker* profile recounts the aesthetic history of Robert Irwin, a sometime Abstract Expressionist painter, who, renouncing one after another of what are commonly considered to be essential elements in art, has come finally to recognize art in perception itself.

> Sitting there in the Whitney's coffee shop, he pointed through the glass wall up at the play of shadows on a facade across the street, and said, "That the light strikes a certain wall at a particular time of day in a particular way, and it's beautiful—that, as far as I'm concerned, now fits all my criteria for art." At the terminus of Irwin's itinerary, when all the inessentials had been stripped away, came the assertion that aesthetic perception itself was the pure subject of art. Art existed not in objects but in a way of seeing. (Lawrence Weschler, "Taking Art to Point Zero," II, *The New Yorker*, 15 March 1982, pp. 88-89.)

p. 13   **"Lovely: through the hole":** The haiku is by Issa (my translation).

p. 14   **some sort of aesthetic sense or "taste":** For example the Abbé J. B. Dubos in France, and Francis Hutcheson in England. A concise history of the concept of "taste" in this period is contained in the two chapters on the Enlightenment in Monroe C. Beardsley, *Aesthetics from Classical Greece to the Present: A Short History* (New York: Macmillan, 1966). Beardsley emphasizes British theorists. The views on taste put forth by Dubos, Pierre Estève, the Abbé Charles Batteux, Voltaire, and others are summarized in Francis X. J. Coleman, *The Aesthetic Thought of the French Enlightenment* (Pittsburgh: University of Pittsburgh Press, 1971).

p. 16 "disinterestedness," "psychic distance," "aesthetic attitude": These terms are associated with a great current of thought running through aesthetic theory of the past three centuries. This way of understanding art, which received full-scale elaboration in Kant's *Critique of Judgment* (1790) and Schopenhauer's *The World as Will and Idea* (1818), is widely regarded as having its origins in eighteenth-century British thought. Beardsley (see note to p. 14) traces it back to Shaftesbury. So does Jerome Stolnitz, "On the Origins of 'Aesthetic Disinterestedness,'" *Journal of Aesthetics and Art Criticism*, 20 (Winter 1961), who sees Shaftesbury's concept of aesthetic disinterestedness as "the first and crucial step toward setting off the aesthetic as a distinctive mode of experience." In Stolnitz's view, this notion—that there is a distinctive mode of aesthetic experience—"was a radically new idea in Western thought" (p. 138). Edgar de Bruyne, however, finds "disinterestedness" in medieval thought (Stolnitz does too, in Thomas Aquinas, but dismisses it as "cursory and undeveloped," p. 131). De Bruyne cites a passage from Scotus Erigena, for example, contrasting one man's desire to possess a beautiful vase with a wise man's appreciation of the vase as a reflection of divine beauty, an appreciation which is uncorrupted by desire: *The Aesthetics of the Middle Ages*, trans. Eileen Hennessy (New York: Ungar, 1969), pp. 117-119. But Erigena assumes that *both* men admire the beauty; the difference lies in the direction toward which they turn their appreciation. Stolnitz's point, I think, holds. Erigena, Hugh of Saint Victor, and certainly Thomas Aquinas can be seen as foreshadowing "disinterestedness," but the "radically new idea" toward which Shaftesbury was moving was the emphasis on the mode of experience rather than the properties of the object. What we see in the eighteenth century, with Shaftesbury, Hutcheson, Burke, Addison, Mendelssohn, and others, is a theoretical shift toward the subject as aesthetic center, a shift which in Kant is fully accomplished. This is not the place to attempt a summary of Kant's complex and difficult aesthetic theory, which concerns itself above all with the basis for aesthetic judgment. See Donald W. Crawford, *Kant's Aesthetic Theory* (Madison: University of Wisconsin Press, 1974); for a brief account see Beardsley, pp. 210-225.

If we want to find a developed theory of aesthetic "disinterestedness" before the eighteenth century, we must turn, not to the scholastic philosophers, in fact not to the Western tradition at all, but to India. Such an approach to art can be seen as implicit in Indian thought beginning with the Upanishads. It is worked out explicitly in the tenth and eleventh centuries, particularly in the commentaries of Abhinavagupta, whose "singular contribution lies in freeing the artistic consciousness from all natural and practical relationships and in investing it with meaning and positive value, the meaning and value lying not in any end outside but wholly within the work itself": Sneh Pandit, *An Approach to the Indian Theory of Art and Aesthetics* (New Delhi: Sterling, 1977), p. 11.

In nineteenth-century Europe, alongside Schopenhauer and his monumental treatment of "disinterestedness," there were the far less systematic but more militant figures associated with aestheticism, who were eager to separate art from utility and morality. "Disinterestedness," given a half twist, became *"l'art pour l'art"* or "art for art's sake"—a weapon that was used to defend art against a materialistic and moralizing middle class. Théophile Gautier set the tone in his Preface to *Mademoiselle de Maupin*, published in 1835: "No, imbeciles, no, you goitrous cretins . . ." He takes on all those whom he sees as making inappropriate demands on art—from religious enthusiasts and defenders of public decency to utilitarians, whether republican or Saint-Simonian socialist. His answer to the utilitarian critics:

> Nothing is beautiful except what is of no use; everything useful is ugly, for it is the expression of some need, and man's needs are ignoble and disgusting, like his poor, infirm nature. — The most useful place in a house is the toilet. (*Mademoiselle de Maupin*, ed. Adolphe Boschot [Paris: Garnier, 1955], pp. 20, 23 [my translation].)

In our century, "disinterestedness" has played a very substantial role in aesthetic theory. Edward Bullough has been particularly influential, supplying a new (and, I'm afraid, somewhat inapt) metaphor for aesthetic experience in his "'Psychical Distance' as a Factor in Art and an Aesthetic Principle," *British Journal of Psychology*, 5 (1913); rpt. in

Bullough, *Aesthetics: Lectures and Essays*, ed. Elizabeth Wilkinson (Stanford: Stanford University Press, 1957), pp. 91-130. Some other theorists working within the tradition of "disinterestedness" have been Charles Mauron, whose understanding of art centers on the "aesthetic attitude," which he describes as contemplating the universe "without any idea of making use of it": *Aesthetics and Psychology*, trans. Roger Fry and Katherine John (London: Hogarth Press, 1935), p. 39; José Ortega y Gasset, *The Dehumanization of Art*, tr. Helene Weyl (1925; rpt. Princeton: Princeton University Press, 1968); Eliseo Vivas, who, in *Creation and Discovery* (New York: Noonday, 1955), describes the aesthetic experience as "intransitive," that is, "so controlled by the object that it does not fly away from it to meanings and values not present immanently in the object" (p. 96), and Panayotis A. Michelis, *Aësthetikós* (Detroit: Wayne State University Press, 1977).

Phenomenology would seem to point in the direction of "disinterestedness." Beardsley observes that "the Phenomenologist's presuppositionless openness to what is presented, suspending practical and theoretical concerns, comes close to being a description of all aesthetic experience" (p. 369). What could be seen as a latent tendency in phenomenology is most fully realized, perhaps, in Mikel Dufrenne, *Phenomenology of Aesthetic Experience*, trans. Edward Casey et al. (Evanston: Northwestern University Press, 1973). Dufrenne begins by distinguishing between the "work of art," the existence of which is not dependent on the fact of being experienced by a perceiver, and the "aesthetic object," which exists only in the experience of the perceiver. Having established this distinction, Dufrenne tells us that "the aesthetic object is nothing else but the work of art perceived for its own sake" (p. 16). The perceiver of a painting, forbidding himself active participation, has "derealized" himself "in order to proclaim the painting's reality." That is: "By becoming disinterested in the natural world which I have left, I have lost the ability to be *interested* in the aesthetic world. I am in it but only to contemplate it" (pp. 57-58).

"Disinterestedness" has also attracted some imposing critics. I have to say "critics," not "criticism," because some of the arguments, to my mind, have been remarkably weak. Santayana, for example, attempts to show that aesthetic enjoyment is not disinterested because it is as "selfishly pursued" as other pleasures. That is, "appreciation of a picture is not identical with the desire to buy it, but it is, or ought to be, closely related and preliminary to that desire": *The Sense of Beauty* (New York: Scribner's, 1896), p. 30. One asks oneself how a mind as subtle as Santayana's could fail to make a clearer distinction between our enjoyment of art, on the one hand, and our desire to procure that enjoyment, on the other—between the quite different states of mind involved in (a) enjoying a concert, and (b) standing in line to buy tickets for it. What Santayana demonstrates is merely that the *pursuit* of aesthetic enjoyment is not disinterested— which goes without saying.

On the other hand, some of the criticism represents a very reasonable response to off-center or overstated examples of the "disinterested" approach. George Dickie, for example, argues that "to introduce the terms 'distance,' 'under-distance,' and 'over-distance' does nothing but to send us chasing after phantom acts and states of consciousness": "The Myth of the Aesthetic Attitude," in *Art and Philosophy: Readings in Aesthetics*, ed. W. E. Kennick, 2nd ed. (New York: St. Martin's Press, 1979), p. 442. Suzanne Langer complains about theories that "begin with an analysis of the 'aesthetic attitude'" and "do not get beyond it." She asserts that "to dwell on one's state of mind in the presence of a work does not further one's understanding of the work and its value": *Feeling and Form* (New York: Scribner's, 1953), p. 34. This point may not be as self-evident as Langer seems to think it is; still it does remind us that "disinterested contemplation" should be seen as essentially a starting point for aesthetic theory, a basis for careful consideration of the art work itself. In any case, it's not my intention here to summarize and comment on all of the various criticisms that have been made of "disinterestedness." What I hope is that the present book will be able to reconstitute this theoretical position in a way that may avoid some of the pitfalls it presents and also forestall much of the misunderstanding it has elicited. Most of all, I hope that this book meets Langer's criticism, by establishing the disinterested nature of aesthetic experience and then getting "beyond it."

We can ask why "disinterestedness," important as it may be in twentieth-century aesthetic theory, has not been even more widely accepted. One reason, I think, is that there has been a tendency, particularly in the earlier part of the century, to tie it to an elitist, aestheticist, hyper-refined attitude that seeks to divorce art not merely from any immediate utility but from "common" human feelings. We have Bell's and Fry's exclusion of ordinary emotions from "pure" art in favor of an elusive "aesthetic" emotion, experienced only by certain persons endowed with extraordinary aesthetic sensibility (see note to p. 74). We get Ortega's assertion that "preoccupation with the human content of the work is in principle incompatible with aesthetic enjoyment proper" (pp. 9-10), and that "Tears and laughter are, aesthetically, frauds" (p. 27). It is Ortega who loftily explains the popularity of nineteenth-century art": it is made for the masses inasmuch as it is not art but an extract from life" (pp. 11-12). This kind of attitude is understandable as a reaction against a sentimentalizing, moralizing, and oppressively realist and "content"-oriented bourgeois aesthetic. Nevertheless, it is somewhat off balance and invites refutation.

There is, I think, another, more fundamental reason why some theorists distrust "disinterestedness." To experience art is to have our attention directed unswervingly toward the work itself. The more we find satisfaction in art, the more grateful we are likely to be toward these art works. The more importance art assumes, not only in our own lives, but in human life in general, the more we are likely to value, even venerate these extraordinary human accomplishments, these masterpieces, which *are* art in so demonstrable a sense that it can seem almost perverse to construct an aesthetic which begins with the perceiver, which finds "art" in an "aesthetic attitude" or in "disinterested contemplation," instead of in the work. Some of those who experience art most deeply may be among the ones who have most difficulty accepting such a theory.

On the one hand, we have the evident primacy and incontestable value of the work of art—on the other, the essential role, in aesthetic situations, of the perceiver, whose experience provides the only workable basis on which art can be distinguished from non-art, the only solid foundation for the very term "aesthetic." Between these two ways of looking at art is a gap which should encourage not partisanship but bridge-building.

p. 16   "When something is perceived": Magda Arnold, "Brain Function in Emotion: A Phenomenological Analysis," in *Physiological Correlates of Emotion*, ed. Perry Black (New York: Academic Press, 1970), pp. 262-63.

p. 16   But aesthetic perception is time out: This does not, as I've said, mean that the self is not involved in aesthetic perception (as though that were possible) nor even that the *ego* is entirely inoperative, but rather that it is operative only in a particular way. In the absence of self-concern, in the absence of appraisal based on a personal future, the ego is left with only an *immediate* relationship with the aesthetic object— immediate and free of self-reference. It's a sort of one-way street, a lovely exploitative relationship: I project my feelings onto the image, but it can't talk back; it can neither intrude in my personal future, nor make personal comments about me (because I'm not home; I'm in the image).

The ego, pursuing its strategies for dealing with unacceptable—and perhaps even merely uncomfortable—thoughts and impulses, can make immediate use of art, not as an instrument but as a direct source of gratification. In fact, aesthetic experience itself looks suspiciously like an ego defense mechanism, though it is no such thing (this, perhaps, is why psychoanalytic theory has never quite been able to comprehend art: a partial answer was always too close at hand). The very projection of our response into the aesthetic image parallels and can accommodate that other projection, which attributes our own threatening thoughts and impulses to someone or something in the external world, and which is a basic type of ego defense. All art, when it's working, involves projection in the aesthetic sense; that is, our entire response is perceived in the image. This overall *aesthetic* projection may or may not include a more specific *ego-defense* projection. Only the most intrepid psychoanalytic theorist would look for ego-defense projection in our response to Bach's "Great" G minor Fugue. *King Lear*, however, is another story. The good daughter invites our empathy, while the bad ones invite projection in the psychoanalytic sense. In this way, art allows us to project conflicting feelings and impulses into a single image where none of them need be charged to our personal account, and where they may even be brought into some kind of satisfactory relationship with each other (if only temporarily).

I don't mean to focus exclusively on a single defense mechanism: projection. There are others that may come into play in aesthetic experience—displacement, for example. We can displace both attraction and aggression to appropriate but less threatening objects. In this connection I think of Dmitry, to whom, two years ago when he was five, I read a fairy tale, "The Devil's Three Golden Hairs." Although he didn't say much about it, he quite obviously enjoyed this tale of the good-luck child who is persecuted by and who eventually triumphs over a wicked king. And he left me in no doubt about the psychodynamics involved when much later that day we passed in the hall and he called out, "Hello, wicked king!"

In this book, I haven't had much to say about the relationship between art and the various ego defenses. Writers with far more knowledge of psychoanalysis than I possess have done so at length. Since I've touched on the subject of children and fairy tales, it will be particularly appropriate to cite Bruno Bettelheim, *The Uses of Enchantment* (New York: Vintage, 1977), which, though it may not present itself as aesthetic theory or even as literary criticism, should be tremendously suggestive to anyone pursuing the subject of art and ego-defense.

p. 19 *Othello:* Several years earlier, oddly enough, I had read Bullough (see notes to p. 16), who uses a similar, hypothetical problem with *Othello* to illustrate his notion of "loss of distance."

p. 20 the short story: I'm aware that in some instances there can be an extractive attitude even when we're reading fiction; it derives not from self-concern but from the *reactive* kind of response described in Chapter Six. In some cases, a fictional work may have little to offer but the reactive excitement of "plot." Overbalancing other elements in the work, this excitement, particularly if it is highly suspenseful, may lead us to race through the perfunctorily done and irrelevant-seeming descriptive passages. We are in a sense editing or condensing the image as we read. In other cases, the problem may lie not with the work but with the perceiver. The reactive plot elements of a story may be tightly integrated into the whole, but the reader may take an extractive approach anyway. Schooled by the kind of fiction I've just described and by TV dramas, the reader may have learned to be impatient with whatever doesn't advance the "plot" and feed a reactive response. In both instances, the work will be inadequately realized in aesthetic terms—in the first case, because of its own deficiencies, and in the second, because of inappropriate habits and expectations on the part of the reader.

Roland Barthes takes a more sophisticated view of this way of reading. He recognizes that "our very avidity for knowledge impels us to skim or skip certain passages (anticipated as 'boring') in order to get more quickly to the warmer parts of the anecdote (which are always its articulations: whatever furthers the solution of the riddle, the revelation of fate)." But Barthes sees this skipping itself as a source of pleasure, since "what pleasure wants is the site of a loss, the seam, the cut, the deflation, the *dissolve* which seizes the subject in the midst of bliss." Therefore, "it is the very rhythm of what is read and what is not read that creates the pleasure of the great narratives": *The Pleasure of the Text*, trans. Richard Miller (New York: Hill and Wang, 1975), pp. 7, 11. Detached from its full context, this point of Barthes's may seem elusive or hyperbolic (somewhat so, perhaps, even *in* its context). But it brings a remarkable, fresh perspective to reading. The way we read—with its stops and starts and changes of speed, its jumps backward and forward, its reveries and absences—all of this in relation to our pleasure in reading (and specifically our aesthetic pleasure) is a subject that has been little studied.

p. 21   "But is there any comfort": These lines are from W. B. Yeats's poem "Nineteen Hundred and Nineteen," *The Collected Poems of W. B. Yeats* (New York: Macmillan, 1956), p. 205. Copyright 1928 by Macmillan Publishing Co., Inc., renewed 1956 by Georgie Yeats.

p. 21   Are there other ways . . . ?: The pursuit of "enlightenment" (a pursuit seen by some as self-contradictory) can, of course, be regarded as an attempt to reduce or eliminate self-concern. Is aesthetic experience temporary "enlightenment?" I don't think we can say that. Art is defined by the frame that separates it from the practical context. This frame is what makes possible the aesthetic liberation of experience. The individual self, the "me," passes from the ever-threatened, ever-embattled frame of its own narrow identity into that other frame, that refuge from the practical context, which is a work of art. But to *live* liberated, not in any refuge but in the midst of the practical context, requires something akin to a de-framing of that very self which we have, since early infancy, learned to establish. The boundaries are retained, you might say, but without their former meaning. They have become as much an inner surface as an outer one. Aesthetic liberation is accomplished by transferring experience from one frame to another more or less parallel frame which is not subject to self-concern. Whereas, if this other "enlightened" sort of liberation reduces or eliminates self-concern, that's because "self" is no longer operative in the way it was.

But I don't want to draw this line with *too* heavy a stroke. For one thing, art does reveal the possibility, within its frame at least, of experience which is full, dimensional, affective, and liberated. Some people may be led to make a connection between this revelation and their "ordinary" lives as they are lived out in the practical context. Others may not, and among them may well be those who have the most continual need of art. Furthermore, though art is not categorically to be regarded as "enlightenment," "enlightenment" itself, insofar as it may involve perception in the absence of self-concern, could perhaps be described as aesthetic. Finally, there is the question of *individual* works of art. There is no reason why a particular painting or poem, in its frame, cannot evoke a more de-framed way of seeing "self," cannot draw what we conventionally see as separate entities into one unified process:

> a hundred summers
> snowmelt rock and air

> hiss in a twisted bough.

(from Gary Snyder, "Burning the Small Dead," in *The Back Country* [New York: New Directions, 1968]).

Art, however, is more likely to evoke such an awareness when the awareness is already attained, or at least latent and ready to emerge, than to create it more or less from scratch.

Chapter Two

p. 23 the entire window scene itself: Not surprisingly, the window has been used on more than one occasion as a way of describing aesthetic perception. Ortega y Gasset (see notes to p. 16) speaks of looking at the windowpane, instead of looking through it to "revel in the human reality with which the work deals." This kind of distinction leads him to regard nineteenth-century realism (a term which for him includes— along with Zola—Chateaubriand, and even Beethoven and Wagner) as "impure," producing works which "are only partial works of art." "All they require," he says, "is human sensibility and willingness to sympathize with our neighbor's joys and worries" (p. 11). I would have suggested to Ortega, if I had had the opportunity, that realism is not in fact "the human reality" which exists beyond the window, but a perfectly acceptable style in windowpanes. The distinction between looking *at* and looking *through* is also to be found in James McNeill Whistler, *The Gentle Art of Making Enemies* (1892; rpt. New York: Dover, 1967), when he argues against confounding beauty with virtue and judging art on the basis of its usefulness: "and thus the people have acquired the habit of looking, as who should say, not *at* a picture, but *through* it, at some human fact, that shall, or shall not, from a social point of view, better their mental or moral state" (p. 138). Some readers of literature, I've found, have a very difficult time looking *at* the window. Each literary work for them is a moral questionnaire: "1, strongly agree . . . 5, strongly disagree." They leap to judge each new character in fiction as though he or she were a prospective roommate.

p. 25   an aesthetic object: I use this term for convenience. But the "object" could be a performance, that is, an event. In fact, one could maintain that the aesthetic "object" is always an event.

p. 32   Coleridge:

> Why are such simulations of nature, as wax-work figures of men and women, so disagreeable? Because, not finding the motion and life which we expected, we are shocked as by a falsehood, every circumstance of detail, which before induced us to be interested, making the distance from truth more palpable. You set out with a supposed reality and are disappointed and disgusted with the deception; whilst, in respect to a work of genuine imitation, you begin with an acknowledged total difference, and then every touch of nature gives you the pleasure of an approximation to truth . . . ("On Poesy or Art," *The Literary Remains of Samuel Taylor Coleridge*, ed. H. N. Coleridge [1836; rpt. New York: AMS Press, 1967], I, 220-21.)

Ortega y Gasset (see notes to p. 16) finds the origin of our "uneasiness" in the presence of such figures:

> in the provoking ambiguity with which wax figures defeat any attempt at adopting a clear and consistent attitude toward them. Treat them as living beings, and they will sniggeringly reveal their waxen secret. Take them for dolls, and they seem to breathe in irritated protest. They will not be reduced to mere objects. Looking at them we suddenly feel a misgiving: should it not be they who are looking at us? (pp. 28-29)

p. 33   "'Worlds on worlds": The opening lines of a chorus from Shelley's drama, *Hellas*.

p. 34   an expectation that *we* bring: Norman N. Holland makes this point in his chapter on "The Willing Suspension of Disbelief" in *The Dynamics of Literary Response* (New York: Norton, 1975). But Holland attaches more importance than I would to the element of "fiction" (as opposed to "fact" or "history") and to the concomitant "suspension of disbelief"—perhaps even more importance than his own theory demands. It is self-concern, not belief, that blocks our aesthetic path. That is why literary journalism can be more successful as art than this fact-fiction distinction would prepare us to believe. Sooner or later, I think, we will have to revise the meaning we commonly attach to "fiction," realizing that the essence of fiction has nothing to do with whether a story is "true" or "made up." Just as it is a needless embarrassment to let our recognition of an object as art depend on its having been created by an artist (so that we have to strip it of its title should that turn out not to be the case), so it seems unnecessary to restrict "fiction" to made-up stories, so that a novel which later turns out to be as uninvented as any autobiography suffers an *ex post facto* change of status.

Unlike fiction, a scientific or historical work presents itself as a series of relatively modest, necessarily limited statements about something else: a virus, let's say, or a revolution. It doesn't claim to present us with the virus or the revolution; on the contrary, this kind of work is always *about* and therefore outside of its subject. Fiction, however, gives us its subject, *realizes* it, makes it happen for us on the page and in our minds. Fiction is not outside of but in its subject, which is this reality it creates for us. The "truth" or "falsity" of this reality in relation to something else outside the work is, for me, beside the point in determining the work's status as fiction. I'm perfectly content to call Erica Jong's *Fear of Flying* a novel and to recognize it as fiction. If someone were to demonstrate that, in fact, "only the names have been changed," I wouldn't rush to reclassify the work as non-fiction.

Is fiction what is "invented," "made up," "not true?" Then we have two problems. One is the novel that turns out to be uninvented. But what about nonfiction? Works of history, biology, psychology, and so on are constructions in language, erected outside of the subjects they describe and in accordance with rules and patterns which may have little to do with these subjects. That's why such works, as it has been repeatedly pointed out, can be seen as "fictions." All the more reason for literary criticism to recognize fiction as a *way* of writing.

It may well be that a history text could be read as fiction in the sense I propose, just as an autobiographical novel could be studied solely for the information it provided about the author's life. But the novel, if it's any good, is much more likely than the history book to be read as fiction, because the author's literary technique does more than merely narrate or describe; it *realizes*: turning the words into a coherent, immediate aesthetic image.

Chapter Three

p. 38   "The nature of the activity of the infant": Donald B. Lindsley, "The Ontogeny of Pleasure: Neural and Behavioral Development," in *The Role of Pleasure in Behavior*, ed. Robert G. Heath (New York: Harper, 1964), p. 18.

p. 38   John Boddy: From his *Brain Systems and Psychological Concepts* (Chichester: John Wiley, 1978), pp. 209, 190.

p. 38   "Like most of its kind": H. J. Campbell, *The Pleasure Areas: A New Theory of Behavior* (New York: Delacorte, 1973), p. 45.

p. 39   "On about the fourth day": Campbell, p. 50.

p. 39   stained glass, gems, fire, fireworks: I'm aware that there are other explanations for our attraction to stained glass, gems, etc. Aldous Huxley, for example, in *Heaven and Hell* (New York: Perennial-Harper, 1956), regards precious gems, which so often appear in descriptions of paradise, as "precious because they bear a faint resemblance to the glowing marvels seen with the inner eye of the visionary" (p. 19).

p. 41 sensory hunger would find *immediate* satisfaction: Ordinarily our needs aren't satisfied by mere perception. It's not the taste of food that fills you up. How popular would a diet be that had you chewing whatever food you liked and then spitting it out? With sex as well, if the mere feel of flesh were all we needed, birth control would be no problem. What is true of sex and hunger is just as obviously true of other kinds of striving. The sight of a check in the mail may be pleasant, but only as a means. It's not the visual perception we want; it's the money. Unlike these needs, a need for sensory stimulation can find its immediate satisfaction in the mere perception of color, sound, and so on. Here the aesthetic object is not an instrument; striving leads us toward it, not away from it.

We could ask what happens if, with sex and food, one does find satisfaction in the immediate perception itself: in the sharp sweetness of an apple, or the sexy play of fingertips —without any leaning-forward toward some further consummation. Wouldn't we want to say that, to the extent that this really happens, the experience has become an aesthetic one? No surprise really. To be absorbed in, given over to, immediate perceptual images, without striving and self-concern— aren't these the privileged moments when sex and eating become aesthetic experience?

It's worth emphasizing, by the way, that aesthetic experience is not utterly passive and perfectly still. This false notion may, for some readers at least, be implied in Schopenhauer's description of the individual who experiences art, as a "pure, will-less subject of knowledge," who exists only as "the clear mirror of the object": *The World as Will and Idea*, trans. R. B. Haldane and J. Kemp (Garden City: Dolphin-Doubleday, 1961), pp. 191-92. In art as in ordinary experience, we tend to explore and to perceive (or construct) relationships. In the case of architecture, we may quite literally explore, on our feet. But even with a painting, our eyes rarely hold to a fixed point; we instinctively explore a visual field. Ordinarily we tend to explore extractively and instrumentally ("What can I use?") But in art we explore in a different way: along pathways of immediate sensory gratification and also

—always in the context of the whole image—by following immediately unfolding patterns which have the reactive, resonant, or cognitive potential that is considered in Book II.

p. 43   A novel—its imagery notwithstanding: It's worth speculating at least that literature may provide sensory gratification of a sort. William Carlos Williams' famous "The Red Wheelbarrow" obviously doesn't provide us with the retinal image of a wheelbarrow. The image he creates is not a *sensory* one in the ordinary meaning of the term; what my eyes actually see are words. On the other hand, it may not be merely a verbal abstraction either. To the extent that I visualize this red wheelbarrow, it may activate areas of the brain that form part of my visual apparatus and may therefore provide something akin to "sensory pleasure." But such speculation lies along one of the many paths that lead out of this particular book and into the realm of neurophysiological research.

Chapter Four

p. 46   they are *referred* into the image: Obviously, this response that we perceive is not physically located in the aesthetic object, nor does it come to us through channels of perception, e.g., eardrum, ossicles, cochlea, auditory nerve, etc. But phenomenologically speaking, we perceive it. This is not so strange if you recall that we are continually perceiving our own cognition of things. I don't see something and then, separately, determine that it can properly be categorized as "horse"; I simply see a horse. The category is referred to or projected onto the perception. But in aesthetic experience it is not merely recognition (in some cases, not recognition at all), but our full cognitive-affective response which, for reasons that are developed in this chapter, is projected into the image. For us as perceivers to disappear into the image means that it is a framework for our consciousness, a framework to which every aspect of our response is referred and which contains this response in its totality. Insofar as our response is *not* contained, the experience may be an aesthetic one, but less completely so or, perhaps, only intermittently so.

p. 46 dumping these terms altogether: For example: E. Duffy, "An Explanation of 'Emotional' Phenomena without the Use of the Concept 'Emotion,'" in *The Nature of Emotion: Selected Readings*, ed. Magda B. Arnold (Middlesex: Penguin, 1968), pp. 129-140.

p. 47 "affective experience itself can be seen as a way of knowing": Robert Ward Leeper argues that emotions themselves "are perceptual processes." He proposes an expansion of the traditional view of perception as a basis for his conclusion:

> What we are working with, when we try to understand the problems of emotions, are problems regarding processes that have a full perceptual character, rather than some simpler or more primitive character. Emotions, we might say, are the individual's perceptions or representations of what he regards as the most significant realities in his life. ("The Motivational and Perceptual Properties of Emotions as Indicating Their Fundamental Character and Role," in *Feelings and Emotions: the Loyola Symposium*, ed. Magda B. Arnold [New York: Academic Press, 1970], pp. 156, 164.)

Chapter Five

p. 56 Are some responses of this type built in?: The mention of built-in responses may put some readers in mind of Jung's theory of archetypes. This may be an appropriate occasion, therefore, to stress that the *resonance* which I am proposing as a central element in aesthetic theory is not to be equated with any archetypal resonance.

Early in *Archetypal Patterns in Poetry: Psychological Studies of Imagination* (1934; rpt. New York: Vintage, 1958), Maud Bodkin describes the results of her own "free play" of association to some stanzas in Coleridge's "Ancient Mariner"—association based on personal experience and also on memories of other works. She comments:

If it is true for other readers also that complexes of interwoven personal and literary reminiscence are formed, and vibrate unrecognized in the background of the mind, contributing again and again emotional signifi-cance to words or happenings that make connexion with them—this would be a truth from which certain results might follow of interest for literary psychology (pp. 32-33).

"Unrecognized" is a key word here. Elsewhere, she states that, "at the moment of completest appreciation [of Col-eridge's poem] no imagery, other than the words"—that is, none of these associations—"is present." But she senses "a whole of far-reaching significance, concentrated like a force behind any particular stanza or line." When "the grasp of poetic apprehension loosens," *then* she can become aware of past experiences, which she seems to recognize "as having contributed something to the preceding unified experience of meaning" (pp. 36-37).

At this point she appears to be moving toward an analysis of something like what I describe as "resonance." But, though Bodkin acknowledges that different individuals will be in-fluenced by different "memory-complexes," it is not the *individual* dimension in experience that she is primarily concerned with. What interests her more are the associations which "may still be reckoned upon as holding good for individuals of widely different nurture and temperament" (p. 38)—that is, the archetypes, set forth in Jungian theory as primordial, universal, and inherited, which are the subject of her book: rebirth, heaven and hell, the mother-goddess, the hero, and so on.

From a Jungian point of view it could be argued that what I call a resonant response to the red stoplight may, in fact, be determined by the role this particular kind of color has played in human, rather than individual, history (I've already mentioned a related theory of Huxley's, in my note to p. 39). Inherited archetypes are certainly an intriguing possibility. But my own tendency is to do without them theoretically (Bodkin herself appears to leave open the question of whether or not they are actually inherited [p.124]). For it just may be that in the course of an ordinary human life there is enough repeated experience of certain sorts, both immediate and vicarious, to establish the kind of psychic residues that Jung regarded as inherited archetypes. In any case, though the study of archetype and myth is a fascinating and immensely productive activity which I would hardly want to disparage, it does present a potential problem from the point of view of aesthetic experience.

The problem is that of reductionism. Insofar as archetypal patterns are regarded as the unconscious "content" of a work, or as its meaning, or even merely as the true source of its appeal, there is a risk of constricting and deadening the individual's own resonant response, rather than enhancing it or opening it up. Maud Bodkin's own approach reveals enormous respect for the individual experience. But it is also possible for archetypal criticism (like many other styles of criticism) to present us with a peremptory and official interpretation of a work or even to leave us feeling that somehow the whole point of reading literature is to see through it to the mythic patterns which animate it. Emphasizing, as I do here, the *personal* nature of resonance by no means excludes a consideration of such patterns, but it encourages us to ground them, as Bodkin does, for example, in her consideration of "The Ancient Mariner," in individual response, and it discourages us from presenting them in reductionist fashion.

Equally important: resonance, as I suggest in Chapter Eight, is a way of responding to the *entire* work of art as a unique entity. I don't think this could properly be said of an "archetypal" resonance. Furthermore, the resonance I describe is obviously less amenable to conceptual description, particularly as it tends to shift its dimensions and its balance from one moment to another. In addition, the study of archetypal patterns seems to have a natural home among the representational arts. What I mean by resonance is characteristic of our response to all arts and is nowhere more purely evident than with absolute music.

Norman N. Holland (see notes to p. 34) takes up the question of mythic "resonance," which, he says, according to myth critics, "comes about because myth taps some sort of collective unconscious, the deepest memories and fantasies of the race." Holland, however, will have none of it: "these are airy nothings psychologists proper have long hooted at." He seeks another explanation for what he agrees is a particularly rich and deep feeling that some mythic material evokes, an explanation which does not require "the troublesome assumption that our RNA and DNA, already so fraught with information, must carry Grimm's fairy tales as well." What Holland comes up with is the ingenious notion that it is not merely mythic material itself but "the myth plus our conscious knowledge of it" that evokes resonance, and that the resonance derives from the sense of "being merged into a larger matrix." He suggests that this sense corresponds to Freud's "oceanic feeling," the psychic state that, according to Freud, precedes an infant's awareness of separation from the mother, and argues that where there is the experience of mythic resonance, "we should expect to find oral elements: motifs of being engulfed, of devouring and being devoured" (pp. 243-44, 261, 248-49). Needless to say, Holland's resonance would be a somewhat narrower category than the one he is attempting to replace.

Can we say then that there is, on the one hand, a "mythic resonance," which may be explainable from Jungian, Freudian, or other points of view and which is to be seen as a response to particular mythic content in (usually) a representational work of art, *and*, on the other hand, "resonance" itself, that is, the aesthetic resonance which I am proposing in Chapters Five, Six, and Eight of this book?

p. 57   resonance, unlike recognition: Some readers may wonder if "resonance," as I use the term, isn't merely "connotation" dressed up in new clothing, with "recognition" standing in for "denotation." Actually, "resonance" and "connotation" are rather different. It may be useful to see just where the difference lies.

"Connotation" has, on occasion, been applied to nonverbal arts: see, for example, Eleanor Metheny, *Movement and Meaning* (New York: McGraw-Hill, 1968). Usually, however, it is thought of in connection with language, as the "secondary" meaning suggested or implied by a term. This meaning involves associations, attitudes, or "overtones," and forms a sort of nimbus around the core of "denotation": the explicit, literal meaning. Resonance, however, is not secondary to some denotative meaning: in fact, it is in no way tied to language, nor for that matter to any system of signs. We can resonate to colors or musical phrases that have no denotative meaning whatsoever.

Resonance is not static; it is not an idea or a meaning but a process. "Connotation" is a semantic (or semiotic) concept; "resonance" is a psychological one. One of the advantages of "resonance" as an element in aesthetic theory is that it allows us to observe what goes on in aesthetic experience without always being forced to fit what we see into the frame of meaning. Some images are compounded entirely or partially out of words, or out of other signs. Some are not. Invaluable as it may be to investigate the interrelationships among signs in the first kind of image, we have to recognize that the aesthetic image itself doesn't merely signify.

Monroe Beardsley identifies one of the chief problems in defining "connotations" as that "of distinguishing connotations from personal associations": *Aesthetics: Problems in the Philosophy of Criticism* (New York: Harcourt, 1958), P.151. Connotative meaning, though marginal and even hazy, is still public and excludes purely private associations. Resonance is not public, though many of us may well have similar resonant responses to a work of art.

A single word can connote, e.g., "booze," "prioritize," "cottage," "honcho," whereas resonance requires the image. Connotation takes its place in ordinary life, as well as in art; it is always there when we use language. Connotation can speak to our self-concern just as denotation can (compare "women" and "chicks"). Resonance, however, is essentially aesthetic. In the absence of self-concern, the aesthetic image is allowed free play among areas of experience linked by no concept or instrumental purpose but only by the image itself (Chapter Seven). These areas of experience surrender, not their identity but their quality, a complex cognitive-affective "elixir" which saturates the image, where it is perceived.

Resonance is a way of responding to the *whole* work as a complex structure of resonant relationships (Chapter Eight). One could try to use "connotation" in that way, but it would be stretching the term to the breaking point. Even Metheny, who applies "connotation" to dance, uses it in connection with discrete elements—dynamic patterns—*within* a dance. And with good reason. Connotations typically are multiple, whereas resonance, though fluid, dynamic, and complex, is always whole.

We can, if we like, see "connotation" as an expansive tendency in language, reaching out from meaning in the direction of resonance, a tendency away from strict denotation and toward a richer, more associative, more personal response. But this tendency is ordinarily held in check by the conceptual, instrumental nature of language. When it is contained within language, we call it "connotation"; it is set free only when language becomes aesthetic image, and connotation can expand and merge into resonance.

p. 58   Recognition, then, is important, to varying degrees: It's worth observing that the boundaries of recognition are not precisely marked. In painting, for example, there are shapes that don't seem to represent anything other than themselves, but also shapes that seem to play with recognition, that appear to lurk just around the threshhold of recognition. Many of Miró's paintings present us with such shapes, which verge on recognizable forms of humans, birds, etc., shapes which are somewhere between "abstract" and "representational." Of course, where the dividing line falls depends very much on who's perceiving. You may unhesitatingly see the Judgment of Paris in a painting where I recognize nothing at all.

p. 59   "Their eyes mid many wrinkles": Yeats, "Lapis Lazuli" (see note to p. 21), p. 293. Copyright 1940 by Georgie Yeats, renewed 1968 by Bertha Georgie Yeats, Michael Butler Yeats and Anne Yeats.

p. 62   an oversimplified view: My overlapping-circle analogy may give a rough sense of the resonant potential in metaphorical images, but beyond that it won't do. Following I. A. Richards, *The Philosophy of Rhetoric* (New York: Oxford University Press, 1936), Max Black stresses the *interaction* which a metaphor brings about. And Black offers his own metaphor for metaphor: the principal subject (Richards' "tenor") is *filtered* or *screened* through the subsidiary subject (Richards' "vehicle"). Describing a battle in terms of chess: "the chess vocabulary filters and transforms: it not only selects, it brings forward aspects of the battle that might not be seen at all through another medium": "Metaphor," *Proceedings of the Aristotelian Society*, 55 (1954-55), rpt. in *Art and Philosophy: Readings in Aesthetics*, ed. W. E. Kennick, 2nd ed. (New York: St. Martin's Press, 1979), p. 326. Black's emphasis on the transforming effect of one term on another is of central importance, I think. The "filter" metaphor has one weakness in that it tends to de-emphasize the evocative importance of the subsidiary subject itself. The "poor and white" foot in Plath's poem is not merely a medium through which we view the speaker's relationship with "Daddy"; it has substantial evocative presence in its own right. Black's idea of filtering is, I suspect, most useful in relation to metaphor as a cognitive strategy in expository writing.

The main problem with "overlap" as a way of seeing metaphor is that its assumption of common characteristics is too mechanical—as though foot-shoe and child-daddy were each a bag of marbles of various types, out of which the metaphor merely drew out all the matching pairs. But no such exact matches are to be had. Furthermore, to bring two terms together, as with child-parent and foot-shoe, can be a demand that we create some new structure as a bridge between the two: a rearrangement, a new vision, a new understanding. What we end up with then is not merely the evocation by metaphor of two separate but in some way parallel experiential areas; these separate areas, brought together, join in creating a new cognitive-affective complex, which itself is not static but dynamic—so that at any instant either of the two areas, or some particular aspect of either, or some new structure created by their interaction, may take on greater, or less, importance in our complex response to the metaphorical image.

The ability of the metaphor not merely to reveal what already exists but to create what has never existed before becomes paramount in the "surrealist metaphor" (e.g., "re-usable dogs" or Breton's *The White-Haired Revolver*), which Richards dismisses as "a contemporary fashionable aberration" (p. 123), but which in Anna Balakian's view "renovates the entire notion of the metaphor": *Surrealism: The Road to the Absolute* (New York: Noonday, 1959), p. 120. The metaphor used to be seen as a way of representing a pre-existing image in the writer's mind. "Now," Balakian states, "the cart is placed before the horse, and it is the unusual metaphor that creates the even more extraordinary image, which is composed of two or more elements having no logical relationship with each other" (p. 121). What this kind of metaphor does, I think, is to demand that we instantly provide a means of relating two incongruous experiential areas, a means which will be framed by our shocked recognition of their incongruity. In some cases, well-established subterranean relationships will be ready to hand, possessing their own dream-logic. In other cases, even that connection will be missing, and from this bizarre mating of terms an utterly new, hybrid "reality" is born. But some of these hybrids are more interesting than others, and to create them, select the most effective, and set them in still more complex, novel, and interesting patterns of relationships is no mere exercise in contradiction, but the work of an artist (an artist who, in this case, might be a painter, sculptor, choreographer, or filmmaker just as well as a writer).

p. 63 "Her thighs slipped away": Federico García Lorca, "The Faithless Wife" ("La Casada Infiel"), trans. Stephen Spender and J. L. Gili, in *The Selected Poems of Federico García Lorca*, ed. Francisco García Lorca and Donald Allen (New York: New Directions, 1955), pp. 71, 73. The original:

> Sus muslos se me escapaban
> como peces sorprendidos,
> la mitad llenos de lumbre
> la mitad llenos de frío.
>
> (70, 72)

p. 64 "lips as raunchy as a swig of grape soda": *The Electric Kool-Aid Acid Test* (New York: Bantam, 1969), p. 99.

p. 65   "It is a cold and snowy night": Robert Bly, "Driving to Town Late to Mail a Letter," in *Silence in the Snowy Fields* (Middletown: Wesleyan University Press, 1962), p. 38.

p. 66   "In the morning dew": Bashō's haiku is translated by R. H. Blyth in his *A History of Haiku* (Tokyo: The Hokuseido Press, 1963), I, 127.

p. 68   "The rains of May": my translation.

p. 69   "Dans l'interminable": The first line is also the poem's title.

p. 69   "And all is seared with trade": from "God's Grandeur."

p. 71   seems so especially real: Actually, I can think of several reasons why an object perceived aesthetically might seem especially real—whether it is a natural object or an art work. First of all, when we see something aesthetically, we're likely to perceive more of it. Ordinarily we may see no more of an object than we need in order to recognize it and perhaps to make instrumental use of it. Aesthetically, however, it's "all there." Second, our sensory enjoyment of the object is likely to be heightened, and this enjoyment perceived in the object will make colors more vivid, textures richer, and so on. Third, as I suggest in the text, our resonant response will take us beyond any narrow concept of the object and will invest what we perceive with the immediacy and abundance of experiential quality. Finally: since, perceiving aesthetically, we are less "businesslike" about what we see—less likely to take it for granted, deal with it in some way, and move on— we may even find ourselves seeing in an object what most people rarely see: its very existence. With a little encouragement from the artist or, in the case of a natural object, from our own receptive state of mind, we may see it as a concrete embodiment of, in Paul Tillich's words, "the astonishing prerational fact that there is something and not nothing": *The Courage To Be* (New Haven: Yale University Press, 1959), p. 40.

Chapter Six

p. 74   **Clive Bell and Roger Fry:** In *Vision and Design* (1920; rpt. Cleveland: World, 1956), Fry summarizes Bell's thesis:

that however much the emotions of life might appear to play a part in the work of art, the artist was really not concerned with them, but only with the expression of a special and unique kind of emotion, the aesthetic emotion. A work of art had the peculiar property of conveying the aesthetic emotion, and it did this in virtue of having "significant form."

Fry illustrates this by supposing two viewers of a religious painting (Raphael's *Transfiguration*): one Christian, the other pagan. For the Christian spectator the work, through its content, will set up "an immense complex of feelings, inter-penetrating and mutually affecting one another." The pagan, however, whom Fry establishes as a person who is either ignorant of or indifferent to the Biblical background of the painting and who is "highly endowed with a special sensi-bility to form," will be excited by formal relationships only:

> We may suppose him to be moved by the pure con-templation of the spatial relations of plastic volumes. It is when we have got to this point that we seem to have isolated this extremely elusive aesthetic quality which is the one constant quality of all works of art, and which seems to be independent of all the prepossessions and associations which the spectator brings with him from his past life.

It is the "attempt to isolate the elusive element of the pure aesthetic reaction from the compounds in which it occurs," which for Fry is "the most important advance of modern times in practical aesthetic" (pp. 295-300). Note, by the way, that Fry's "aesthetic reaction" is independent of associations from past experience. I should think it *would* be elusive.

Chapter Seven

p. 79 "Vernon Lee" (Violet Paget) and Theodore Lipps: Empathy in Lee and Lipps is an attempt to explain our response to art *in general*; here I use the term, in its common sense, in con-nection only with *reactive* response. What is most valuable in their theories, from my point of view, is an emphasis on the perceiver's tendency to experience a merging or identity with the aesthetic object. But both were less fortunate, I think, in the importance they attached to imitative or mimetic elements in the perceiver's response. See Lee, *The Beautiful* (London: Cambridge University Press, 1913). Lipps, "Empathy and Aesthetic Pleasure," trans. Karl Aschenbrenner, is reprinted in *Aesthetic Theories: Studies in the Philosophy of Art*, ed. Karl Aschenbrenner and Arnold Isenberg (Englewood Cliffs: Prentice-Hall, 1965), pp. 403-12. Both an excerpt from *The Beautiful*, and Lipps, "Empathy, Inner Imitation and Sense-Feelings," trans. Max Schertel and Melvin Rader, are reprinted in *A Modern Book of Esthetics*, ed. Melvin Rader, 3rd ed. (New York: Holt, Rinehart, 1961).

p. 81   "Not, I'll not, carrion comfort": from Gerard Manley Hopkins, "Carrion Comfort."

p. 81   "Hardly was Candide in his inn": This translation of Voltaire's *Candide* is by Peter Gay (New York: St. Martin's Press, 1963), p. 165.

p. 86   "ORONTE: Others have praised my sonnet": Molière, *The Misanthrope and Tartuffe*, trans. Richard Wilbur (New York: Harvest-Harcourt, 1965), p. 41.

p. 87   "But such a bulk": *The Dunciad*, II, 39-50.

p. 88   Jarry's King Ubu: In his "Preliminary Address" at the first performance of *Ubu Roi*, Jarry said: "you are free to see in Mister Ubu as many allusions as you like, or, if you prefer, just a plain puppet, a schoolboy's caricature of one of his teachers who represented for him everything in the world that is grotesque." Particularly in view of the fact that the play arose out of schoolboy teacher-mocking, this statement of Jarry's might suggest that he himself, at least, saw Ubu in essentially aggressive rather than redemptive terms. All of which makes it especially interesting to read what Jarry wrote for a program distributed at that same first performance: "Mister Ubu is an ignoble creature, which is why he is so like us all (seen from below)." Both texts, translated by Simon Watson Taylor, are in *Selected Works of Alfred Jarry*, ed. Roger Shattuck and Simon Watson Taylor (New York: Grove, 1965), pp. 76, 80.

p. 91   "camp" and "camping": Susan Sontag, "Notes on Camp," in *Against Interpretation and Other Essays* (New York: Laurel-Dell, 1969), pp. 283-84.

Chapter Eight

pp. 109-110   Jack Kerouac's *On the Road:* (New York: Signet-New American Library, n.d.); "desirous of everything" (p. 9), "the holy void" (p. 143), "We zoomed" (p. 27), "She sighed" (p. 48), "Beyond some trees" (p. 138).

Chapter Nine

p. 122   "Your ugly token": from "Upon a Dead Man's Head."

p. 123   Theodore Adorno makes a comparable criticism: in his *Introduction to the Sociology of Music*, trans. E. B. Ashton (New York: Seabury, 1976), pp. 25-26. I wonder what Adorno would have said about the popular music which appeared later in the sixties and which broke through at least some elements of the standard form: let's say "Time Has Come Today," by the Chambers Brothers. I suspect he would still have disliked it. Adorno was not an admirer of popular music after Offenbach and Johann Strauss—and he had reservations about *them*.

Chapter Ten

p. 139   "An accident is perhaps the only thing": Igor Stravinsky, *Poetics of Music in the Form of Six Lessons*, trans. Arthur Knodel and Ingolf Dahl (New York: Vintage, 1956), p. 56.

p. 141   "the gold coin": Henri Bergson, *An Introduction to Metaphysics*, trans. T. E. Hulme (1913; rpt. New York: Liberal Arts Press, 1955), p.23.

p. 145   "the particular history of their encounters": Herbert Marcuse, *The Aesthetic Dimension: Toward a Critique of Marxist Aesthetics*, trans. Herbert Marcuse and Erica Sherover (Boston: Beacon, 1978), p. 5.

p. 146 *taming them* : Sontag (see note to p. 91), p. 17.

p. 146 "The painter goes through states of fullness": *Artists on Art: From the XIV to the XX Century*, ed. Robert Goldwater and Marco Treves, 3rd ed. (New York: Pantheon, 1958), p. 421.

p. 147 "seemingly cumbersome preliminary theorizing": Don McDonagh, *The Rise and Fall and Rise of Modern Dance* (New York: Mentor-New American Library, 1970), pp. 209-10.

p. 147 Paul Valéry has said: *The Creative Vision: Modern European Writers On Their Art*, ed. Haskell M. Block and Herman Salinger (New York: Grove, 1960), pp. 35-36.

p. 147 Joyce Cary tells of a story: *Writers at Work: The Paris Review Interviews*, ed. Malcolm Cowley (New York: Viking, 1959), pp. 63-64.

p. 148 "The true life, life at last uncovered": Marcel Proust, *A la recherche du temps perdu* (Paris: La Pléiade, Gallimard, 1954), III, 895 (my translation).

p. 150 William Burroughs . . . Louis-Ferdinand Céline: *Writers at Work: The Paris Review Interviews*, 3rd ser., introd. Alfred Kazin (New York: Viking, 1967). Burroughs: "I would go on writing for company. Because I'm creating an imaginary—it's always imaginary—world in which I would like to live" (p. 174). Céline: "If I had money I'd never write. Article number one" (p. 95).

p. 151 purposefully and carefully kept secret: See Edmund Carpenter, "Silent Music and Invisible Art," *Natural History*, May 1978, pp. 90-99.

p. 154 a backstage where you put things together: Edgar Allan Poe, in "The Philosophy of Composition," *Selected Poetry and Prose of Edgar Allan Poe*, ed. T. O. Mabbott (New York: Modern Library, 1951), didn't hesitate to apply the metaphor to poetry:

> Most writers—poets in especial—prefer having it understood that they compose by a species of fine frenzy—an ecstatic intuition—and would positively shudder at letting the public take a peep behind the scenes, at the elaborate and vacillating crudities of thought—at the true purposes seized only at the last moment—at the innumerable glimpses of idea that arrived not at the

maturity of full view—at the fully matured fancies discarded in despair as unmanageable—at the cautious
selections and rejections—at the painful erasures and
interpolations—in a word, at the wheels and pinions—
the tackle for scene shifting—the step-ladders and
demon-traps—the cock's feathers, the red paint and the
black patches, which, in ninety-nine cases out of the
hundred, constitute the properties of the literary *histrio.*
(pp. 364-65)

The century that followed Poe's has brought with it artists
who not only fail to shudder at letting the public take a peep
backstage, but whose art plays with, straddles, or in some
way calls into question the backstage-"out front" division.
For example: when I last saw Daniel Nagrin give a solo dance
concert, the audience entered the theatre to find him already
seated near the back of the stage, putting on make-up. Then,
while people were still coming in—before "curtain time"—
he did warm-ups, still in full view. Between numbers, he
would change shoes or costume on stage, while talking
informally to the audience. And, during intermission, he put
on a carpenter's apron and, still on stage, hammered together
a stool, which he auctioned off after the show for a charity of
the audience's choosing. None of this, however, strikes me as
an attempt to undermine the aesthetic image. Nagrin, who
even presented as one of his dances the tenacious, repetitive
process of choreography itself, is (in my mind) a very great
artist, who may demystify his art in an admirable way, who
may broaden his image to include an extraordinary range of
experience, including his own experience as a man who
comes to the theatre to dance on stage in front of us, but
who has never given me the feeling that he has let go of his
art or lost his sense of the overall image that is being
created. On the contrary, his art is so strong that "dance" is
projected out into areas where we are not accustomed to
recognizing it. What we find then is not that Nagrin has
taken us backstage, but rather that he has brought a certain
amount of backstage into his image in order to encompass a
broader experiential structure than the traditional conven-

tions of dance and theatre allow. Instead of dance as a seemingly magical alternative to "life," he shows us dance growing out of life, dance as a mode of living.

p. 155 "And at this clamor almost everyone": Rainer Maria Rilke, *The Notebooks of Malte Laurids Brigge*, trans. M. D. Herter Norton (New York: Norton, 1949), p. 161.

Chapter Eleven

p. 163 Diderot demanded that actors be cold and calm: Denis Diderot, *Paradoxe sur le comédien* (Paris: Garnier-Flammarion, 1967).

p. 163 "mere puppets in motion, not people": *"Your Isadora": The Love Story of Isadora Duncan and Gordon Craig*, ed. Francis Steegmuller (New York: Random House, 1974), p. 47.

Chapter Twelve

p. 168 Schopenhauer: Erich Heller, "Arthur Schopenhauer," in *¡Viva Vivas!*, ed. Henry Regnery (Indianapolis: Liberty Press, 1976), pp. 276-77.

p. 168 Flaubert: Francis Steegmuller, *Flaubert and Madame Bovary: A Double Portrait* (London: Collins, 1947), p. 114.

p. 168 Oscar Wilde: "The Critic as Artist," in *Intentions* (New York: Brentano's, 1905), p. 128.

p. 169 an anti-bourgeois "counterculture": Two historical studies that cast light on the relationship between aestheticism and bohemia are César Graña, *Bohemian Versus Bourgeois: French Society and the French Man of Letters in the Nineteenth Century* (New York: Basic Books, 1964), and Richard Miller, *Bohemia: The Protoculture Then and Now* (Chicago: Nelson-Hall, 1977). For an account of the connections between aestheticism and utopian socialism in nineteenth-century France see Donald Drew Egbert, *Social Radicalism and the Arts: Western Europe* (New York: Knopf, 1970) pp. 145-158.

p. 172 Beaumarchais's *Marriage of Figaro*: My account of the struggle over this play is taken principally from Frédéric Grendel, *Beaumarchais ou la calomnie* (Paris: Flammarion, 1973), pp.

399-429. I have translated Grendel's quotations from Louis XVI and Beaumarchais (p. 400). The part played by "*Malbrough s'en va-t-en guerre*" is described in Georges Lemaître, *Beaumarchais*, (New York: Knopf, 1949), pp. 275-79. "Malbrough," incidentally, is the tune we know as "For He's a Jolly Good Fellow."

p. 173   Napoleon certainly wasn't inclined to deny it: Grendel (see preceding note), p. 413. Grendel asks: "And whom would Napoleon send to the asylum today? No one, I'm afraid" (p. 416). My translation.

p. 173   Hitler . . . *Rienzi* . . . Bayreuth: William Carr, *Hitler: A Study in Personality and Politics* (London: Edward Arnold, 1978), p. 139.

p. 173   a shell-shocked flier: Richard Grunberger, *A Social History of Nazi Germany 1933-1945* (New York: Holt, Rinehart, 1971), p. 386.

p. 182   an ally in the world out there: Someone might object that our subjectivity is not, in fact, out there in the aesthetic object. That's quite true. But what matters is that we perceive it there—and, equally important, that there is an object which is capable of evoking and receiving it.

p. 183   unreconstructed subjectivity: In speaking of subjectivity, I'm not referring, it should be clear, to that me-ness which is merchandised to the affluent: *Self* magazine, $500 weekend seminars on self-realization, and so on: the whole furniture store of "personal space"—all of which, among its other functions, (a) answers the question, "What do we sell people after the refrigerator is full and the stereo has been installed?" and (b) rationalizes a situation which might otherwise produce "liberal" guilt and even social activism.

pp. 183-184   Herbert Marcuse: (see note to p. 145), pp. ix, 46, 41, 38.

p. 184   The "accursed" (*maudit*) artist: Adolfo Sánchez Vásquez, *Art and Society: Essays in Marxist Aesthetics*, trans. Maro Riofrancos (New York: Monthly Review Press, 1973), p. 117.

p. 185   "An integral part of his personality": Carr (see notes to p. 173), pp. 139-40.

Chapter Thirteen

p. 189 "The most decisive feature of capitalist society: Georg Lukács, "The Old Culture and the New Culture," trans. Paul Breines from "Alte und neue Kultur," *Kommunismus*, I (1920); rpt. *Marxism and Human Liberation: Essays on History, Culture and Revolution* by Georg Lukács, ed. E. San Juan, Jr. (New York: Delta-Dell, 1973), p. 6.

p. 189 "Whereas objects establish relations with human beings" Sánchez Vásquez (see note to p. 184), p. 190.

p. 192 "the novel, the sensational and the conspicuous elements": Lukács (see note to p. 189), p. 8.

p. 198 "There is no special artist class": "The Artist and his Art in an Australian Aboriginal Society," in *The Artist in Tribal Society: Proceedings of a Symposium held at the Royal Anthropological Institute*, ed. Marian W. Smith (New York: Free Press of Glencoe, 1961), p. 7.

Chapter Fourteen

p. 203 "To know the plum tree": (my translation).

p. 205 Ilya . . . when he was much younger: Jerry Farber, *The University of Tomorrowland: A Book of Essays* (New York: Pocket Books-Simon & Schuster, 1972).

p. 209 "There's a barrel-organ carolling": Alfred Noyes, "The Barrel-organ," in *Collected Poems* (New York: Frederick Stokes, 1913), I, 80.

p. 212 "a literal usurpation": Roger Shattuck, "How to Rescue Literature," *The New York Review of Books*, 17 April 1980, p. 29.

p. 215 To make no contribution or to give them watered-down teaching: This is not to say that it may not be wise in certain situations to pull back and give the class more room. Occasionally you may feel a class relying on you in too dependent and passive a fashion, and then your own diminished presence may induce them to take more responsibility in the learning process.

p. 220   This question of evaluation: I'd like to offer a distinction with respect to evaluation. There are two sorts. One is an important part of the teaching process; oriented toward the future not the past, it is open, provisional, and personal, that is, devoid of institutional authority. This type of evaluation, for example, might take the form of written comments directed to the student about a project that she has done. It answers a pedagogical question: what can I say that will be of use to this person? The other kind of evaluation is professional and institutional; it may have reference to the future but is primarily an assessment of what has taken place. It could take the form of a letter of recommendation, a decision to accept or reject a thesis (or any student work), or an offer, or refusal, of employment. This second type also includes all grading. Now this type of evaluation, which is, as I've said, professional, ought to have a limited range of application. General students, whose involvement with an art is not professionally oriented, needn't be subject to this kind of evaluation (at the very *most*, perhaps, some sort of Credit/No Credit decision: that they have or have not made some basic investment in a course). And even graduate students are hardly benefited, nor are standards maintained, by grading. Like most of my colleagues, I've been on various staffing committees; and, though I always look with interest at applicants' letters of recommendation, professional histories, self-descriptions, written work, and so on, the idea of checking their grades seems like the silliest thing in the world.

p. 221   **Sontag:** (see note to p. 91), p. 17.

p. 223   **Stravinsky:** (see note to p. 139), pp. 66-68.

Epilogue

p. 235   "'Tis with our judgments": Alexander Pope, *Essay on Criticism*, I, 9-10.

Index